THE
DEFENSE
NEVER
RESTS

THE
DEFENSE
NEVER
RESTS

by F. LEE BAILEY

with HARVEY ARONSON

STEIN AND DAY/*Publishers*/New York

For my sons, Ben, Brian, and Scott; whether the calling of any of them should be in the legal profession or elsewhere, they will have much to do. Despite my best efforts and all the good intentions with which the road to hell is paved, I must anticipate that my own court will adjourn with many injustices yet to be corrected.

Copyright © 1971 by F. Lee Bailey and Harvey Aronson
Library of Congress Catalog Card No. 70-179487
All rights reserved
Published simultaneously in Canada by Saunders of Toronto, Ltd.
Designed by David Miller
Manufactured in the United States of America
Stein and Day/*Publishers*/7 East 48 Street, New York, N.Y. 10017
ISBN 0-8128-1441-X

FOURTH PRINTING, 1972

CONTENTS

ALONE

The Carolina coast was below me: white and gleaming in the afternoon sun. I leveled off about a mile above the earth and swung the Sabrejet parallel to the coast, looking for a beach picnic to buzz or a pair of young lovers to startle. Then I glanced at the instrument panel and saw the red warning light flashing: FIRE.

There had been trouble with our Sabrejets—planes catching fire on takeoff and costing pilots their lives—but I hadn't worried about that when I left the runway seconds before. I was a fighter pilot and chief legal officer for a Marine unit based at Cherry Point, North Carolina. I was twenty-three years old and I was punching holes in a sparkling sky; enjoying myself while putting in the necessary time for flight pay. And I guess I was protected by the rationale that enables any pilot to keep going after he's seen a buddy killed in a crash—*it must have been pilot error, it could never happen to me.*

Only now, on a sun-splashed day in 1955, a red warning light was saying that it could happen to me. I had to make a decision: I could use the ejection seat and bail out, or I could shut down the engine and try for a dead-stick landing.

If I bailed out, there was the possibility that the airplane might crash in a populated area. True, the region was sparsely settled, and I could always point the ship to sea. But there was no guarantee that it wouldn't turn and come back to shore. And suppose the parachute was defective— the terminal velocity of a free-falling human being is 125 mph. Then I remembered the words of an old navy lieutenant who had been my instructor in all-weather school. "A ground bum," he had said, "is a guy who points the nose down the moment he gets in trouble, because he knows he doesn't belong in the sky. A pilot climbs like hell, knowing that altitude is both time and insurance, knowing he'll never get hurt as long as his plane doesn't hit the ground."

I grabbed the microphone and yelled "MAYDAY" as loud as I could. I hauled back on the stick, turned toward the base, and yanked the throttle back to idle cut-off almost in the same instant. I had made my decision— a flame-out approach.

Essentially, a jet airplane is a flying gas tank powered by a blowtorch, and I would have bailed out if the fire warning light had remained on when I cut the power. But it went out, and the air was silent. I had enough altitude, and the runway at Cherry Point is the longest in the world —I landed without difficulty. When I got out of the cockpit, I was soaked with sweat and figuring to myself that I had earned a full year's flight pay by saving the government a million-dollar jet fighter.

Later, after the plane had been towed into a hangar and checked, I talked to an old maintenance chief. He said there had been no fire, just a short in the warning system.

"But I bet you thought about poppin' out, Lieutenant," he said with a grin, "what with all the fire trouble we've been having lately."

"A passing thought, Sarge," I said in the best tradition of the fearless fighter pilot. "Just a passing thought."

His reply was appropriate if not eloquent: "Horseshit."

I can still feel the excitement of that moment of decision a mile above the earth. If I ran a school for criminal lawyers, I would teach them all to fly. I would send them up when the weather was rough, when the planes were in tough shape, when the birds were walking. The ones who survived would understand the meaning of "alone." If I understand anything, I understand that. I've been a pilot for seventeen years.

I am also a criminal lawyer.

1

The Torso Murder
and
Other Beginnings

1. *ORIGINS*

In Omaha recently, Andy Crane, a copilot, found himself explaining his line of work to a new acquaintance. "I fly a Learjet for F. Lee Bailey," Andy said. "You know who he is, don't you?"

The man thought for a moment, and then nodded. "Yeah," he said. "F. Lee Bailey. Wasn't he one of the Chicago Seven?"

I plead innocent. To his credit, the man knew I had something to do with courtrooms; I like to think he simply had his rebels mixed up.

Specializing in criminal law makes me a rebel by profession; our system requires that mavericks stand for the defense. Otherwise, pity the poor accused. Kids in grade school are told by their teachers that we have the most impeccable system of criminal justice in the world. Our educators and leaders have been saying so for years, and most people believe it. I see a lot of these people. It is with a good deal of indignation, fright, and consternation that they walk into my office and say, "I have an indictment here that falsely accuses me of such and such. I'll pay you a big retainer, and I'd like to know how soon I'm likely to be acquitted." I tell them that because they spend too much time reading the newspapers and watching Perry Mason, they think they're hiring a magician instead of a lawyer. And I usually add something like "I suppose you think that your innocence is a factor in the probable outcome of this case?" Invariably, the answer is "yes." Whereupon I explain that not only is innocence less than a guarantee that there will be a favorable outcome, but, as the wheels of justice grind on, innocence becomes progressively less relevant.

That's why the defense lawyer has to be a maverick; he has to be able to buck the system to make it work. "A trial lawyer in a contentious case is a paid professional fighter," I once told a reporter. "The one word that comes closest to what he ought to be is 'renegade.' That's why most good criminal lawyers are loners. A hundred years ago you saw them walking down some dusty street with a couple of guns, shooting people. That's all gone. Now it's more refined."

The idea of this book is to tell you about my dusty streets, so I'll keep the biographical data to a minimum. As of this writing, I am thirty-seven—I think of myself as thirty-seven going on sixty-seven. I was born June 10, 1933, in Waltham, Massachusetts, where my father was an advertising man forced to work for the WPA and my mother ran a nursery school. I am married to my former secretary, an intelligent, unreasonably attractive blonde whose given name is Froma, but who is best known as Wicki; we have a son, Scott Frederic, currently eight. I own a home in Marshfield, Massachusetts, and I fly a lot.

What else? Well, the "F" in F. Lee stands for Francis, and we'll let it go at that. I enjoy telling jokes, I'm lefthanded, I used to play hockey, and I never take vacations—doing nothing bores me. My law firm, Bailey, Alch and Gillis, has its headquarters in Boston, but there are associates in almost every state. I prefer cases that offer whopping fees and/or professional challenge. My favorite cases are the most challenging—the ones that have something to do with improving the system, with changing the law. As for fees, ours have ranged from zero to close to a million dollars. (We recently sent out a bill for that amount, and someday we may even collect it all.) About thirty percent of our cases wind up in the red—because either the expenses outweigh the fee, or the clients don't have the money. A current client, Captain Ernest Medina, is a case in point; the government gave him seventy-nine dollars for his defense.

As for my route to the criminal bar—well, I like to claim its unorthodoxy as one of the reasons for my success. When I graduated from prep school and was accepted at Harvard, my ambition was to become a writer. I was sixteen at the time and unfortunately—or, perhaps, fortunately—I was thoroughly incapable of academic dedication. After two years of getting by on "Gentleman's C's," I joined the Navy and enrolled in flight training.

Next came two experiences that pushed me from literature to law. The first was reading *The Art of Advocacy* by Lloyd Paul Stryker, an eminent New York trial lawyer, during a Christmas leave. The book, which takes the position that the defense lawyer is a dying species, attempted to interest young men in trial skills. It interested me as nothing had before. I still find it fascinating.

The second experience was the U.S. Marine Corps, to which I transferred after graduating as a naval aviator. I wanted to fly jets, and this was almost guaranteed in the Corps. I was assigned to a fighter squadron in Cherry Point, North Carolina, and as my secondary duty, I asked for assignment to the unit's legal office. I was made second assistant legal officer, which is comparable to being a taxi-squad quarterback. But then the first assistant legal officer died in a Sabrejet crash. And the chief legal officer's wife threatened to leave him if he kept flying. He wanted her more than his wings, and Lieutenant Bailey suddenly found himself chief legal officer. For the next two and a half years, until my discharge in 1956, I prosecuted, defended, judged, reviewed, and investigated cases. Although I worked within the framework of the military court-martial system, I also obtained a working knowledge of civilian practice—in the course of checking civilian court proceedings involving Marines, I had become friends with a local trial lawyer named Harvey Hamilton. He was the first teacher I ever had, and one of the best.

I moonlighted as an investigator for Harvey and also functioned as his apprentice. I saw his cases being put together in the pretrial stages, and I sat at the counsel table with him in court. When I told him I had decided to become an attorney, Harvey gave me both his approval and a piece of advice that should be passed on to anyone else who makes that decision: "You'll have to train yourself. Law schools have all but abandoned the education of trial lawyers, and the sad truth is that you'll graduate knowing very little more about the art than you do now. What you have to do is go to work for someone who's in court every day. Do that even if you have to pay him for the education. Cut classes if you have to, but *go to court.*"

In September, 1957, I began the formal study of law at Boston University. And on the day school started, I opened a business called "Investigative Service." This seemed a necessary step if I wanted to follow Harvey's advice—I'd gotten nowhere trying to join the staffs of Boston trial lawyers as even a nonpaid investigator. The surprising truth was that the city's trial lawyers did very little investigating.

The investigative service flourished. The money helped a great deal, and I supplemented my school work: as an investigator, I literally went all the way through trial with whatever lawyer was using our service. I learned the distinction between information and evidence in a way no school could teach. I saw good cross-examination and bad cross-examination, bluffs that worked and a lot that didn't. And the biggest lesson I learned was that nothing is more important than solid pretrial investigation. No matter how skillful the lawyers involved in a case, the winner is almost always the one who is best prepared, best able to put the evidence before the court. That's why the bureau that began as a law student's part-time venture is very much in operation today. It is, in fact, the backbone of my criminal practice.

Which pretty well takes care of preliminary data. Except to say that I live an accelerated life, but the action keeps me going. I enjoy being F. Lee Bailey.

2. *THE TORSO MURDER*

The woman's body had been scooped up in pieces from the Merrimack River, an otherwise innocent stream that winds through northeastern Massachusetts. The head was never found, which gave the newspapers a ready-made title: "The Torso Murder." The body was identified as that of Betty Edgerly, a Lowell, Massachusetts, housewife. Within a few weeks her husband George was indicted for her murder.

In the spring of 1960, I was finishing law school and preparing for my bar exam. All I knew about the Torso Murder was what I read in the papers. But less than a year later, I was to tell the members of a jury why they should not send George Edgerly to the electric chair. The most sensational murder case to hit Massachusetts in years would mark my first appearance as a trial lawyer. And I would enter the trial when it was already in progress—after half the evidence had been heard.

I was admitted to the bar on November 16, 1960, and for the first few months the investigative service paid the rent for my Boston office. By the following February, when the Torso Murder trial was making headlines, I had fewer than ten open files in my legal drawer.

One of them was that of Willard Page, a man accused of rape almost four years after the crime. The polygraph—or, as it is popularly and mistakenly called, the lie detector—was shaping up as an important part of Page's defense. A polygraph test had indicated that he was innocent. But in Massachusetts, like most states, polygraph results are not admissible as evidence unless both sides agree. In Page's case, the prosecution was understandably reluctant. So as I saw it, there was only one thing to do— set a precedent and establish new law by getting Page's test before a jury. After doing a great deal of research on the polygraph, I had arranged for a panel of experts to come to Boston and testify to its reliability. The trial was set for May.

Meanwhile, the Edgerly trial was titillating the public as the lurid sort of details that never fail to make news come out. Betty had once served time for rolling GIs; George was a philanderer of the first order. But the banner headline that struck me as sensational was straightforward enough: "Edgerly Flunks Lie Detector Test." A polygraph examiner had testified that Edgerly had taken a test whose results indicated his guilt. At first I thought my precedent had been set. Closer reading of the story showed that this was not the case. Under the mistaken impression that the test results favored Edgerly, his chief defense counsel, John H. Tobin, had asked that they be admitted.

The following day I got a phone call from Charlie Zimmerman, the highly experienced polygraph examiner who had tested Willard Page for me. He said the Edgerly defense wanted some quick advice on how to cross-examine the lie detector "expert" who had done in Edgerly. This was during the weekend; the cross-examination was to start on Monday. At Charlie's suggestion I went on Sunday to see John Tobin, who had suffered a seizure of some sort late Friday afternoon and was resting at his home in Cambridge. John told me what had happened, and it was clear that he was not just being outmaneuvered by the prosecution. In poker terms, he had been sandbagged.

During their investigation, police had given Edgerly two polygraph tests. Edgerly told Tobin about them, and the lawyer called Captain Michael Cullinane, the state police polygraph examiner, to check the results. Cullinane, a police officer with a well-deserved reputation for honesty, said the tests were inconclusive.

At the trial, however, one of the investigating officers spiced his testimony with repeated references to some "tests" Edgerly had taken. He was careful not to say "lie detector tests," as this would have been automatic grounds for mistrial. But the implication was clear—Edgerly had been tested on the polygraph, and the results were being withheld. Tobin then made what seemed to him to be a foolproof move; he demanded that the tests be produced. He was surprised when prosecutor Frank Monarski agreed.

Now Cullinane took the stand. He repeated what he had told Tobin: the tests had been too inconclusive to warrant any opinion. And, yes, Edgerly had been cooperative in taking them. Tobin at that point had every reason to believe that his strategy in calling for the test results had paid off.

Then the prosecution called Augustine Lawlor, a Lawrence, Massachusetts, pharmacist. A graduate of the Keeler Polygraph Institute in Chicago, Lawlor was acquiring testing experience by working free for local authorities. Lawlor testified that he, too, had tested Edgerly. He exhibited several charts and said that in his opinion, Edgerly had "not told the truth" when he denied complicity in his wife's murder.

Tobin turned angrily to his client and asked him why he hadn't mentioned the Lawlor tests. He had forgotten about them, said Edgerly. Besides, he'd been told they just represented practice for the examiner and that they proved nothing.

15

Up to this point, the prosecution had been the underdog. Now, it looked like a winner—and George Edgerly looked like a candidate for the electric chair.

Unless, of course, the defense could shake Lawlor's testimony in cross-examination.

I told John Tobin everything I knew about the polygraph, a fairly simple device first used in crude form about 1920. The modern polygraph has three components that measure physiological changes in the person being questioned. The first component is a replica of the standard blood pressure cuff used by doctors. But whereas the physician's device has a small dial that records the readings and is attached to the cuff itself, the polygraph's cuff is attached by a rubber tube to a stainless steel pen. Every time the subject's heart pumps, the pen moves up. As the blood flow ebbs, the pen moves down. The pen records on a moving paper chart that, when the test is complete, will show any changes in the subject's blood pressure as well as any variance in the frequency of his pulse beat. Both of these are significant in detecting deception.

The second component is an accordion-like expandable rubber hose that is fastened around the chest. A piece of rubber tubing connects the hose to a second steel pen on the machine. When the subject inhales and his chest expands, the pen moves up. When he exhales, it moves down. The regularity of his breathing can then be studied after the test is complete. Changes that coincide with psychologically stimulating questions can strongly indicate deception.

The third component, the galvo or GSR, measures what is known as the galvanic skin response. It consists of a highly sensitive galvanometer capable of measuring the flow of a minute electrical current. Two electrodes are placed on the skin, and the instrument measures the amount of resistance that the skin offers a current passing from one electrode to the other. This, too, is recorded by a steel pen, which swings from the top of the chart to the bottom, indicating the changes in conductivity. There are various theories about why the galvo is significant in reading truth, but I think it's fair to say that no one really knows. The most common view is that lying induces perspiration, which affects the skin's conductivity. Whatever the reason, the galvanometer is of proven value, especially with certain individuals. When a person is a good galvo reactor, many examiners will say that the other two components need not be used. Conversely, some people can tell blatant lies without significant galvo reactions.

This, then, is the machine itself. On the whole, it is dependable; the critical factor in any polygraph test is the examiner. In the United States, polygraph examiners range from experts who rarely err to rank amateurs who should be locked up for posing as experts. There are no formal educational requirements, and only fifteen or sixteen states license examiners. Consequently, in any state where examiners are not regulated, anybody can buy a machine and put up a shingle. That is why attorneys and police officers should choose polygraph examiners as carefully as most people choose doctors and accountants. A first-rate polygraph examiner must have intelligence, skill at interrogation, and considerable knowledge of both psychology and physiology.

To begin with, there are the questions. The examiner must be equipped with the known facts of a case. The right questions must be asked in the right way. The questions must all be answerable with "yes" or "no." And they should be written out before the machine is activated. The subject should at least know the areas the questions will cover. For one thing, an unexpected question may cause a reaction that has nothing to do with deception. For another, the very fact that a subject anticipated a question will cause him to build emotionally toward it and react all the more emphatically when it comes.

Because of the pressure on the upper arm's artery caused by the blood pressure cuff, tests are limited to no more than seven minutes. The subject sits with his back to both the examiner and the polygraph, so that he won't be distracted by the fluctuation of the pens. As each question is posed, a mark is made on the moving graph indicating the place where it was asked. Then a second mark is made indicating whether the subject answered "yes" or "no."

Finally, it is up to the examiner to interpret the finished chart correctly. The term "lie detector" is a misnomer; "truth verifier" would be more accurate. Essentially, the polygraph has a single function—it separates those who have told the whole truth from those who have not. This is all it can do. Anyone can pass a polygraph test—all he has to do is tell the *whole* truth. A person can tell the *literal* truth and still show deceptive responses.

By way of illustration, suppose John, suspected of killing Mary, is asked: "Did you kill Mary?" John didn't do it, but he knows who did. Or he had a secret desire to knock her off. Either way, he may react very much as if he were the killer. And he will not be able to clear himself until he tells the examiner everything.

Although civilian courts regard the polygraph as a threat to the jury system, it is widely used by law enforcement agencies and by military and industrial authorities. In some places, a suspect who passes a police polygraph test is automatically eliminated as a potential defendant. This makes good sense because it eliminates the need for indictment and trial, an experience from which few people recover even if they are acquitted. They may have been found not guilty, but so far as much as the public is concerned it was just a case of some smart lawyer getting them off. This is a flaw in our system that could be remedied with proper use of the polygraph. Maybe, I told John Tobin, the Edgerly case could help.

John Tobin was seventy-two years old; he was tired and ailing, and the trial had etched new lines of strain across his face. I was twenty-seven, a young fighter hot for combat. We talked for several hours about the polygraph. Then John stared at me.

"Lee," he said, "would you be willing to come into the case to cross-examine this guy Lawlor? I don't think there's another lawyer in Massachusetts who would recognize a lie detector if you dropped one on him. I think you could help us."

I had reason to hesitate. In the Page case, I was fighting to prove the polygraph's reliability—now Tobin was asking me to cast doubt on the results of a polygraph test. But offering me a chance to appear in the Torso Murder case was like offering the advocate inside me a slice of the moon. I said "yes."

It was evening when I left Tobin and returned to the small apartment across the street from my Boston office. I knew more than most lawyers about the polygraph, but all my research had been done from a positive viewpoint; I had never concentrated on attacking a test or its examiner. I had to go back to the books, and I had one night to do it in.

My ability to cram, a hangover from student days, stood me in good stead. So did my friends. I called Dan Bloomfield, then my chief investigator, and Phil Halloran, a law school classmate. We sat in the apartment drinking coffee and reading books on the polygraph; then Dan and Phil briefed me on the material they had studied. When we finished, the third pot of coffee was empty and the sky was getting light. It was time to get ready for court.

I put on a black suit and vest, shined my shoes, and dumped an armful of polygraph texts and some magazines into a briefcase. On the way to my first appearance as a trial lawyer, I forgot the polygraph. Instead, I reviewed everything I knew about the most devastating weapon in the trial lawyer's arsenal—cross-examination.

We all cross-examine. Parents cross-examine children, executives cross-examine subordinates, politicians cross-examine aides and each other. But for the trial lawyer, cross-examination is a deadly specialty. Through his questions, he must destroy the evidence amassed against his client—he must diminish it, limit it, explain it away. As the prosecutor tries to build, the defense counsel tries to tear down. Attorneys who don't understand this should stay out of court.

Unfortunately, they're in court every day. Most law schools teach little or nothing about cross-examination. There should be courses in the methods and principles of cross-examination, and the courses should be followed up with practice sessions. Instead, the new lawyer must learn cross-examination in real trials at the expense of real clients. To me, this makes about as much sense as it would make to let medical interns practice surgery on living people instead of cadavers.

Good cross-examination also suffers at the hands of public misunderstanding. This achieves serious proportions because it is the public that fills our jury boxes. Too many jurors are waiting for Perry Mason; they expect the lawyer to bring the witness to a point where he cries out that the defendant is innocent, that *he's* the one who killed the go-go dancer. Well, it happens—on television.

In fact, the first rule of cross-examination is DON'T. Unless the witness has said something that can be used against him, unless there is a chance that the effect of his testimony can somehow be diminished, a lawyer should smile and say: "No questions."

Until a witness is firmly committed to a definite statement or position, he can parry a question or sidestep it with some kind of explanation. The cross-examiner's first task is to pin down all that the witness claims to know about the subject and all that he says he doesn't know. What he doesn't know is equally important because it is often from the lack of evidence that reasonable doubt must flow.

Obviously, the witness has made some commitment under direct examination. But this testimony usually is brief and lacks detail. So before going on the offensive, the cross-examiner must ask questions patiently and methodically until the witness has taken some position, either positive or negative, as to everything he knows about the matter in dispute. The most common error lawyers make in cross-examination is that of immediately attacking a witness who has not been sufficiently pinioned. The result is that the witness escapes.

The cross-examination of an expert witness, which is what I was about to do, poses added problems. He's a professional who understands the trial process; he knows how much he can get away with; he knows how to answer questions. And usually, though not always, he is thoroughly versed in his field. Give an expert a broad enough question, and he may bury you. That's why a trial lawyer has to be a crammer; he has to know his stuff well enough to catch any weakness on the part of the witness.

Such was my task with Augustine Lawlor, the small-town druggist who in the space of two days had come to represent a pivotal point in my life. As I walked up the steps of the old East Cambridge courthouse that icy February morning, I thought about the drawbacks. I hadn't seen Lawlor's test charts, I had never met him, I knew little of his background or his capability as a witness. I had never cross-examined anyone before a jury. I had been in practice for less than three months.

The courtroom that was my first arena might have been built in England in the 1800s. It was high ceilinged with dark mahogany furnishings, an antique defense table, an ornate judge's bench. The acoustics were ridiculous; many of the thrill-seekers in the spectator section could barely hear what was happening. But the room was jammed all the same.

John Tobin was home in bed, and his associate counsel, Clem McCarthy, took me to the chambers of Judge Edmund R. Dewing, where I obtained permission to appear for Edgerly. The district attorney, John J. Droney, shook hands warmly; he didn't seem to think I could hurt his case.

In the courtroom I met George Edgerly. He sat in a wire cage, a barbaric contraption used until a few years ago in all Massachusetts capital cases. Edgerly, I soon discovered, had a quick sense of humor, an excellent memory for details, and an almost clinical attitude toward the trial. He made $10,000 a year as an auto mechanic, and his boss described him as both skilled and dependable. He was also a man of the world, at least his world. Some of the trial's most colorful testimony had come from his wife's sisters, who described trips George had taken with them, going into such details as who had stayed with whom in various hotels.

Edgerly examined me from inside his cage. "You think you can tear this lie detector guy apart?"

"I don't know," I said, "but I'll sure give it a try."

"Okay," he said. "I hope you know what you're doing. He sure doesn't or he would of never said I was lying. I didn't kill my wife."

For the moment, I had to take Edgerly at his word. I had to presume that Augustine Lawlor had made a mistake, or that he hadn't gone far enough in his testing. I might at least be able to establish that although Edgerly's reactions did not show innocence, neither did they prove guilt.

Now court was in session, and Augustine Lawlor and I faced each other. Lawlor was in his middle thirties, scholarly-looking, very erect. He didn't seem the least bit nervous. I introduced myself to the jury, explained that John Tobin was sick, and summarized the testimony Lawlor had given on Friday.

"Mr. Lawlor," I said, "it is correct to say that the so-called lie detector, or polygraph, does not detect lies. Is that right?"

Lawlor hesitated, glanced at Frank Monarski, and then answered. "Yes, that's correct."

I saw the jurors react. Monarski had laid very little foundation for the polygraph technique in his direct examination of Lawlor, and the jurors were startled by what seemed to them a surprising disclosure.

It was essential to establish what polygraph texts Lawlor, as an expert, might regard as authoritative. Unlike a lay witness, an expert is permitted to give an opinion or conclusion. If he endorses a text or professional publication in his field, he may be questioned closely on it, and may say something that contradicts the book. In many instances he will have a hard time explaining the contradiction.

Very few books have been written on the subject of polygraph testing. The one generally considered most authoritative was written by Fred E. Inbau, a Northwestern University law professor, and John E. Reid, one of the country's top examiners. I showed a copy of that book to Lawlor and asked whether he had read it.

"I've read most of it," he said.

"Do you regard it as authoritative?"

"No," said the prosecutor's expert. "I do not."

"Tell me, Mr. Lawlor, is there any book on the subject of polygraph testing that you regard as authoritative?"

I walked to the defense table and put my hand on a stack of about eight books. I'm sure Lawlor thought all of them were books on the polygraph, which is precisely what I wanted him to think. A few of them actually were.

"No . . . no, I can't think of any such books."

"Have you written a book on the subject, by chance?"

"No, I haven't."

"Have you written any articles for any of the police or crime detection publications?"

"No." He was beginning to look irritated.

"You have of course read such articles, and know that a number have been published from time to time?"

"Yes, I have read some of them."

"Are there any articles you regard as authoritative?" I reached into my briefcase and began to draw out magazines.

"No. There are none that I remember that I regard as an authority in the field."

Gus Lawlor seemed immovable. But I had another lever.

"I understand, Mr. Lawlor, that you use a Keeler polygraph?"

"Yes."

"You regard the Keeler as a reliable instrument, do you not?"

"Yes, I would say so."

"And you consider the Keeler company as expert in the teaching and manufacturing of polygraphs, is that correct?"

"Yes."

"What model do you use—would it be a 6303?"

"It is."

There was something else I wanted to establish here. "That, by the way, is a *three*-pen machine, isn't it?"

"Yes."

"Now then, when you bought your instrument, did you receive a handbook on its use and the administration of polygraph tests published by the manufacturer?"

"Yes, the handbook came with it."

"Good. Now, having in mind your opinion that the Keeler company knows what it's doing in the field of polygraph testing, wouldn't you say that at least their handbook on how to run the instrument is an authoritative publication?"

Lawlor sighed. He had to commit himself. "Yes," he said, "the handbook is authoritative."

"You have read the handbook, of course?"

"Yes."

I moved close to the witness stand and showed him a standard handbook for a Keeler 6303 polygraph. "Your copy is just like the one I am holding here?"

"It is."

"And it is your practice, no doubt, to conduct your polygraph examinations in the manner that this handbook recommends?"

"Well, yes," he replied. "I go by it pretty much."

I had pinned him down on one item. And then I used another basic tactic of cross-examination: I dropped the subject. There was something in the Keeler handbook I intended to use, but not while Gus Lawlor was thinking about it.

"With respect to your practice as a polygraph expert, Mr. Lawlor, I take it this is not a full-time occupation?"

"No," he said, "it's not full-time."

"You are a *druggist* by profession?"

"I am a pharmacist."

"You make most of your income from the business of druggery—er, excuse me, pharmacy?"

"Yes."

"And when I say most of your income, I mean ninety-nine percent. Would that be correct?"

Lawlor nodded.

"That is because, is it not, you are not *paid* for the testing you do?"

"I run my tests free, yes. I have an interest in law enforcement."

"Many other examiners run tests for law enforcement officials, do they not?"

"Yes."

"And many of them charge for their testing, true?"

Again, Lawlor nodded.

Now I was ready to get back to the handbook. Prior testimony had suggested that due to an excess of boozing—and, by innuendo, wenching—

Edgerly had not been in the best shape during some of the interrogation sessions. "Mr. Lawlor," I asked, "it is true, is it not, that on the morning you tested George he appeared to have, shall we say, a bit of a hangover?"

"He may have."

"Well, he told you that he hadn't slept much the night before, isn't that right?"

'I believe he mentioned it."

"You wanted the tests to be as accurate as possible?"

"Of course."

"And you wanted the tests to be fair to Edgerly, didn't you?"

"I always try very hard to be fair to the subject."

I turned to the counsel table, and scooped up the Keeler handbook. "In this book," I said, waving it at him, "in this very book it says that in any proper polygraph test the subject must be well rested and in good physical condition. You know that, don't you?"

Lawlor glanced at Monarski. "I believe it says that."

"And you agree that this is so, don't you?"

"Yes, I suppose so."

"But you nonetheless ran a test on George Edgerly, knowing that he had neither complete rest nor good physical condition?"

No answer.

"In a *murder* case, Mr. Lawlor, did you run this polygraph test knowing that the subject was not fit physically? Did you do that in a *murder* case?"

"I was not told that it was a murder case," he answered frostily. "I thought it was a missing persons case."

"Do you mean, Mr. Lawlor—do you mean that when you tested this defendant you did not know that he was supposed to have killed his wife? Is that what you mean?"

"Well, yes—in a sense. I mean, I could only go on what I was told."

"Of course," I said sympathetically. "Had you known that this was a murder case, and that you might be called upon to testify, you would have insisted on more stringent conditions for the test, wouldn't you?"

Yes, said Lawlor, he would have. I decided to stop.

It was almost time for the morning recess. I had not yet said anything about Lawlor's test charts, although I had been dying to get a look at them. "By the way, Mr. Lawlor," I said, "do you have with you those graphs, or whatever they are, that you made when you ran the *missing person* test on the defendant?"

Lawlor produced two polygrams.

At 11:30 A.M., after an hour and a half of cross-examination, Judge Dewing called the morning recess. I had fifteen minutes to study the charts and the lists of questions that had been put to Edgerly.

23

A close look at the charts showed that Edgerly had a right to complain. They were much too inconclusive to warrant any opinions, expert or otherwise.

When the recess was over, I took Lawlor through a description of the principles of polygraph testing and we discussed the three components of the machine. Lawlor had used the blood-pressure cuff and the pneumograph, but not the galvanometer. Actually, earlier machines had no galvo and some examiners questioned its usefulness. But I was not about to point that out.

"You told us your machine had three pens, Mr. Lawlor?"

Lawlor looked uneasy. "Yes," he said. "It has."

"And when you attended the Keeler School you were taught to use all three?"

"Yes."

"I notice that in testing the defendant you elected to omit the galvanometer that you earlier explained. Is that so?"

"No, I didn't use it."

"Tell the jury why."

I was taking a chance. Generally, cross-examiners avoid "what," "when," "where," "why," and "how" questions, all of which give the witness, especially the expert, far too much latitude. But I felt that there was no way for Lawlor to talk himself out of the corner into which I had pushed him.

"I believe," he said, "that the galvanometer adds very little to the test and may in fact confuse it. It is nowhere near as dependable as the other two components, and I don't like to rely on it."

"You were taught how to use it?"

"Yes."

"Would it be fair to say, Mr. Lawlor, that your reason for omitting the use of the GSR is your concern that you might not be able to competently determine the results of its tracing? That you really don't understand it?"

"That is not the reason at all. I can read it perfectly well!"

I turned to his charts, which I had pinned to the blackboard next to the witness stand so that the jurors could see them. There is nothing more frustrating for a juror than to have a lawyer go into a long discussion of some photograph or document the jury cannot see.

With the charts in view, I asked Lawlor to point out the responses where he felt Edgerly had not told the truth about his wife's disappearance. He indicated several.

"Do you believe, Mr. Lawlor, that the defendant's name is George?"

"Why yes. . . . I have no reason to believe otherwise. . . ."

"Would you point to that portion of the chart where you put the question to him: 'Is your name George?' "

Lawlor took the pointer and complied. "I see that when you asked this question there was a rise in the defendant's blood pressure," I said. "Do you say that the defendant's answer was untruthful?"

"No," said Lawlor, "I do not consider that to indicate deception."

"But his blood pressure did rise, as your chart indicates?"

"Well, yes, it did rise some—but not neecssarily deception."

"Might his, er, poor physical condition account for the change we see here?"

"Yes, it very well could."

"To be fair, then, might we not say that the same poor physical condition could account for all of the similar responses we see on both of these charts?"

Lawlor was boxed in. The word "fair" challenges the heart of an expert's integrity.

"It could," he conceded, "but in my opinion there is a difference between the responses to the various questions. . . ."

I'm sure that he was more than willing to explain, but I wasn't about to give him the chance. If Monarski had been fully briefed on the polygraph, he might encourage Lawlor to elaborate on redirect. For instance, Lawlor could discuss the pneumograph pattern, which showed somewhat more damaging reactions than the blood pressure lines. As it was, Monarski decided to let well enough alone. I stopped, and there was no redirect examination.

If I had done nothing else, I'd pleased my client. "That was pretty good," George Edgerly said. "How about sticking around until the case is over?"

I thanked him, but told him I had just come in to handle the polygraph evidence, and that I was sure John Tobin would be back with him soon. The judge called a recess for lunch, and I was through with the Edgerly case. At least, I thought I was.

I lunched with two friends, feeling both glad and sorry that the encounter with Lawlor was over. In any case, I thought, I hadn't made a fool of myself. And I had established some ground for doubt.

I couldn't resist returning in the afternoon as a spectator. I wanted to hear McCarthy's opening statement. He told the jury the defense case would be built around the testimony of George Edgerly himself. Using the testimony of other witnesses as to when and where they had last seen Betty, he would show that Betty had been seen alive after the time of death claimed by the state.

I was about to return to my office when John Tobin called to say he'd had favorable reports about the Lawlor cross-examination. Would I like to stay with the case and handle some of the witnesses?

The trial had been going on for two weeks, and a lot of ground had already been covered. But it was like asking a kid singer who's been playing roadhouses if he'd like a shot on the *Ed Sullivan Show*.

I didn't need any urging to say yes.

My first asignment from John Tobin was to handle a witness I'll call Louis DuBois. Although his real name appears in the trial transcript, I'm changing it to spare him any more misery than he's already suffered. Louis DuBois put himself on the line in coming into the case, and what happened to him was a damned shame.

DuBois was a figure out of Betty Edgerly's checkered past. She and DuBois were ex-business associates; he had been sentenced to jail, along with Betty, for rolling GIs some years before. After his release, DuBois went straight. He married, got a steady job, and won the respect of his neighbors, most of whom were unaware of his criminal record.

When the Edgerly trial opened, DuBois had a difficult decision to make. He had seen Betty Edgerly on the street in Lowell six weeks after she was supposed to have been murdered. He had gone to the police at the time, but his involvement was not made public, and the defense knew nothing about him. Appearing as a witness would mean his exposure as an ex-convict, notoriety and perhaps shame for his family. But if George Edgerly got the electric chair, Louis DuBois would always wonder whether his testimony could have made a difference. When the trial was in progress, DuBois contacted the defense and told his story.

He repeated it on the stand, and he was a beautiful witness. His manner was quiet but forthright, and his answers were convincing. He testified that when he was agonizing over the consequences of getting involved in the case, he had first gone to a priest for advice. The priest had gone with him to the Lowell station house.

Monarski stepped forward to cross-examine, a piece of paper in his hand. He looked confident.

"You claim, Mr. DuBois," he said, "that you talked with Lieutenant Wilson in the presence of this priest, is that so?"

"Yes, I did."

Now Monarski waved the piece of paper at DuBois. "Have you at some time signed a statement for the Lowell police?"

DuBois looked down. "Yes, I did."

"Is this your signature at the bottom of the statement?"

DuBois nodded.

"And in this statement do you not say that you did not get a good

26

look at the woman you thought was Betty Edgerly on the day in question, and could never be sure that it was she?"

DuBois nodded again, and Monarski sat down. It was my turn. DuBois had never told me about the statement, and I had to try to repair the damage in redirect examination. Almost sobbing, DuBois testified that police had told him to sign a statement or else. They said that exposure of his past could only bring him trouble, that the best way to stay uninvolved was to become a "nonwitness." He signed the statement.

But now he had chosen to get involved. He was willing to say under oath that the statement to the police was a conscious falsification, and that his testimony was fact. It took courage, which I felt had to impress the jury.

John Tobin agreed with me, but he began an intensive search for the priest who had accompanied DuBois to the precinct house, and who had since been transferred to a parish outside the state.

Tobin also asked me to handle the direct examination of George Edgerly. Edgerly's testimony was crucial. If the defendant sits on the stand, invariably he is his own star witness—if the jury believes him when he says he didn't do it, his acquittal is certain.

Obviously, the questioning of George Edgerly was a rare opportunity as well as a challenge for a young lawyer just starting to practice. And it was a chance to do something for John Tobin. There was a real fear on the part of everyone involved in the trial that the strain of taking Edgerly through his story could be too much for John.

There were also manifest drawbacks in my taking on the assignment. I had not seen half the trial. I was not aware of what evidence had had the greatest impact on the jury. I could read the transcript, but if I spent the time studying all seventeen hundred pages, I would have little if any time to go over the case with Edgerly. And that was vital for both of us— for me, because the facts as the defendant knows them are often quite different from the facts supplied by the other witnesses; for Edgerly, because if I put him on the stand cold, he would have trouble knowing what I was driving at with each question.

Except for occasional references, I decided to forget about the transcript. I would stick with Edgerly himself; he had both an excellent memory and, for a layman, an almost uncanny sense of what was significant as evidence. I would let George do it—I would rely on him to tell me what testimony had been given that required explanation or rebuttal.

All through that night, and the next two nights, my secretary (and wife-to-be) and I worked with Edgerly. The jailkeeper and his wife, who lived on the prison grounds, let us use their home and even helped keep us going with coffee and sandwiches. I questioned Edgerly, and Wicki took down everything in shorthand. Bit by bit, we assimilated the facts of the Torso Murder case.

The background was relevant. George and Betty Edgerly had had more a truce than a marriage. If it was correct to say George strayed, you would have to say Betty traveled. She was likely to disappear for days and then return home without any explanation of where she'd been. George's motto on these occasions was live and let live; he didn't ask questions.

The night she disappeared, they had gone to dinner at a restaurant not far from the coast. This was in December, 1959, and it was snowing as they drove home. Although they had not argued, Betty was sullen on the ride back and seemed upset. George suspected that she might have been having an affair at the time, and that this could have caused her moodiness. But if he was right, he had no clue to the identity of the other man.

As they were driving through Lowell, their car got stuck on a grade on the slippery road. George left Betty in the car and went to get help. At the top of the rise, he spotted an orange truck plowing the street but was unable to flag it down. When he returned to the car he found it empty. He looked around for Betty and called her name. What the hell, he thought, Betty had disappeared on him before. This time, he never saw her again.

Edgerly insisted that he had no reason to kill his wife and added that the prosecution had failed to show any strong motive. He told us Betty had some friends who might have been involved in the sale of narcotics. There was a possibility that she had come to know too much about their operations and was killed as a potential risk. But he didn't have enough solid information for us to put this theory before the jury.

Edgerly also discussed the testimony that had already been given by other witnesses. His perception and grasp of nuance were amazing as he went into details of who said what, how they said it, and how the jury reacted. For long stretches I simply listened, occasionally nodding at Wicki to indicate that something should be underlined.

When we left the jail the first night, we had more than enough material for the first day's testimony. Since there wasn't time to have the shorthand notes transcribed before court opened, I got permission from Judge Dewing to allow Wicki to sit at the counsel table with me. The press immediately named her "Della Street."

Edgerly was on the stand for two days. He told his story the way he had told it to me at the jail; not a fact was changed.

When Monarski's turn to cross-examine came, the tension in the courtroom reached a high point. All the curious were waiting to see whether George Edgerly would crumble. Monarski, experienced and capable, carried a thick pad of notes. He probed for inconsistencies, he searched meticulously for shadows of doubt. When the cross-examination began, Edgerly was up against the wall. When it ended, he had stood up well.

The next morning I got a phone call from an attorney for whom I had conducted investigations. He made a few remarks about young lawyers who start at the top with murder cases, and then came to the point. He was calling for a woman client who was afraid her name was about to come out in the Edgerly case. Around the time of Betty Edgerly's disappearance, his client had gotten somewhat stoned in a bar and had left with a drinking companion. They stopped on the way home and found themselves together in the back seat of the car he was driving, but their attempted coupling was halted by his discovery that she was having her period. Later she learned that her new acquaintance had borrowed the car from an old buddy—George Edgerly.

At this point in his narrative, the attorney, a man I both liked and respected, paused and asked whether the story rang a bell.

"Sure," I said. "The prosecution put in evidence that blood was found in the back seat of George's car, and hinted strongly that it was Betty's. I've got to prove it wasn't. The boyfriend's going to testify."

"Look, Lee," he said, "the girl is in the middle of a messy divorce, and this could ruin her. Leave her name out of it, can't you? The way it looked in the papers, you've got it beat anyway."

"For chrissake, Ed," I said, "I can't leave out any evidence that might explain the blood. Suppose I don't put it in and they convict him? What do I do then? Go to the judge and ask for a new trial because I deliberately withheld some evidence?"

"Oh, come off it," he said. "It's not going to be that important. They haven't identified the type of blood or anything, have they? This is a decent girl who never even met Edgerly. Why do you have to drag her through the mud?"

"I'm sorry, Ed. This guy has to testify. He won't mention the girl's name, but Monarski can demand it on cross. There's nothing I can do."

"Oh bullshit!" he yelled, and hung up.

Actually, the favor he asked was not unreasonable. Many times, a lawyer will try to avoid hurting an innocent third party. But not when the defendant's life is at stake. I put the evidence in, and I presume the woman suffered some embarrassment. Defending a murder case is one of the best ways I know to lose friends.

At Edgerly's urging I had turned up another witness who saw Betty after she was supposed to have been killed. The witness was sure of his identification; he testified he had been dancing with her. We also brought in the weather reports for the night Betty disappeared and the records of a snow-removal contractor—an orange plow had been exactly where Edgerly said it was that night. After tying up as many loose ends as possible, we rested our case.

Monarski announced that he had a rebuttal witness, and the Torso Murder case took another twist. The witness was Lieutenant Wilson of the Lowell police—the officer to whom Louis DuBois had gone with a priest to report spotting Betty Edgerly on the street.

"The whole story is false," Wilson told the jury. "DuBois did not come to me and report seeing Betty. There was never such a meeting with the priest."

It was hard to imagine that a police officer would lie about such a matter. But I found it even harder to believe that Louis DuBois was lying.

I turned to Leonard Mullen, an associate defense counsel who was a longtime colleague of Tobin's. "We'd better find that priest fast," I said. "If the jury believes this cop, they'll have to believe we dreamed up DuBois. They might convict on that alone."

I stood up to cross-examine Wilson.

"You did meet Mr. DuBois at some point, Lieutenant?"

"Sure," said Wilson. "I took his statement where he said he didn't see Betty Edgerly. But that was after we found her body, long after."

"And you do know the priest he claims was with him when he met you, do you not?"

Wilson nodded. "I know him. He was a good friend. But I never met him with DuBois."

Challenging Wilson on the statement that DuBois said he had been pressured into signing, I failed to rattle him. Wilson, it seemed, had put the prosecution back in the lead.

There was other rebuttal, but nothing comparable to Wilson's testimony. All of us were depressed, except Edgerly. He was furious. "Where in hell is that priest?" he raged.

By that evening the priest had been located in upstate New York. He wouldn't discuss the case by phone, but he would come to East Cambridge the next morning. All we could do was wait. We had no sure way of knowing whose credibility he would destroy—Lieutenant Wilson's, the cop's, or Louis DuBois's. We did know that if he destroyed Louis DuBois, he would also probably destroy George Edgerly.

The next morning we waited at court for half an hour, but there was no word about what action the priest had taken. Then a court officer summoned us to Judge Dewing's chambers. John Droney and Frank Monarski sat against one wall; Tobin, McCarthy, Mullen, and I sat against the other.

"Gentlemen," said the judge, "I have conferred with this priest at his specific request, and because, as I understand it, both sides wished me to do so. Is that correct?" We nodded.

"He has told me that he does know Lieutenant Wilson, and that he does know Dubois. I have explained the conflicting testimony, and he says that Wilson is not telling the truth, but that what DuBois has said is completely true."

It was impossible for the defense to keep quiet in the face of such good news, but Judge Dewing stopped us short.

"Just a minute," he said. "It's not quite that simple. It appears that Lieutenant Wilson called the Father last night, and asked him not to come to this court because he would be destroyed by the Father's testimony. The Father feels that this was in the nature of a priest-penitent disclosure and is unwilling to testify to this fact. Indeed, he is not anxious to testify at all, and since he did not come here under subpoena, he may not be compelled to testify. Any suggestions?"

I knew what I wanted. I wanted the priest put on the stand. I wanted Wilson's hide. The penalty for perjury in a capital case was life imprisonment, and that was what the lying bastard deserved. On the other hand, I felt that a clergyman ought to have protection against having to testify to something told him in confidence.

Tobin, however, had been around a great deal longer than I had, and he knew juries better. He agreed to compromise with a stipulation—a statement, agreed to by opposing counsel, which could be used to replace testimony. Ordinarily, it is not an agreement as to the truth of what it states, but only means that if the witness is called, such will be his testimony. Either side may then argue that the testimony stipulated to is not the truth.

"That seems like a sensible solution," said Judge Dewing.

Tobin was sure that a simple statement to the effect that the priest did recall the stationhouse meeting and corroborated DuBois in every important detail would be enough.

I realized Tobin was probably right, but I didn't want to give in completely. "John," I whispered. "You can bet they want a stipulation more than we do. Only it will close the evidence. If we present final argument this afternoon, Monarski will have all night to pick through it and give us the business in the morning. Let's agree to stipulate if they'll agree to suspend until tomorrow."

He grinned at me. "Very good," he said. "You'll be a lawyer yet." He explained our terms, and the prosecution agreed. The jury was informed in open court that if the priest had appeared, he would have corroborated DuBois. As dramatic endings go, it wasn't bad. Now only the final shouting remained, and we had to decide who would shout for George Edgerly. In some states, each lawyer involved in the case is allowed to make his own summation; in Massachusetts, each side gets just one summation and one man.

I wanted to be our man. Maybe it gets back to that question interviewers invariably ask me: what makes me run? I burn, dammit, that's why. I like to run. But this was John Tobin's case, and I knew the decision wasn't mine to make.

When we asked Edgerly how he felt, he left it up to John. "If you feel up to it," he told Tobin, "you're my lawyer. But if you want the kid to do it, it's okay with me. I don't want you to kill yourself with this case."

Tobin was silent for long minutes. Finally, he turned to me. "You think you know the evidence well enough to sum it up—even the part you didn't hear?"

"I think I do." I had read the transcript and had gone over all the testimony with George.

"All right," he said. He seemed tired and a little relieved. "We'll come to your office tonight and go over it with you. You make an outline of what you think should be covered. You'll do the talking."

By the time we met, I knew my way. I'd learned long before the Edgerly trial that the best defense is a good offense. So far as I was concerned, Edgerly had been arrested and indicted simply because no other suspect could be found, and because it was politically expedient to come up with *some* solution to a frightening crime. It was not entirely irrelevant that a number of officials, including the district attorney, had been up for election between the time Edgerly was indicted and tried. To the public, mere arrest implies solution—the general feeling being that the law enforcement agencies have done their job, and the trial is just a game. And the American people do not equate jury acquittal with innocence. That's one of the reasons a criminal lawyer doesn't win popularity contests.

And so the Torso Murder case came down to a bitter cold March morning when I stood before a packed courtroom and looked from one juror to another—hoping I was finding something receptive in each face. "Ladies and gentlemen," I began, "this is the beginning of the end of the Edgerly Case. . . ."

I spoke for two hours; it was the longest summation I have ever given, and probably the longest I will ever give. I covered all the aspects of a criminal trial that I knew; I went into the responsibilities of the jury, of counsel, of the judge. I turned over every piece of evidence. I castigated Wilson and his prosecution allies for everything they had done, especially for the rebuttal perjury. I denounced political influence. At one point, I walked over to the D.A. and shouted: "Here's a man so callous as to try to put a man in the electric chair for something he didn't do just in order to get reelected." I denounced everything but the American flag.

When I sat down, Tobin patted me on the shoulder. "That was good," he whispered.

I was physically whipped; I was almost glad to let Monarski have the floor. He argued skillfully, picking at weaknesses in our case. At times I felt like jumping up and reminding the jury that the prosecution, not the defense, shouldered the burden of proof. When he finished there was a brief recess, and then Judge Dewing gave his charge.

Our system calls for the jury to determine what the facts are, and then to apply to those facts whatever law the trial judge describes as appropriate. Unfortunately, we operate ass backward. Before the jurors have been able to discuss the testimony or vote on it, they're flooded with more rules of law than a bright law student might be expected to learn in a month.

Looking at the transcript, I would have a difficult time picking out a solid error in Judge Dewing's instructions. But at the time, they seemed slanted toward the prosecution. The judge was a former prosecutor, and perhaps it was his inflections that bothered me. Perhaps it was my own fervor as a defense lawyer. Whatever the reason, I took exception to the charge on the ground that it was slanted in favor of the state. The judge nodded without comment. He knew such an exception was meaningless under Massachusetts law.

The jury went out shortly before 4:00 P.M. Observing what was considered local tradition in East Cambridge, I walked across the street to wait in the Esquire Bar.

The press was there in force, its members in the relaxed frame of mind that is their style when juries are out. They took pity on a young advocate who was breaking his back to look casual and not having much success. They even bought the drinks, perhaps recognizing that whereas their pay was miniscule, mine was nothing at all.

The court officers in East Cambridge all know enough to call the Esquire when a jury comes in. Whenever the phone rang, I jumped in my seat. At about 7:00 P.M., Eddie Corsetti of the *Boston Record-American* nudged me and said: "Quit worrying. The jury will be in at two in the morning with an acquittal."

Other reporters varied in their estimates of time and verdict. Most of those who bet on conviction figured it would be in the second degree. I kept fidgeting and drinking Scotch. I had done little boozing in the service, and I couldn't afford liquor while I was in law school. But I drank like fourteen fishes while the Edgerly jury deliberated. Interestingly enough, the liquor had little effect on me. Perhaps it had something to do with tension. Or with adrenalin. All I know is that most trial lawyers drink. And the good ones can hold their booze.

33

Hours later, the phone rang for what seemed the thousandth time. The jury was ready. In the courtroom, we waited for the judge to come back from his hotel. When he finally ascended the bench and the jurors filed into their box, it was two o'clock in the morning.

The clerk took the written verdict from the foreman of the jury. He read it, turned toward the jury, and asked: "Mr. Foreman, how say you? Is the defendant guilty or not guilty?"

The next second bordered on forever. And then: "We find the defendant, George Edgerly, not guilty."

The exhilaration mounted slowly. Shouting, back-pounding, and then it all broke loose and I was soaring. I was all alone in a velvet sky, and the weather was wonderful. How about that Eddie Corsetti? I would buy him a drink, and one for Wicki, and one for myself, and . . .

EPILOGUE

The night had been a melange of television cameras and microphones and gin in paper cups and George Edgerly wearing the only grin in the room bigger than mine. But now it was the morning after the verdict, and my phone was ringing. "Lee," said a voice, "the power company just cut off our electricity. You haven't paid the bill for three months."

The following Sunday, my mother was in church. One of the front-row spinsters approached her and said she had read about me in the papers.

"Yes," said my mother, full of pride. "Lee just tried a murder case."

"Well, it's nice that he has some cases," said the spinster. "I suppose when he's starting out, he has to take whatever kind of cases he can get."

3. THAT'S THE MAN!

It was a November night in 1956. The car door was yanked open; and the dashboard light came on. A man in a dark jacket was pointing a .45 automatic at Roger Saloman and Janet Sullivan, two teenagers parked in a wooded area on the outskirts of Worcester, Massachusetts. He ordered them out of the car and marched them across a dirt road. Then he slammed Roger across the back of the head. As the boy crumpled unconscious to the ground, he grabbed Janet and started tearing at her clothes. When she tried to fight him off, he smashed her in the mouth with the pistol, knocking out two of her teeth. He raped her, and disappeared into the woods.

After obtaining medical treatment, Roger and Janet told their story to police. They described the rapist: he had crew-cut brown hair and was about five feet seven, their own height. They went over hundreds of mug shots of known sex offenders, but could not find the face of their attacker.

Three and a half years later, on June 28, 1960, Roger and Janet were parked at a drive-in restaurant in Worcester. When Janet noticed another couple waiting for service about twenty feet away, she took a second look and nudged Roger. "Do you see who I see?"

Roger looked up from his milkshake to the man in the other car. "My God, you're right. It does look like him." They watched the man a while longer, made a note of the car's license plate number, and went to the police. They were almost sure they had just seen their assailant.

The car checked out to a gas station attendant named Willard Page. The law lost no time putting the boot to him. He was picked up without being told what crime he was accused of. Before attempting a formal identification, the police led him into an interrogation room and had Roger and Janet look at him through a one-way mirror. Then he was put in a lineup with several other men, none of whom even slightly resembled him. By this time Roger and Janet were positive. That's the man, they said.

They had originally described the rapist as brown-haired and about five seven. Page—who denied any knowledge of the attack—was more than six feet tall and had long, curly blond hair. But he was charged with rape and with assault with a dangerous weapon, and locked in jail.

I had taken my bar examination the day Roger and Janet spotted

Page at the drive-in. My introduction to the case was as an investigator—a few days after Page's arrest, his brother-in-law called our service. I was going to Canada to take a few days off, and I turned the case over to Dan Bloomfield. "This one looks like a weirdo," I told him.

When I returned, I was surprised to find Dan excited over the Page case. "Dammit, Lee," he said, "I think this guy's innocent, and he's going to be convicted."

Page, who served as an M.P. in Germany, had been discharged from the Army shortly before the teenagers were attacked. Photos taken of him a few weeks before and after his discharge showed him with long blond hair. Then there was the height discrepancy between the victims' original description of their assailant and Willard himself.

Still, Dan felt that Page would be convicted because Roger and Janet would stick to their guns. "Page makes a good appearance, but those kids are more than a match for him," he told me. "They're sharp, they're a handsome pair, and I'm sure they think they're telling the truth."

Of course, Page would take the stand and deny everything. But he had the best reason in the world to lie—his freedom was at stake. There was no reason for Janet and Roger to lie. And jurors usually tend to believe eyewitness identifications—another weakness in our system. Mistaken identifications are the greatest single cause of wrongful convictions. Every time someone is convicted on an uncorroborated eyewitness identification, the odds are fifty-fifty that justice has miscarried.

In recent years, the U.S. Supreme Court has limited the circumstances under which lineups can be used, a step in the right direction. Lineup identifications are among the most vicious practices permitted by our system. The idea is for the eyewitness to pick someone out of a group of people similar in size, dress, and appearance. But the victim of a violent crime rarely knows for sure which of even two look-alikes was his assailant. In many cases the victim, confused and excited, has neither the time nor the capability to memorize the attacker's features. Often the attack takes place in the dark. And where a gun is involved, the victim rarely sees anything other than its muzzle.

A lineup, bad news in itself, becomes criminal when police pull tricks like the sneak peek afforded Roger Saloman and Janet Sullivan. This is as much a fraud on the court as is perjury, but it happens. Or there are times when the officer running the lineup tries to help the witness out with a little whispered advice. "Take a good look at the third guy from the right, we've got other evidence that he's the one."

So Willard Page looked like a loser because two sincere young Americans were willing to swear he was a vicious rapist. An alibi? As yet, Page didn't have one, which was to be expected—how many people can say with certainty where they were on a particular night more than three years ago? And even when an alibi exists, it's not much help, unless it includes unimpeachable witnesses. A man's wife testifies that on the night of the crime he was home with her watching television; the average juror figures the wife is probably lying to save her husband from imprisonment. The juror neither remembers nor considers the fact that *he* was home watching television with his wife that same night. And in Massachusetts, there's an extra twist—the jury must be instructed to scrutinize alibi evidence very carefully on the grounds that such evidence may be the result of connivance, subornation, or perjury. That's like sending a batter up to the plate blindfolded, but it's the law.

"We'll need something awfully good to get anywhere," I told Dan Bloomfield. "Unless he was confined in a hospital or in some other place where records are kept, anything you find will be highly suspect. I don't think Page is going to win his case on alibi. And by the way, how is he fixed financially?"

"He doesn't make much, he's got domestic problems, and his relatives aren't all that well fixed, although I'm sure they'll scrape the barrel for him. But my inclination is to make the effort even if we have to put most of it on the cuff—this man needs all the help he can get."

"I'll go along with that," I said, "but I'd hate to find out later that he's taken us for a ride." Then the idea came to me. "How do you think he'd react to a lie detector test? They used to work pretty good when I was in the Marine Corps."

"I don't know," Dan said, "but let's find out."

A day or two later Page came into my office with his sister and her husband. He fit Dan's description—tall and lanky with long, curly blond hair and eyes that crinkled when he smiled. I asked him if he was willing to take a lie detector test. "Sure," he said. "The police asked me to take one when they first brought me in, but when I agreed they dropped the whole idea."

"The police," I said, "are double bastards. They sandbagged the lineup, and then passed up a polygraph test that would have told them right away whether you were guilty. Police turn suspects loose every day on the strength of lie detector tests. I'll set it up next week."

The test showed that Page was a highly reactive subject. It also showed that he was clean. Asked whether he had raped a girl named Janet Sullivan, he showed no reaction at all. "He's a cinch to nail where his involvement is either total or none at all," said John Conrad, the highly experienced examiner who administered the test. "He doesn't know anything about the affair."

Page had the wrong attitude from the beginning; he suffered from the delusion that because he was innocent he would be acquitted. Now he figured he was home free, that the case would be dismissed. After all, the police had asked him to take a lie detector test; it made sense that they'd be willing to accept the one he'd just taken. I began his education in practical justice by explaining that police are apt to show flexibility where polygraph tests are concerned. If they want to announce that a suspect has been cleared, they say he passed a lie detector test with flying colors. But if a suspect they have decided to prosecute passes a test on his own, they say it's not admissible in court.

When I suggested that Page's lawyer show the test results to the district attorney and ask that a polygraph exam be given by the state police, we were told that state police wouldn't test anyone after he had been arrested. Ideally, police should have a continuing interest in determining a man's innocence. But expediency dictates otherwise. The prohibition probably was motivated by fear of a false arrest action, or by the embarrassment of having to prosecute someone cleared by a police polygraph test.

Nevertheless, the polygraph was becoming focal in Page's defense. Several days before I was to be sworn in as an attorney, I got a call from Page's sister. Would I take over the case? Page's lawyer felt he didn't know enough about the lie detector to try to get the test results into evidence. After checking with him, I agreed. I had just gotten my license, but why start small? Why not make law in my first case? Massachusetts had never sanctioned polygraph evidence, but it had never refused it either. I would try to get Page's test before a jury.

I had plenty of enthusiasm if little financial resource (as I remember, we had less than $200 to work with), and I started writing every polygraph authority I knew of. I described Page's plight, I explained what I was trying to do for the polygraph. The response was good. Little by little, we began to compile an impressive list of witnesses for the trial.

Meanwhile, I had another idea—hypnosis, a technique that would later produce a dramatic encounter with the Boston Strangler. I had heard of people demonstrating total recall under hypnosis; if Page were hypnotized, he might remember where he was the night of the assault. Hell, we had nothing to lose.

Dr. Robert Mezer, a prominent legal psychiatrist and one of my former law school professors, agreed to hypnotize Page. And things started looking good for the home team. Under hypnosis, Page went back in time. He believed that on the day of the attack he had attended the grand opening of a new bowling alley in the Worcester suburb of Shrewsbury. He even supplied the names of people who were there and might remember his presence. Dan hurried to Shrewsbury to check out the story. There had been a grand opening, all right. The day of the week was correct. So was the month of the year. But there was just one problem: the bowling alley had opened exactly seven days before the attack on Roger and Janet.

Back to the polygraph. We became lay experts on polygraphs and law; we analyzed almost every judicial decision relevant to the device. There were some cases where test results had been admitted by agreement of both sides, but only one in which results had been received into evidence because the judge was satisfied as to their reliability. And that had not resulted in any change of law. The criterion, going all the way back to a 1923 decision, continued to be "general scientific acceptability." Turning those words around, we'd have to prove that polygraph testing was accepted by "science generally."

Consequently, the authorities I would produce as witnesses had to be impeccable. And they were; I lined up what amounted to a polygraph all-star team, five experts willing to try and win one for Page and the polygraph. I also enlisted the aid of Charlie Zimmerman, the man who would send me into the Edgerly case a few months later. Charlie has popped in and out of my practice ever since our first meeting—most recently, he has figured in the defense of Captain Ernest Medina.

At the time I met him, Charlie was a German national who had come to Boston to take the chief examiner's post with one of the country's most successful polygraph-testing companies, Scientific Security Inc. Trained by the U.S. Army as an examiner, he had worked for Interpol and aided police agencies across the country.

When he got my letter, Charlie called the office to offer his help. I visited him the next day and learned more about the polygraph in three hours than I had in the past three years. I showed him John Conrad's charts on Page, and he said they were good. "But are they good enough for a jury?" he asked.

"What do you mean?"

"Well," he said, "these are good enough for any examiner to read. But they require some interpretation. I don't think many experts would quarrel with John Conrad's opinion, or doubt that Page is telling the truth. But for laymen you need something, how do you say, *dramatic.*"

"But Page didn't react because he's innocent! How can you have a dramatic nonreaction?"

Charlie laughed. "You can't. That's the point. There should be a strong reaction on some other question, not connected to the case, which would show that when asked about an area where he does have concern, his response is strong. That is proof he didn't rape the girl, because if he had he would have reacted strongly. That's what you want to show a jury. And a judge, too."

He wanted to give Page another test. I had one reservation. "Suppose Willard hasn't ever done anything that will make him respond dramatically?"

"Don't worry," he said. "Page has done something. So has everyone, including you." He winked. "Listen, including me."

Page went to Charlie's office the next week. He had been there about two hours when Charlie phoned me. "Come on over," he said, "I want to show you something."

When I arrived, Charlie motioned me into his office past an exhausted Willard Page. "Look at this chart," he said.

I immediately spotted a picturebook response near one end of the strip. The blood pressure had skyrocketed, the pulse had accelerated, the breathing had almost ceased, and the galvo needle had deflected sharply. Any one of these alone would rate as a strong response. Together they constituted what Charlie calls a home run.

"What question produced *that?*"

Charlie handed me the list. "Number five."

Strike out! The question was: "Did you ever rape anyone?"

"Jesus," I said. "Don't tell me. Please don't tell me."

"Wait a minute before you shoot yourself," Charlie said, looking like Santa Claus about to give the elves a day off. "Look at three, seven, and eight." They were: "Did you rape Janet Sullivan in November, 1956?" "Did you hit Roger Saloman with a pistol in November, 1956?" "Have you lied to me about your involvement in the Sullivan rape?"

The response to each question was a smooth and regular tracing—not even a hint of a reaction.

"Now look over here." Charlie picked up a second chart and pointed to the spot where question five had been asked again. This time, there was no reaction.

"I don't get it."

Charlie was having fun. "It's simple. First, Page didn't rape the Sullivan girl, and the best proof is the comparison of questions three and five on the first chart. Second, he was once *accused* of rape when he was an M.P. in Germany, and that's what triggered the reaction to question five. He told me about the incident. So when I asked him question five again, there was no reaction. That's about as solid a test as you can get."

"What do you mean he was 'accused' of rape in Germany?" I said. "How do you know he was only 'accused'?"

"He gave me the details," said Charlie, "and they make sense. I know from when I was in the police. All kinds of GIs were accused of rape by German girls, and it got to the point where we gave each girl a polygraph test to see if it was even worth picking the man up for questioning. Also, Page told me he was cleared by both the military and the local police, and I tested him on this fact. He tested clean."

As Charlie's explanation sank in, I began to get excited. "Can you get some confirmation of this from the military or the German police?" I asked. "It's a helluva point—I see what you mean by a dramatic reaction."

Page's trial was scheduled for early 1961. For the most part, we were ready as we were ever going to be. We'd had no luck in corroborating Willard's story, but I felt the test might still be effective. Dan had lined up most of the witnesses who could help us as to the facts in the case. He had checked into the background of the victims, but Janet and Roger were the model young Americans they appeared to be. As for the battle of the polygraph, I had one more move to make—I filed a motion asking that the commonwealth be ordered to give Page a lie detector test of its own.

That motion, heard before Judge Edward DeSaulnier, marked my first appearance in a Massachusetts court as a lawyer. I argued that since other suspects were given polygraph tests by the state police, the refusal to give one to Page represented illogical discrimination. To my surprise, the judge ordered that Page be tested right away. That evening the *Boston Globe* ran a small story on page two under the heading, "Court Grants Odd Request."

Mike Cullinane tested Page, and—as was the case with George Edgerly—said the results were inconclusive. I wasn't particularly surprised; I knew Mike was a conservative examiner. Still, it would have been interesting to see what the state would have done if Mike had agreed with John Conrad and Charlie Zimmerman.

The trial was less than a week off when the district attorney's office said the case would have to be postponed to make way for an overload of cases in which defendants had been marking time in jail for lack of bail. I rushed to Worcester to argue before Judge DeSaulnier for an immediate trial. I explained that it had not been easy to assemble my panel of unpaid experts and arrange their transportation; that Page had been unable to find employment with a rape charge hanging over his head; that it had been more than six months since his arrest, and justice demanded a trial without delay.

Judge DeSaulnier was unimpressed. He not only said "no," he chewed my tail as it had not been chewed since preflight training. The judge was an ex-marine. Years later, I appeared before him in a bank robbery trial. "Why didn't you tell me you were a marine back when we had that Page case?" he said. "I never chew out marines, I thought you were some navy type."

Actually, the judge had done me a good turn. The Page case would not come to trial until the first week in May. In the interim, I would be called into the defense of George Edgerly.

Willard Page's trial got off to a fast start before Judge Eugene Hudson. I was able to reassemble my panel of experts, and a jury was formed in double time, thanks to another of the quaint customs practiced in my home state. We take the first twelve warm bodies—except in a capital case, jurors are asked *no questions*.

Janet Sullivan and Roger Saloman testified and held up well. In my cross-examination, I leaned hard on three points: an interval of more than three and a half years would dim even the best memory, their original descriptions were at great variance with Page's appearance, and the preview the police had allowed through the one-way mirror was a dishonest trick. I couldn't shake them. No matter what, they insisted that the man who attacked them on that night in 1956 was the slim blond man in the courtroom. Willard Page. No one else.

After the cross, court was adjourned until the following day, when the judge would hear what my expert witnesses had to say.

We met that evening in the conference room of attorney Peter Princi, who had been a client when I first started the investigative service. We sat at a long table, my experts and I: Dr. LeMoyne Snyder, Dr. Robert Mezer, Dr. Hudson Jost, Major Charles N. Joseph, Lynn Marcy, Charlie Zimmerman, John Conrad, and myself.

LeMoyne Snyder, a doctor, lawyer, and polygraph examiner from California, had worked with Erle Stanley Gardner in the Court of Last Resort, an organization devoted to righting miscarriages of justice. A former chief physician for the Michigan State Police, Dr. Snyder specialized in criminal pathology. As a lawyer, he would be able to compare the polygraph's reliability to forms of scientific evidence that *were* considered admissible.

Hudson Jost, now head of the psychology department at the University of Arizona, had been working with the polygraph for twenty years and knew as much about the theoretical psychology of the test as any man alive.

Robert Mezer, the psychiatrist who had hypnotized Page, had taught medicine and law at Harvard and Boston University. He would be able to explain a matter that some considered vital in polygraph testing—the extent to which mental illness might interfere with a test's accuracy. More to the point, he could testify that Page suffered no such illness.

Lynn P. Marcy was chief staff instructor at the Keeler Polygraph Institute in Chicago, where many of the country's police examiners are trained. As a student, Marcy had maintained one of the highest averages in the institute's history. He had spent the five years since his graduation teaching and doing advanced research.

Charles N. Joseph, a retired army major trained both at the Keeler Institute and the army's polygraph school at Fort Gordon, Georgia, had given polygraph tests all over the world. In more than twenty years as an army examiner, he could not recall a single case in which a suspect cleared by a test had subsequently been prosecuted in military court.

I looked from one to the other and thought about what that moment meant. If the testimony of these men couldn't win the polygraph its rightful place in our system of jurisprudence, whose could? And failure could mean that Willard Page and others like him—men who should never have been brought to trial in the first place—might spend years locked away from the world. And where, then, on God's green earth was justice?

Charlie and John showed their polygrams, which were closely examined by the other experts. All agreed that Willard Page had never raped Janet Sullivan. We covered the testimony each man would give, and that was that. Later, I stayed up for two hours in my apartment studying polygraph material and going over my presentation.

The next morning, the courthouse halls were crowded with reporters, photographers, and would-be spectators. In the courtroom, the jurors were absent. Judge Hudson had excused them—explaining with classic understatement that he had to hear some questions "of law." We were on.

Leading off was LeMoyne Snyder. His experience predated that of the other experts, and he had a reputation as a superb witness. His approach was simple. The polygraph was an uncomplicated device; there was little that could go wrong. Medically, its principles were sound. Legally, he was familiar with the standards of reliability imposed on types of scientific evidence that were admissible in the courts—X rays, electrocardiograms, ballistocardiograms, and so on. A machine measured something happening or existing in the body, and an expert interpreted the results. Reliability varied only with the expert's skill. Such was the case with the polygraph. When Dr. Snyder finished, prosecutor John Driscoll asked few questions. LeMoyne knew too much about his material.

Jost testified next. Using numerous examples, he described how the polygraph's components could point out deception. He also explained the psychological theory as to why this was so. He, too, had no problem with cross-examination.

I had planned to call Dr. Mezer next, but when Jost finished, I decided to hold off Mezer for a later punch and called Lynn Marcy. I wasn't sure how Marcy would do, but if he faltered, I could come back with Mezer.

Marcy was fine on direct examination. He estimated that he had given polygraph tests to about five thousand people. He had followed through on most of these cases and found that most people who passed the tests were exonerated, while most of those who had failed wound up showing that they were guilty or had knowledge of the crime. He could recall no proven error in any of the five thousand.

Driscoll was smiling as he started his cross. He threw out a couple of light questions, and then picked up a printed pamphlet. "Mr. Marcy," he said, "what is a synapse?"

I didn't know the answer, and I didn't know how many polygraph experts would have.

Marcy's eyes never flickered as he stared at Driscoll out of his horn-rimmed glasses. "A synapse," he said, "is the point of connection between two neurons in the nervous system, where an impulse passes from one nerve to another."

Judge Hudson looked at Driscoll. "Is that definition correct?"

The prosecutor nodded. "Well then," said the judge, "I think you'd better smile, Mr. Driscoll. Yes, smile indeed."

To his everlasting credit, Driscoll smiled.

The remaining pieces fell quickly into place. When I tried to qualify Dr. Mezer, the judge stopped me. "I know this witness," he said, "He has appeared before me in other cases. He is very well qualified. Proceed." I did, and Mezer demolished false notions about the effect of various mental conditions on polygraph tests. He said that psychotics might be unsuitable for testing, especially if they suffered delusions. But otherwise, the polygraph was eminently reliable. And, in any case, Page was not psychotic.

John Conrad explained his charts on Page, and we described the wide use of the polygraph by law enforcement agencies. As a final witness I called Captain Mike Cullinane. He wasn't exactly happy about being a defense witness, but he affirmed that state police used the lie detector to eliminate suspects. He said his test on Page had indicated neither guilt nor innocence.

Judge Hudson declared a recess while he decided whether to admit the tests into evidence. I waited with mixed emotions. Above all, I wanted Page acquitted. And I was certain we would win if the judge let the jury hear the polygraph testimony. But Massachusetts trial judges do not report their decisions, and no trial judge's ruling is binding on another judge. A favorable ruling by Judge Hudson did not necessarily mean a precedent would be set. The only sure chain of events that could produce a precedent would be an adverse ruling, a jury conviction, and a reversal by the Massachusetts Supreme Court. As you might imagine, this was not a sequence that interested Willard Page.

The judge's decision wasn't long in coming. He ruled out the polygraph evidence without giving any reason. But he indicated that he had been impressed by the testimony—which provided a glimmer of hope for the future as far as polygraph admissibility was concerned. And in any case, our appeal was well preserved.

An appeal, though, would not affect the present. My job was to win acquittal for Willard Page. And I would have to do it without the tests on which he had registered his innocence.

In the absence of scientific evidence, we concentrated on old-fashioned testimony. I called Page's barber, who testified that Page's hair had never been brown or crew-cut. The family priest testified that he had known Page most of his life, and that he had always had long blond hair. Page's sister testified that he had been living with her and her family at the time of the assault, and that he had never owned a pistol. She also said he had never worn a jacket of the sort described by the victims.

Then Page took the stand. He was emphatic and forthright as he denied any knowledge of the attack. And he held firm under cross-examination. But as he stepped down from the stand, I saw troubled looks on the faces of some of the jurors. I imagined that they were wondering why, unless Roger and Janet were absolutely sure of their identification, they had been willing to swear under oath that Willard Page was their attacker.

It was time to sum up. I stressed the facts we had gathered, attempting to be forceful but not emotional. Although I'd never seen John Driscoll try a case before, a local lawyer had told me that he was likely to pull out all the stops in summation. Accordingly, I told the jury that emotion on the part of counsel was inappropriate to the trial process. What's more, I said, it was often an indication that the lawyer had doubts about the strength of his own case.

Driscoll got off to a businesslike start, and I began to think my little stratagem had been in vain. But as he got near the end, style overcame content. His face reddened and his voice rose; he pounded his cane on the floor and fairly bristled with indignation over the cruel and vicious rape suffered by Janet Sullivan. As Driscoll stormed to a close, one of the men in the first row of the jury box looked at me and winked.

Judge Hudson's charge was fair and straightforward: Roger had been assaulted and Janet had been raped. Was the assailant Willard Page or someone else?

It was shortly after lunch when the jury went out. It was spring in New England, and the day was warm and clear. It was Friday, there was the promise of a pleasant weekend. Judge Hudson had a summer home on Cape Cod, and I couldn't blame him if he was thinking about it. I sat with Willard and his family and chewed my nails.

The jury stayed out. At 5:00 P.M., Judge Hudson decided to leave

45

for the weekend. He ordered that the jury continue its deliberations. If there was a verdict, it would be sealed until Monday morning.

I went back to Boston, where I spent the weekend second-guessing myself and worrying. If Page were convicted, what would I say to him? How should I frame an appeal? Should I have called more experts? Were there any cracks in the foundation we had laid? Would the Supreme Court turn us down because it felt, as appellate courts had felt in the past, that the polygraph was a threat to the jury system? There were questions, but few answers.

Monday morning came, and the questions persisted. A court officer told me that the jury had sealed its verdict late Friday after deliberating for eight hours. That had to mean there had been stubborn arguments both for conviction and acquittal. I tried to remember how the jurors had looked as they filed out. I couldn't.

There was the ceremony of the sealed envelope, and the living theater of the short dialogue between the clerk and the jury foreman.

"What say you, Mr. Foreman, is the defendant guilty or not guilty?"

A half-smile puckered the foreman's face. "We find the defendant not guilty." Page's sister moaned with relief behind me. Page nodded his thanks to the jury, took a couple of deep breaths, and stepped free from the prisoner's box.

As I drove back to Boston, I turned on the car radio. A local station was reporting the verdict. The announcer was excited, and so was I. The Supreme Court of Massachusetts would not get a chance to rule on the polygraph, but I had no regrets. There would be another opportunity, another case. My job—as well as the job of judge, jury, and law-enforcement officers—was to make the system work. This time, at least, it had.

4. *WOULD YOU DEFEND A GUILTY MAN?*

The rate of acquittal for all the cases I have handled is between sixty and seventy percent. For the forty homicides I have handled, the rate is much higher. One client pleaded guilty in the murder of a teenage girl. Only three of the accused killers I have represented were convicted. I'm not saying I have never gotten a guilty man out of prison on a point of law or that I have not won acquittal for a guilty man. But in none of those three convictions was it proved beyond a reasonable doubt that the defendant had committed murder. When there isn't the slightest doubt that my client committed the crime, he pleads guilty. Otherwise, we fight.

Even if I know a client is guilty, it's not that simple. The question that laymen put to me most frequently is: "Would you defend a guilty man?" Or, "How can you defend a man you know is guilty?"

The questioner is rarely satisfied with my answer. He sees no justification for defending someone who really did it. He can afford to play the moralist, it's not his neck on the guillotine. If lawyers were to shun every case in which they knew the defendant was guilty, there would be no courts. Every person who was arrested and indicted would go right to jail unless his defense counsel judged him innocent.

Guilt, like most things, is scarcely ever black or white. Yes, I have defended a number of men I knew to be guilty. Two were acquitted. One of them was James Martin, and his story is indeed a case in point.

I met Jimmy Martin in the summer of 1961. His cousin, a former classmate of mine, had asked me to take his case. Jimmy could have posed for a Pepsi-Cola ad; he was a good-looking eighteen-year-old with rosy cheeks, clear blue eyes, and curly brown hair. He didn't look as if he were capable of murder, but few people do. And under sufficient pressure, any one of us is capable of killing another human being.

Jimmy was accused of an especially ugly slaying—the murder of an elderly nurse in Roxbury, one of Boston's poorest suburbs. She had been found dead on a church lawn, her uniform ripped open and the back of her skull crushed.

The night of the incident Jimmy, who had finished a pint of Southern Comfort, was standing drunk on the sidewalk near his home. He spotted the nurse, crossed the street in front of her, stooped as if to tie his shoe, and then suddenly shot up with a haymaker right to her eye as she was about to pass. She fell to the sidewalk, and Jimmy grabbed her pocketbook and ran. There was thirty-eight cents in the purse, but Jimmy had committed an unarmed robbery, an offense punishable in Massachusetts by a maximum sentence of life imprisonment.

As Jimmy fled, the woman got to her feet and continued walking toward the hospital. Meanwhile, Jimmy threw up some of the whiskey and began to feel sorry about the attack. He decided that the only way he could make amends would be to help her. He caught up with her in front of a church whose front lawn was surrounded by a rough stone wall. Still drunk, he tried to tell her that he would help her to a hospital. The woman told him to leave her alone, but Jimmy was adamant about

47

carrying her to the hospital. Although she was small and light, she struggled in his arms as he picked her up, and they fell to the sidewalk. The back of her head struck the stone wall.

Jimmy hauled her onto the church lawn beneath an oak tree. He tried unsuccessfully to have intercourse with her. That was all he could remember.

When the woman's body was discovered, an investigation led police to Jimmy within a few days. Held for several hours without food or a chance to consult with a parent or lawyer, he confessed that he was involved and told his story. When he first talked to me, he said that his mind had been a blank and that he couldn't vouch for the accuracy of what he had told police.

The case was a legal nightmare. If it were found that Jimmy had caused the woman's death—even unintentionally—in the commission of the robbery, then it was felony murder, which carried a penalty of life imprisonment or death. If the victim had died as a result of attempted rape, that too was felony murder—punishable by death only.

I believed that Jimmy Martin was guilty of robbery and attempted rape, and that the woman's death was accidental. My belief was based on his own story and on the medical examiner's findings that the crushed skull was the cause of death and that the nature of the injury was consistent with the woman's having fallen against a stone wall. But I knew a jury might be too repelled by the facts of the case to draw such fine distinctions.

I arranged for Jimmy to be examined by psychiatrists, who found that he suffered from epilepsy, and that the fits were triggered by alcohol. It was determined that he was not competent to stand trial, and in the fall of 1961 he was confined to the state prison hospital at Bridgewater.

Four years later, hospital authorities reported that he had shown unusual improvement and could be brought to court. The chess game began.

My first move was an attempt to persuade the district attorney to accept a manslaughter plea. I pointed out that changes in the law during the four years Jimmy was hospitalized probably would void his confession. Without the confession, there was little evidence linking him to the nurse's death. Furthermore, we had a strong case for insanity; some of the state's own psychiatrists were convinced that Jimmy had been unable to control his actions at the time of the incident. I didn't want Jimmy convicted of murder, but I didn't want him acquitted by reason of insanity and sent back to Bridgewater, which was more dungeon than hospital. On the other hand, I felt he needed supervision and continued medical help. He had already served four years toward a sentence. If he were allowed to plead guilty to manslaughter, he could be closely supervised during a long probationary period.

The district attorney felt that even without the confession he had enough to force me to defend on insanity grounds. In order to show insanity, I would have to admit Jimmy's complicity. No deal, he said. We would go all the way. I urged the trial judge to accept the manslaughter plea without the district attorney's consent, but he refused.

The trial opened in December, 1965. The judge was Frank J. Murray, an extremely able jurist who would subsequently be named to the U.S. District Court. The prosecutor was assistant district attorney Jack Mulhern, a former Boston College hockey star and a skilled lawyer.

Mulhern presented his case quickly and without fanfare. There was no nonsense; Judge Murray ran a tight court. "Gentlemen," he would say whenever Jack or I seemed puzzled by one of his rulings, "this is a courtroom, not a classroom. Proceed."

As expected, Jimmy's confession was excluded because it had been "extracted" from him under circumstances that showed it to be clearly involuntary. There were no eyewitnesses to the incident. One person had seen Jimmy near the woman, but no one had seen him kill her. When the state rested, it was obvious that its case was weak.

To show insanity, I would have to give the state's case a boost. I had no desire to put Jimmy Martin in the electric chair by proving what the state had been unable to show. On the other hand, the defense could rest without raising the insanity plea, but that might be equally dangerous. In an effort to create a third alternative, I approached Judge Murray in the lobby.

"How about a bifurcated trial in the California manner?" I asked him. "Let the jury decide if he's guilty, and if they convict him, we'll try the issue of sanity."

"I like the idea," the judge said. "And if this case were not capital I might do it. But that's not the law, and it seems to me a question for the Supreme Court, not me."

"We take no position, ladies and gentlemen," I said in my opening statement, "as to whether or not the defendant committed the crime. That's for you to decide. But if you find that he did do it, upon the evidence I am about to present you should also find that he was insane, and therefore not responsible for his act."

The opening left some of the jurors looking puzzled, and I couldn't blame them.

My problems became obvious when I called Dr. Robert Mezer to testify. He had been working with Jimmy since his arrest, and I was counting on him to show that Jimmy was mentally ill. But I had to be very careful. I couldn't ask him a question that would give Jack Mulhern a chance to drag in the confession on cross-examination.

"Doctor," I asked, "do you have an opinion as to whether or not, on June 26, 1961, the defendant was suffering from any disease or defect of the mind?"

Mezer was also taking it slow. "I have an opinion," he said.

"Please let us have it."

"Objection," said Mulhern.

"Sustained," said Judge Murray.

Mulhern and I approached the bench. "I think I'm entitled to that evidence," I said. "If permitted to answer, Dr. Mezer would say that on the day in question, Martin was suffering from schizophrenia and alcoholically triggered epilepsy, each of which is a mental disease and defect."

"No," said the judge. "I won't permit that question. If you wish to show a defense of insanity, you may ask the doctor to assume that Martin committed the crime, and then inquire as to what his mental condition was —whether it affected his ability to know right from wrong, and so forth."

"The effect of that ruling is that in order to raise insanity, I have to admit guilt," I said.

"You may view the situation any way you choose," he said. "I have ruled."

I asked for a recess, and explained our dilemma to Jimmy. Which way did he want to go?

"That stuff's all over my head," he said. "Do whatever you think is best."

When court reconvened, I asked to see Judge Murray in his chambers with Mulhern and the stenographer. I had one more idea. "I would like to make a statement for the record, if your honor please," I began as we settled into our chairs, "after which the defense will rest."

Judge Murray looked at me sharply, but there was the hint of a smile in his eyes.

"The decision to rest the case at this time," I said, "is mine alone and not that of the defendant. In my judgment, his mental condition, youth, and lack of education are such that he cannot understand the avenues open to him and the attendant risks.

"It is my opinion that the state has failed to make out a case, and on the present state of the record the jury should not be allowed to convict of the principal offense. If I proceed to advance my insanity plea along the lines required by the court, I will in essence be proving the guilt of my client. Because I am an appointed lawyer I do not feel that I have the right to do this. Further, I object to a proceeding where the state can put in half a case, and force the rest of the proof out of a defendant who wishes to avail himself of a collateral defense."

The statement was as important as any I would make in open court, and I pushed a little harder. "In addition," I said, "I do not feel that there is now before this jury any evidence at all of rape-murder. A conviction of that crime would require that the defendant be executed. I will not subject him to that jeopardy. Experience has taught that operating within the archaic rules of our present insanity law, juries are apt to reject the insanity defense even where the medical evidence is overwhelming in support of it, especially where the crime is as grisly as this one. Our Supreme Court has sustained convictions where all the psychiatrists testified that the defendant was insane, and this despite the rule that the burden of proving sanity is on the prosecution, not the defendant. In view of all of these defects in our system, I am forced to rest at this point; I do not waive the defendant's right to his insanity defense, and he does not. If he is convicted of murder in any degree, I will take the position that he is entitled to a new trial. As evidence that the defendant is not attempting to unconscionably escape punishment, I will state that our offer to plead guilty to manslaughter is still open."

What happened next was up to Judge Murray. He looked out the window for a few minutes, and then made his decision. "In the circumstances," he said, "I am satisfied that counsel's position is correct. We will split the trial. You gentlemen will give your arguments on the merits, and I will charge. If the defendant is convicted, we will not record the jury's verdict. We will litigate the issue of sanity, and resubmit the case, after further arguments and charge, on the sole issue of guilt or insanity."

My summation was brief. I emphasized the gaps in the state's evidence and the many areas for reasonable doubt. Jack was also brief; without the confession he had little evidence to discuss. The judge's charge was crisp and precise; there was no sense in trying to note errors for future objection.

The jury was ready with its verdict in just a few hours. "Guilty," said the foreman. "Guilty—of assault and battery." There would be no need for an insanity defense. And Jimmy had already served more time in jail than the charge carried.

The following day, I saw the judge at a local restaurant. He would pass sentence the next morning. He mentioned that he had heard very little of the psychiatric evidence. "I'm concerned about releasing this boy if he's still dangerous," he said. "The court will appreciate all the help you can give it in disposing of this case."

I felt the same way about Jimmy's release, and so did Jimmy. At the sentencing, I suggested a solution "It is apparent," I said, "that the defendant has served more time in jail while awaiting trial, four and one half years, than he can be given for his conviction of assault and battery—three years. However, counsel has no desire to see him released to absolute freedom if he is not ready, or if he will be a threat to the community. The defendant agrees. Therefore, I submit affidavits setting forth what is known of his present mental condition and suggest that he be sent for further

51

evaluation to a state mental hospital." I added that the proposal had Jimmy's consent.

Judge Murray read the affidavits and agreed. He committed Jimmy for thirty-five days' observation. At the end of that time, the hospital reported that his condition was relatively good. Jimmy was released, and has been in no trouble since.

EPILOGUE

Would I defend a guilty man? In a real sense, Jimmy Martin was guilty—if not of murder, than of something more than a simple assault and battery. In a technical sense, however, he may not have been guilty—there was ample evidence available to show he was not mentally responsible for whatever he did that day.

Was justice done? That question is personal and subjective, and each of you can answer it for yourself. But the question of whether he should have been defended in every possible way is not personal or subjective. It is professional and legal. And any lawyer worth his license would answer it the same way.

II

The Exoneration of Sam Sheppard

1. *DOCTOR SAM*

As the shooting of Stanford White was the crime of the early 1900s, the murder of pretty, pregnant Marilyn Reese Sheppard, found beaten to death the morning of July 4, 1954, was the crime of the '50s. More than ten years later, the Sheppard case would serve as model for the popular television show, *The Fugitive.* The big difference was that Dr. Richard Kimble, the hero of *The Fugitive,* was at large; Dr. Samuel Sheppard served ten years in jail that no court could ever give him back.

It was not simply the murder; it was also the trial that followed. If there is a classic description of the case, it came in a dissenting judicial opinion written by James Finley Bell, then a judge of the Ohio Supreme Court, which upheld Sam's conviction in 1956: "Mystery and murder, society, sex, and suspense were combined in this case in such a manner as to intrigue and captivate the public fancy to a degree perhaps unparalleled in recent annals. Throughout the pre-indictment investigation, the subsequent legal skirmishes, and the nine-week trial, circulation-conscious editors catered to the insatiable interest of the American public in the bizarre. Special seating facilities for reporters and columnists representing the local papers and all major news services were installed in the courtroom. Special rooms in the Criminal Courts building were equipped for broadcasters and telecasters. In this atmosphere of a 'Roman holiday' for the news media, Sam Sheppard stood trial for his life."

I met Sheppard on November 18, 1961, two days past the first anniversary of my admission to the bar. We were in the visiting room of a prison in Marion, Ohio; Sheppard, a tall, good-looking man with close-cropped gray hair and the bearing of a regimental commander, had already spent more than seven years in jail for a crime he never committed. From our first handshake, I believed in his innocence. It took more than five years to get him the two things he wanted most—freedom and vindication.

The background to this story of crime and wrongful punishment was as comfortably all-American as Sam Sheppard himself. The son of an osteopathic surgeon, he'd grown up on a tree-lined street in Cleveland Heights, Ohio. As a high school senior, he was voted both class president and outstanding athlete. He attended Western Reserve University and the Osteopathic School of Physicians and Surgeons in Los Angeles, and he served a residency in neurosurgery at Los Angeles County Hospital. In 1951, he came home to practice and prosper. By the age of thirty, in 1954, he was making $30,000 a year. He had his own office in Cleveland and worked with his two older brothers and his father in the Sheppard Clinic in Fairview Park. He was also in charge of neurosurgery at the family-owned Bay View Hospital in Bay Village, which his father, Dr. Richard A. Sheppard, had founded in 1948.

The aura of social and material well-being that surrounded Sheppard would add to the public animosity that followed him throughout his arrest and conviction. He was the boy with the silver spoon who grew up into the man who had it made. Married to his teenage sweetheart, Sam had a seven-year-old son; a four-bedroom house set on a wooded tract that included a small sand beach on Lake Erie; a used Lincoln Continental and a Jaguar; and a fourteen-foot aluminum outboard co-owned with Spencer Houk, a friend and neighbor who was the part-time mayor of Bay Village.

In the summer of 1954, Sam and Marilyn had been married for nine years. The surface of the marriage was smooth. The young Sheppards' close family circle included Sam's parents and his brothers and their wives and children. About a month before the slaying, Sam's parents had hosted an especially happy family dinner at which Marilyn announced she was pregnant again.

Sam enjoyed his work, and maintained his interest in sports; Otto Graham, then quarterback for the Cleveland Browns, was a good friend. Both Sam and Marilyn were water-ski buffs and played tennis and golf. And they took part in community life. Marilyn was active in church work and belonged to the Bay Village Women's Club; Sam served as the village's police surgeon. There were potluck suppers, dances, and a full social life marked by get-togethers with such people as Spencer Houk and his wife Esther, and Don and Nancy Ahern, a young couple who also lived nearby.

There were problems, too. Her son Chip's birth, unusually painful, had left Marilyn traumatized. And living in fear of another pregnancy for several years had blunted her sex drive. In 1951, soon after the Sheppards came home to the Cleveland area to stay, Sam became involved with twenty-one-year-old Susan Hayes, a trim brunette medical technician at Bay View Hospital. The affair continued into the winter of 1953, at which point Susan moved to California. Sam saw her again in March, 1954, when he and Marilyn took a trip to Los Angeles. While Marilyn was at a ranch some three hundred miles north of the city, Sam spent four or five nights with Susan at the home of friends.

As Sam would later tell it, his relationship with Susan was "a purely physical arrangement of convenience." It was, he said, a matter of need, not love. According to Sam, his wife was aware of the situation, and although she was less than delighted by it, her attitude was one of tolerance. "Marilyn knew about this relationship, but she understood and recognized why it had developed," Sam would write in his book, *Endure and Conquer*. " 'Look,' she once told me, 'I know my father has had a mistress ever since I've been able to walk, but that woman has been closer to me than my stepmother.' It gave her a little insight regarding our own situation."

Sam said he loved Marilyn, and he never considered divorcing her. By the spring of 1954 Marilyn had conquered her sexual fears, and so far as Sam was concerned, the affair with Susan Hayes had ended in March. But a "friend" of his had alarmed Marilyn with a false story indicating that Sam was thinking about divorce. It wasn't until three weeks before the murder that the Sheppards talked everything out. After that, wrote Sam, their life took on a "new hue." They lost themselves in the good life, Chip, and each other. "We were surprising ourselves by how very much in love we were," he said.

On the afternoon of July 3, the Sheppards went to the home of Don and Nancy Ahern for cocktails. Sam had to cut the visit short to answer a call from Bay View about a boy who had been hurt in an auto accident. He went from the hospital to his home, where the Aherns and their two children were dinner guests. After the kids had eaten, the grown-ups had a leisurely meal on the porch overlooking the lake. Ahern took his children home to bed and returned to the Sheppard house, where he listened to a baseball game on a radio in a corner of the room while the two women watched a movie on television. Sam sat near the TV set, half watching the movie and half listening to the ball game. Marilyn sat in his lap for a while with her arms around him; Nancy Ahern made Don give up his game and come over and sit in her chair. Later Sam moved to a couch, stretched out facing the TV set, and fell asleep. It was the sort of thing you could do only among friends.

At about 12:30 A.M., the Aherns left. Nancy said later that she watched Marilyn lock the door facing the lake, but did not see her bolt the door facing the road. Sam vaguely remembered Marilyn trying to wake him and telling him she was going upstairs to bed. He dozed off again on the couch. And as he slept, the good times ended.

There is no way of knowing precisely how much time elapsed, but Sam next became aware of the world around him when he heard Marilyn moaning or screaming his name. His reaction was that she might be having convulsions like those she had suffered during her first pregnancy. Only half awake, he rushed up the stairs, which were dimly lit by a light in the

57

hall. He would tell his story of what happened next many times, and the essentials would remain constant.

As he entered the bedroom, he heard Marilyn moaning and saw a "white form," or someone in a "white garment," standing next to her bed. He could not tell whether it was a man or a woman. Then, he was struck on the neck from behind. Sometime later he came to, facing the bedroom doorway. Sitting up, he spotted the gleam of the police badge on his wallet, which was lying on the floor. As he leaned over to get it, a sharp pain ripped through his neck. He went to the bed, where Marilyn lay in a welter of blood. He looked at her and took her pulse. His vision was blurred, but it seemed to him that she was dead. Still not fully conscious, he went into Chip's room and somehow assured himself that his son was all right.

As he left, he heard a noise downstairs, seemingly coming from the front part of the house, which faced the lake. Hurrying down, he caught sight of a figure between the front door of the house and the screen door of the porch, or possibly just past the screen door. Apparently both doors were open. He ran toward the figure, but lost sight of it on the steps leading to the beach. When he got to the beach house landing, he saw the figure on the shore, raced down the last few steps, and tackled the intruder. His impression was that he was grappling with a man with a large head. There was a short struggle, during which he felt as if he were being choked.

His next memory was of coming to on the beach with his feet in the waves and his head facing the shore. He made his way back into the house and staggered up the stairs to the blood-spattered bedroom, looked at Marilyn again. He felt disoriented, trapped in a terrible dream. He may have walked about; he rechecked his wife.

Finally, the reality of her death sank in. He went downstairs trying to think of what to do, whom to call. Spencer Houk's number popped into his mind, and he called him. The Sheppards and the Houks were not so close as they had once been, but Sam, as police surgeon, still saw the mayor frequently. And the Houks only lived a few hundred feet away. According to Houk, the call came at 5:45 A.M. "For God's sake, Spen, get over here quick," Sheppard said. "I think they've killed Marilyn."

When Houk and his wife reached the Sheppard home, Esther went upstairs while Houk stayed in the den with Sam, who was bare to the waist with his trousers still soaking wet and his face bruised and swollen. Drawers had been pulled from Sam's desk, and articles from his medical bag were strewn on the floor. Houk said he asked Sam what had happened, and Sheppard answered, "I don't know exactly but somebody ought to do something for Marilyn."

Upstairs, Esther Houk walked into a room of blood—it had stained the walls and the floor, spotted the spread of Sam's otherwise undisturbed bed, and gathered in pools on Marilyn's bed, where she lay dead with her pajama tops rolled up around her neck, her head and face crimson with cuts. A coroner's report would show that Marilyn had suffered thirty-five separate wounds, most of them on the face and head, and some on the neck and hands. Esther hurried downstairs and shouted to her husband to call for help. Houk phoned the Bay Village police at 5:58 A.M., and then called Sam's brother Richard.

Seconds after he arrived, Richard took a knife from the kitchen and ran upstairs, thinking that perhaps Marilyn could be revived with cardiac massage. When he saw that nothing could be done, he returned to the den. "She's gone, Sam," he said.

Houk later claimed that Richard said either: "Did you do this?" or "Did you have anything to do with this?" and that Sam answered, "Hell no"; Richard testified that he was positive he never said such a thing. "I could not have," he said, "because it never entered my mind that my brother could have killed his wife." In his book, Sam said the gist of Richard's comments was that he should try to pull himself together and remember what happened.

Cleveland police were called, and Sam's other brother, Steve Sheppard, and his wife, Betty, also arrived. The brothers examined Sam, who had broken teeth and a severe neck injury. Then Steve and Betty drove him to Bay View Hospital in their station wagon. Newspaper reports that the Sheppards had spirited Sam away and kept him immune from investigation in the family hospital were to take no account of the fact that police at the scene made no objections as Steve drove off with Sam, or that authorities were able to question Sam three times on that day of the murder, or that one Cleveland detective accused him of the slaying before the day was over. ("I don't know what my partner thinks," said the detective, "but I think you killed your wife.") Nor did it matter that police put Sam through a full-scale grilling four days later at the hospital without counsel being present. No matter what, the stories persisted—all of them spreading the idea that Sam Sheppard was wealthy and influential enough to get away with murder.

The leader of the rat pack nipping at Sam's heels was one of Ohio's most influential citizens, Louis B. Seltzer, editor of one of the state's largest newspapers, the *Cleveland Press*. Almost from the beginning, Seltzer seemed sure that Sam was guilty. Or, as he later put it in his autobiography, "I was convinced that a conspiracy existed to defeat the ends of justice, and that it would affect adversely the whole law-enforcement machinery of the County if it were permitted to succeed. It could establish a precedent that would destroy even-handed administration of justice."

And so Seltzer threw due process to the headlines. There are what the fourth estate likes to call "hard-hitting" stories and editorials, and there are also hatchet jobs. On a comparative basis, what the *Cleveland Press* committed was a series of ax murders.

All of the Cleveland papers featured the case, as did dailies throughout the country. Sensational aspects such as the Susan Hayes affair were reported with the attention to prurient detail that even family newspapers reserve for matters pertaining to sex. The editorials were even worse. On July 16, Seltzer got the *Press* rolling with an editorial, headed "The Finger of Suspicion," that said the murder probe was being stymied by "the hostility of Bay Village officials to any 'outsiders' in the case," and cited "the unusual protection set up around the husband of the victim. . . ." The editorial blamed this protection on Sam's lawyer, William Corrigan. The first step that should be taken, it said, was a meeting of all law enforcement agencies involved. A meeting was held the next day, and Cleveland Mayor Anthony J. Celebrezze suggested that the city police department take full charge of the case.

The *Cleveland Press* editorial on July 20 consumed the top quarter of page one, running beneath the five-column headline "Getting Away With Murder." Seltzer, who wrote the editorial himself, described it in his autobiography as "a calculated risk—a hazard of the kind I believe a newspaper sometimes in the interest of law and order and the community's ultimate safety must take." This one said that the case was studded with "fumbling, halting, stupid, uncooperative bungling-politeness to people whose place in this situation completely justified vigorous searching, prompt and effective police work" and went on to assert: "It's time that somebody smashed into this situation and tore aside this restraining curtain of sham, politeness, and hypocrisy and went at the business of solving a murder—and quit this nonsense of artificial politeness that has not been extended to any other murder case in generations." That night, the Bay Village council passed a resolution setting up a $5,000 fund for the murder investigation and instructing Houk to ask the Cleveland police to take over.

On July 21, the papers called for an inquest. The *Cleveland Press* led the charge with an editorial headed: "Why No Inquest? Do It Now, Dr. Gerber." The next day, Cuyahoga County Coroner Samuel Gerber got a three-day inquest under way. During the hearing, Sam's attorney was ejected from the room as spectators saw him off with catcalls. If he was the villain, Gerber was the hero. At the conclusion of the inquest, the white-haired coroner was surrounded by women, some of whom kissed him.

On July 26, the *Press* ran a front-page editorial: "Why Don't Police Quiz the Top Suspect?" And on July 30, Seltzer published another of his personal compositions. Originally entitled "Why Isn't Sam Sheppard in Jail?," the headline was changed in the final edition to: "Quit Stalling—Bring Him In." That night Sam Sheppard was arrested at his parent's home. It was carnival time in Bay Village as the public ran wild on the lawn, and news photographers took flash pictures through the windows of the house. When the police led Sam out the front door, a path had to be cleared to their car. The people massed on either side cheered.

The grand jury indicted Sam on August 17, and his trial opened a month later. Before the trial had even begun, the judge, Edward J. Blythin, told a reporter that Sam was "guilty as hell." The verdict of guilty of second-degree murder came as no surprise. On December 21, Judge Blythin sentenced Sam to life imprisonment.

It wasn't until after the trial, when authorities turned the keys to Sam's house back to Corrigan, that his attorneys were able to gather evidence. Corrigan hired Dr. Paul Leland Kirk, a nationally known criminologist from the University of California, who turned up some fascinating evidence pointing toward Sam's innocence. Among other things, he determined that the killer was left-handed (Sam was not), and that a large spot of blood on the closet door was neither Sam's nor Marilyn's. He said that Sam's story was consistent with the known facts, and that the technical evidence presented by the prosecution had been worthless. But petitions for a new trial on the basis of Dr. Kirk's findings were turned down by the courts, as were other appeals over the years.

Sam's mother had shot herself, and his father died of cancer less than a month after his conviction. In jail, Sam wrote to his son, worked as a four-dollar-a-month surgeon, and participated in a research program by allowing doctors to inoculate him with live cancer cells. He took part in athletics, made and sold religious jewelry, and earned the respect of his fellow convicts.

He survived, but the years in jail were bitter ones. Our system had failed him. None of the appeals succeeded. He was in prison for something he hadn't done. Think about that; think about what it must be like to pull time for no reason. Think about the anger, the frustration. Think about what it must have been like to be Sam Sheppard, the man who had everything and then woke up one morning to find himself in a void that got blacker and blacker.

Hope became as fragile as bone china, but he hung on. And on a raw, cold day in November, 1961, I became his lawyer. I had all the necessary requisites: I was young, I was idealistic, and I was a little naive.

2. *THE SECOND TIME AROUND*

When Sam Sheppard first stood trial, I was flying Sabrejets for the Marine Corps. Despite the headlines, the case made no particular impression on me. And by the time I was licensed to practice law, Sam had already served six years in jail.

In August, 1961, I was in Chicago, lecturing at the Keeler Polygraph Institute. Paul Holmes, the author of the recently published *Sheppard Murder Case,* had made inquiries at the school for a lawyer who could supervise a lie detector test for Sam. He was referred to me.

"Ohio doesn't want the truth about Sam Sheppard," he told me. "Unless you understand that, you won't be able to help him."

I read Paul Holmes's book and I was furious—at what the state of Ohio had done to Sam Sheppard, and at the way appellate courts had perpetuated the injustice. Paul had covered the trial for the *Chicago Tribune,* and his book was an outstanding job of reporting. It was also a forceful indictment of the system. "I saw it all," Holmes wrote, "and for what it is worth I think the whole business rubbed luster from American jurisprudence, and is, in its most literal and reverent sense, a God-damned shame."

That November Holmes gave me a letter of introduction to Steve and Richard Sheppard. "I've done a little checking," he said, "and I'm recommending to the Sheppards that they ask you to represent Sam. This case needs somebody with imagination, and it needs somebody with a hell of a lot of stamina."

I flew to Cleveland, where Steve Sheppard met me at the airport. There were a lot of strong figures in the Sheppard case; Steve was the strongest. A white-haired, bespectacled man in his early forties, he was not about to stop fighting for what most people considered a lost cause.

Steve and I stayed up until after midnight discussing the possibility of obtaining a polygraph test for Sam. I said that if I couldn't force one by bringing public pressure to bear on Ohio Governor Mike DiSalle, I might be able to do it through court action. At six the next morning, we drove down to the Ohio State Correctional Institution in Marion to see Sam.

When he came into the visiting room, I was surprised. I had not expected him to be as spirited, or, for that matter, in such good physical condition. That first visit with Sam lasted a couple of hours. Bill Corrigan had died the past summer, and Sam needed a lawyer. He was understandably dubious about our chances of success, but he was more than willing to take a polygraph test. And he was grateful that someone was willing to try a new tack for him.

"I'll charge you a whopping fee," I said, "but I'll help you earn the money to pay for it."

"If you can get me out," Sam said, "I'll work for ten years solid, and give you everything I make over the bare minimum I need to live on. Frankly, I don't think you can do it, but if you're willing to try, I'm willing to have you."

"Well, don't pack your suitcase yet," I said, "but keep your clothes clean. Police have been playing games with the polygraph for too long, they know god-damn well it's dependable. If you pass that test you're going to get out."

In order to pass the exam, he had to take it. I needed permission to enter the Marion Correctional Institution with a polygraph and a good examiner and give Sam a thorough test. In fairly short order, I began to understand what Paul Holmes meant when he said that Ohio didn't want the truth.

I tried a couple of avenues. Soon after taking the case, I suggested to Steve Sheppard that I see Louis Seltzer. "Look," I said, "the bad guys in this are obviously Seltzer and his *Cleveland Press*. I have a feeling that when we ask Mike DiSalle, who is a very humane man, to permit this test, Seltzer is going to tell him not to allow it, and Mike is going to turn me down. Let me go to Seltzer first and show him a way to be a winner. I'll tell him, 'Mr. Seltzer, why don't you back this test. During the investigation, Sam refused to take a test suggested by police. I think he had good grounds, but your paper made hay out of it. So now you could back a test, and say that you were always in favor of reaching the truth. If Sam flunks, it vindicates your entire position. And if he passes, you're completely protected.' Seltzer might go along with it."

"If Louis Seltzer walks out of this clean," said Steve, "It's going to be tough to swallow. But I'll buy it."

When I called Seltzer, he asked why I was seeking him out in this matter. "I have nothing to do with the Sheppard case," he said.

"Historically," I said, "you've had a great deal to do with it, and I think your influence is still considerable. I'd like very much to set up a meeting."

Seltzer made an appointment for me to see him at his office. When I walked in he was flanked by his city editor, I believe, and his managing editor. I outlined my position, and Seltzer listened very carefully without saying anything. His editors did the talking. They said they had checked me out, and as far as they were concerned I was a fresh kid. I was probably a front for *Argosy* magazine, which had shown interest in the Sheppard case, or for Erle Stanley Gardner, whose Court of Last Resort had given lie detector tests to Steve and Richard Sheppard and their wives in 1957. (Gardner's group had found that all four Sheppards were telling the truth in denying any attempt to cover up evidence for Sam, and in expressing their belief in Sam's innocence.) They said I wouldn't last two weeks as Sam's lawyer, that I just wanted to get some publicity and duck out. And in any case, they certainly weren't going to go along with anything I said.

When they were through, I turned to their boss. "Mr. Seltzer," I said, "there's something I want you to know. You have almost every advantage in this case that a man could have, and you're going to influence the governor to make an unjust decision if you can. You're probably going to win at least the first three rounds. But you're an old man, and I'm twenty-eight. You've got the money and the influence, but somehow, someday, I'm going to beat you. And when I do, I'm going to hold you up to scorn and ridicule. And you better hope you die before I do it, because then I'll only be destroying your image instead of you as a person. If you survive, you'll be held up to scorn by your own colleagues, who'll be quick to admit that you went too far. That's what you have facing you, and that's the price you'll pay for turning down an honest man who made you a reasonable offer."

Louis Seltzer stayed silent, but I saw the look that crossed his face. I mentioned the incident to a couple of people, and, of course, Seltzer and his boys denied it. But to this day, it's one of my most vivid memories of the Sheppard case.

I lectured on the case at colleges throughout Ohio, and appeared with Steve on radio and television shows to publicize Sam's right to a polygraph test. On a Mike Douglas show we gave a test to comedienne Dody Goodman, who knew the identity of the replacement for Jack Paar on the *Tonight Show*. We gave her a few choices, including Johnny Carson; she denied all of them. But on the basis of the polygraph test, we picked Carson. During the show, we asked viewers if they thought Governor DiSalle should okay a test for Sam, and their calls—which ran nine to one in favor of a test—literally blew out the switchboard.

But the friends I made for Sam in Ohio did not include the officials who could give him a chance to put his honesty on the line. The polygraph request was rejected by the warden at the Marion Correctional Institution by the state commissioner of correction, and by Governor Michael V. DiSalle.

The next step was to carry the battle into court. I brought suit to force the commissioner of correction to let me into the Marion jail with a polygraph. Both sides filed briefs, and we argued before the Ohio Supreme Court. On December 27, 1962—almost a year after I had become Sam's attorney—I got my answer. In a poorly reasoned decision that made no mention of an analogous California case, the Ohio Supreme Court refused to intervene. The court said that it had no power to step in, that the question of letting polygraph experts into the prison was strictly a matter for the warden to decide.

In effect the court was saying, "we can't do anything because there is no precedent." I felt there was a precedent in the California case, in which a lawyer had obtained a writ of mandamus forcing a sheriff to allow his client to be hypnotized. But even without a precedent, the court's opinion was not sufficient answer. As long as he cries out his innocence, any man is entitled to all the help he can get. And both lawyers and judges should jump at every chance they get to correct even a *possible* wrong.

Was Sam Sheppard guilty? The public was beginning to wonder—the response I got at lectures and after television appearances showed that. But officials were another matter. When I started speaking on Sam's behalf, a police officer in Cleveland had told me: "If Sam Shepard is innocent, I don't want to know it." I was coming to realize how many members of Ohio's power structure felt the same way.

We had gone as far as we could in the state courts without getting anywhere. Now we would go all the way in the federal courts. We would attack the original conviction.

I hired three Harvard Law School students—the two who stuck with it were Steve Hoskins and Don Sweeney—and gave them copies of Paul Holmes's book. "Read it," I said, "and then I'll tell you the claims of error I want to bring on a constitutional basis." There were also 9,808 pages of trial testimony and briefs to go through, and go through them they did.

At this point in the Sheppard case, the *fact* of Sam's innocence was of no help to him. All factual questions had been settled by the jury that convicted him. If the jurors had erred, their mistake could not be corrected on the basis of fact. The only way Sam might win his freedom was by our showing an error of law—a mistake in the way accepted rules had been applied in his case, a mistake that violated the Constitution of the United States.

It took Steve and Don almost two months to furnish the necessary material for the twenty-nine-page complaint of habeas corpus, charging that Samuel H. Sheppard had been deprived of his constitutional rights. In all, the complaint listed twenty-two violations, including the following:

Sam had been arraigned without his attorney present, despite the fact that counsel had been retained. Authorities had refused to delay the arraignment until counsel could arrive.

The *Cleveland Press* had "deliberately and with malice" printed articles and editorials in the weeks following the murder that implicated Sam and criticized law enforcement officials for failing to make an arrest. The influence of the *Press* and its editor, Louis Seltzer, "coerced law enforcement officials into fraudulently and maliciously" forcing an inquest and arresting Sam.

Despite the hostile publicity disseminated by the media, and encouraged and generated by law enforcement officials, a request for a change of venue had been denied. Also, repeated motions to postpone the trial "until the prejudicial effect of massive and sustained hostile publicity" had subsided were denied.

Jurors' names had been published thirty days before the trial started, and the jurors were not sequestered once it was under way.

During the trial, Judge Blythin had not sufficiently warned jurors to disregard opinions, rumors, advice, alleged information, and pressures to which they were exposed.

Both Judge Blythin, who was running for reelection, and Assistant Prosecutor John J. Mahon, who was seeking election to the bench, had been "overly attentive to the wishes of news media which might commend or criticize" them.

The impounding of Sam's home by authorities had prevented the defense from obtaining evidence in his behalf.

During their deliberations, the jurors had been allowed to make telephone calls from the hotel where they were locked up.

Two officers had been allowed to testify that Sam had refused to take a lie detector test.

Such were the specifications. I filed the petition for a writ in April, 1963, and the timing couldn't have been better. Three decisions that had just come out of the U.S. Supreme Court broadened dramatically the entire law of habeas corpus. In effect, the nation's highest court said that trial judges were not adequately guarding the rights of accused persons, and that state supreme courts were falling down as watchdogs. The rulings empowered federal judges to check into every aspect of criminal trials involved in habeas corpus appeals.

I filed the petition before Federal District Court Judge Mel G. Underwood in Columbus. He was less than sympathetic. "Counsel," he told me in open court, "give me reasons why I cannot dismiss this writ without reading it."

As reasons I named the three latest cases out of the United States Supreme Court.

Judge Underwood went back to his lobby and read the decisions, and when he returned, he'd changed his mind. "I see you've got a point," he said.

He failed to act, however, and the case dragged on. Finally, in December, Judge Underwood assigned the petition for a writ of habeas corpus to Carl A. Weinman, chief judge for the Southern District of Ohio. Judge Weinman had a reputation as an especially able jurist, and he wasted little time getting started. He called a pretrial conference for January 17.

In terms of freedom, 1963 had been a frustrating year for Sam Sheppard. There had been little action in the courts, and he had failed in an attempt to win parole. But I began to feel that 1964 would be different.

More than ever before, Sam hoped so. The need for freedom was a burr in his soul. Chip was approaching young-manhood, and Sam longed to be with him. And there was something else.

Ariane Tebbenjohanns had come into Sam's life.

3. *FROM GERMANY WITH LOVE*

Near Christmas time in 1962, I got a letter from West Germany containing 1,000 marks for the fight to free Sam Sheppard—$250, the largest donation from any one person we had received for Sam's defense fund. I was impressed, and, to say the least, curious. I asked Steve Sheppard if he had ever heard of the sender, Ariane Tebbenjohanns. Yes, he said, she was a German woman who had been corresponding with Sam for the past three years. As a matter of fact, Steve had just received a letter from her saying that she planned to come to the United States soon to visit Sam.

Such was my introduction to a love story that could only have made sense in the truth-is-stranger-than-fiction context of Sam Sheppard's life. To Sam, as their correspondence developed, Ariane Tebbenjohanns came to represent everything that life outside prison had to offer. In his book, he described his feelings when she sent him a snapshot: "To me, she was Sophia Loren, Doris Day, Marilyn Monroe, and Liz Taylor all wrapped up in one. No, that is an understatement—she was unique, and life once again began to take on some meaning."

Anyone would have found Ariane impressive. At thirty-three she was a glamorous blond divorcee easily able to afford mink in winter and the Riviera in summer. During the years I knew her, I felt that even in the afternoon she was the sort of woman who was always dressed for evening. Sophisticated and well educated, she was almost as fluent in English, French, and Italian as she was in her native German. She was extremely strong-willed; she knew how to take care of herself. And yet, she was also a romantic. Her correspondence with a man convicted of murder was the stuff of which pulp-magazine romances are made, and maybe that was its fascination—it was also the stuff of dreams.

Ariane, the daughter of Oskar Ritschel, a wealthy industrialist, grew up in Düsseldorf. She was the only child of her father's second wife, but she had a half sister, Magda, twenty years her senior, from Ritschel's first marriage. When Ariane was an infant, Magda married a man who would rise to great power in the monsterdom of Nazi Germany: Josef Paul Goebbels. Goebbels was Magda's second husband; her first had been a Jewish businessman.

According to Ariane, her father was neither a Nazi nor a Nazi sympathizer, and visits from Magda and Goebbels often ended in shouting matches between Ritschel and the propaganda minister. Once, she said, Goebbels left the house yelling that Herr Ritschel would be in a concentration camp if he weren't Goebbels's father-in-law. When Ritschel died in 1941, the Nazis boycotted his funeral.

Although she was a member of the Hitler youth organization as a child, Ariane said she was never a Nazi. When the war ended, she was only fifteen. As for her brother-in-law, he followed his leader in death as he had in life. The day after Hitler and his mistress, Eva Braun, committed suicide in a Berlin bunker, Josef Goebbels took his own life and those of his wife and children.

After the war, Ariane and her mother remained in Düsseldorf, where they had a home and income from a trust fund left by Ritschel. In 1951 Ariane married Olaf Tebbenjohanns, a member of a steel manufacturing family. Their marriage ended in divorce in 1957, leaving Ariane with a four-year-old daughter.

In 1954, Ariane read about Sam Sheppard in a magazine she picked up in her dentist's waiting room. She decided that Dr. Sheppard was being pilloried by the press and railroaded into jail because he had been unfaithful to his wife and because he had committed the additional sin of being well-to-do. Hours later, she was still thinking about it.

The case stayed in Ariane's mind. Dr. Sheppard was innocent; she was positive of it. How could the American people permit such a miscarriage of justice? The guilty verdict was wrong, and someone should set it right. Ariane became obsessed with the Sheppard case to the point that her friends told her to stop talking about it, there was nothing she could do.

In the winter of 1959 she wrote Steve Sheppard at the Sheppard Clinic, expressing her sympathy for the Sheppard family and asking if she could communicate with Sam. It was not the first letter Steve had received from a woman seeking to correspond with his brother; now and then, Steve would bring these letters to Sam to cheer him up. But somehow, Ariane's letter seemed different. There was a sense of taste to it, a certain dignity. At Sam's request, Steve wrote her back. "I regret that Dr. Sam is unable to receive letters directly from you nor is he able to answer you," he wrote, "but if you will allow me I shall be pleased to carry messages to him when I visit him each month. Perhaps he will want me to write you on his behalf from time to time."

And so a three-cornered correspondence began. Ariane sent her letters—which she wrote in white ink on parchment-like red paper—to Steve, who brought them to Sam. During each visit, Steve would take notes on Sam's answers. Usually he would use the notes as the basis of letters he would send to Ariane. Other times, he would simply send the notes. In 1961 Sam was transferred from the Ohio Penitentiary to the Marion Correctional Institution, where he was allowed to write Ariane directly. Her letters, however, still had to go through Steve—she was not permitted to write Sam at the prison until 1962.

As the correspondence continued, the relationship between two lonely people became stronger. Sam would carry Ariane's most recent letter with him, reading it as many as six times a day. He also carried a lock of her hair. When he sent her a picture and signed it "all my love," he realized that he was caught. As for Ariane, she tried to keep romance out of her letters, but she knew something was happening to her. In the summer of 1962, she wrote in her diary: "The idea sounds abnormal, but I've become so obsessed with the thought of Sam that everything else seems insignificant. Even my beautiful Riviera and the crazy life I lead here are no longer attractive."

In January of 1963, Ariane Tebbenjohanns arrived in the United States. Blonde and beautifully tailored, she looked like the sort of woman who would be at home in Palm Beach. But her most prized possession was a letter from the superintendent of the Marion Correctional Institution in Ohio, giving her permission to visit a prisoner named Sam Sheppard.

At nine o'clock on the morning of January 29th she showed up at the prison with a dozen fresh doughnuts and a bag of bread and sandwich makings. Sam didn't know she was arriving that particular day, and he thought he was being kidded by the guard who came to tell him that a fine-looking blonde in a mink coat was waiting for him in the visiting room. When he walked into the room and saw her, he smiled and asked for a kiss. Ariane kissed him on the cheek, and he knew she was real.

Ariane's reaction? Well, she was a romantic. "As soon as I saw him," she told Steve Sheppard later, "I knew that he loved me, and that I loved him."

The visit lasted four and a half hours. They laughed, talked, ate, held hands, and filled the drab room with excitement as prison guards watched through a glass wall. It was a fairy tale with a twist—the prince was locked up in the tower, and the princess had come to rescue him. Commitment was inevitable. Sam had not touched a woman's hand or smelled perfume for more than eight years. And, quite literally, Ariane was meeting the man of her dreams. Sam gave Ariane a dove on a silver chain that he had made in prison; Ariane gave Sam an Indian head gold piece on a golden chain. The exchange of gifts symbolized their engagement. If the scene had taken place in a movie made in the '30s, a full string orchestra would have played "The Prisoner's Song." It may have been the best moment of their lives.

A week later, a hearing was held in Columbus before the Ohio Pardon and Parole Commission on a clemency petition the Sheppard family had initiated before I entered the case. Steve called to tell me about the engagement and ask if it would be all right for Ariane to attend the hearing. I said fine, and so Steve broke the news about Ariane and the engagement a day before the hearing. When I brought Ariane to the commission headquarters for the hearing, the flashbulb-and-shouted-question-coverage was the sort of thing usually reserved for new movie stars and visiting royalty. Ariane was an instant celebrity, and she enjoyed the attention. Her name was a headline word. That, too, is the stuff of dreams.

At the hearing, I begged the commissioner's pardon for the furor stirred by Ariane's involvement. I explained that she was no publicity stunt; that she had been corresponding with Sam for three years; that they planned to marry if and when he was released from prison. In asking for commutation of his sentence, I cited his voluntary participation in the cancer research project, and his development of a prison school for practical nurses. I also described an incident in which he had saved an inmate-patient's life in the jail hospital.

I was frank about my own feelings. "I would rather he stayed in jail so I can litigate and prove him innocent," I said. "If he is freed, the question of guilt becomes moot." But I added that I was asking for clemency because Sam wanted out. "I'm his attorney, not his soul," I said.

That night, Ariane appeared on several radio and television programs in Columbus. On one, she was asked if she would be willing to accompany Dr. Sheppard to a town in India, where a philanthropist had expressed a desire to build a clinic for him. When she answered that she'd go anywhere with him, cheers filled the television room at the Marion Correctional Institution.

The next day, the publicity turned sour. The press found out that Ariane's half sister had been the wife of the infamous Dr. Goebbels. Headlines. Newscasts. And, in most cases, guilt by association. It didn't matter that Ariane had been a teenager when the war ended, or that her father had disagreed violently with his high-ranking son-in-law. The woman who had come from Germany to see Sam Sheppard was probably a Nazi too. And the romance must be a publicity stunt.

Two days after the hearing, the Pardon and Parole Commission voted unanimously not to recommend clemency for Sam Sheppard. Governor James Rhodes turned down our petition. And prison authorities got into the act. State Corrections Commissioner Maury Koblentz visited Sam at Marion, forbade further visits by Ariane, and deleted her name from Sam's mailing list. "You better send that blonde back to Europe," he said. Sam had some angry words for him. But opposition is a classic element in a boy-meets-girl story; if anything, Sam's feeling for Ariane was strengthened by it. The day after Koblentz's visit, Steve and Betty Sheppard visited Sam and brought along a couple of engagement rings. Sam picked one out, and Steve gave it to Ariane for him that evening.

In the next few weeks, Sam's situation in prison worsened. First, a letter Ariane had written to Sam at the Marion jail was returned as undeliverable. Ariane, unintimidated, had the letter published in the *Columbus Dispatch*. Soon afterward, Koblentz had Sam transferred back to the Ohio Penitentiary in Columbus, a maximum security prison. Sam, put in arm, neck, and leg chains for the transfer, was placed in solitary confinement when he first arrived at Columbus. Koblentz said that he had ordered the transfer because of violations of prison rules surrounding Sam's romance with Ariane, and that it was "the continuing efforts by persons related to or associated with Sheppard to defy or circumvent, directly or indirectly, an order, which revoked the visiting and mailing privileges of Mrs. Tebbenjohanns."

At the Ohio Penitentiary, fellow convicts and visitors smuggled letters out for Sam. Next Sam used simple codes so that he could include messages to Ariane in letters ostensibly written to his family and to me. At first, every third word in each sentence was a part of the message. Later, he switched to a four-two system. I was not aware of the code at the time; I just sent Sam's letters on to Ariane as he had asked. If I had deciphered the messages, I would have found little evidence of intrigue. One message read: "My destiny rests with you. You're the pride of my life and delight of my existence. I love you."

Ariane returned temporarily to Germany, where she soon received a black bra and panties that Sam had a freed convict buy and send to her. In his book, Sam explained that the gift was symbolic—"it was my way of saying to her that I wasn't a vegetable any more." When May came, it was her birthday and her fiance reverted to more traditional imagery. He saw to it that she received twenty-six long-stemmed, red roses.

In July, after tidying up her affairs, Ariane came back to the States, rented an apartment in a Cleveland suburb and bought two cars—one for herself and another for Sam. She got license plates for Sam's car and kept it ready in the garage.

I visited Sam whenever I was in the area. Finally, the battle for his release came before Judge Carl Weinman.

4. FREEDOM

Judge Carl A. Weinman sat behind a long mahogany table in his chambers facing the attorneys for the state of Ohio and for Sam Sheppard. It was January 17, 1964, and the judge was holding a pretrial conference to expedite proceedings in our petition for a writ of habeas corpus. The book on Judge Weinman was that he was a strong-minded judge with a knack for cutting through chaff and getting right to the grain. He lived up to his reputation.

"Gentlemen," he said, "this appears to be an immensely complex case. We're going to handle it with decorum and minimal publicity, and we're going to handle it correctly. I hereby order counsel to sit down and examine the record and agree on everything they can conscientiously agree on."

The state was represented by John Cianflona, a first-rate veteran, and David Kessler, a young lawyer who was as fair-minded as he was able. Kessler and I went through the whole transcript of Sam's trial. Kessler, obviously indignant at what Judge Blythin had done to Sam, wound up agreeing with most of what I alleged. He didn't throw in the towel by any means, but he didn't hold me up on nit-picking points.

There were additional conferences, we agreed on some stipulations, and I began work on a series of briefs. Meantime, Judge Mel Underwood, who had remanded the case to Judge Weinman, made an interesting comment to John Cianflona. "The reason I transferred this case to Weinman," Underwood told John, "is because somebody's going to have to let this poor bastard out, and I don't want to be the one to do it."

It soon became obvious that the state was worried. On February 24, no less an old Sheppard adversary than Cuyahoga County Coroner Samuel Gerber announced that he was recommending to the state attorney general that Sam be given parole when his case came up in the fall. What's more, said Gerber, he would not oppose parole prior to that time. Then Louis Seltzer's *Cleveland Press* joined the sudden forgive-and-forget movement by recommending that penal authorities match the coroner's "objectivity." Around this time, messages were transmitted to Sam through the prison chaplain saying that all he had to do to get out was to file another plea for clemency with the parole board. The chaplain apparently oversold the proposition—he had Sam believing that parole officials were begging him to accept clemency. Instead of filing a regular petition, Sam sent the board a note that was short in length and tone. It eventually drew a return notice saying that a rehearing of his parole appeal was not in order.

I was in New York during this period, but before Sam could refile a regular appeal I flew to Columbus for a short talk with him. Steve Sheppard told me that the state had communicated to Sam through the chaplain that "if he'll unload you as counsel, they'll commute his sentence to manslaughter and let him out." It was obvious that somebody up there hoped by giving Sam parole to prevent the habeas corpus action. So far as I was concerned, Sam deserved exoneration as well as freedom. I called Ariane, and she told me she was going to tell Sam to go along with the deal—she wanted him out right away. I tried to convince her that he was going to come out on the writ in the next few months, although I couldn't say just when. We had a hell of an argument. It ended by my telling her that I was going to Columbus to see Sam, and that I would do everything in my power to undermine her advice because she didn't know what she was talking about.

When I saw Sam, he said that to be so close to freedom when the courts had failed him over and over again presented an almost irresistible temptation. And then he asked the question most men in his position would have asked. "If I do it your way," he said, "can you guarantee that I'm going to get out?"

"Ethically, I can't guarantee you anything," I said. "But I'm practically assuring you that you will get out, and that's a long way for me to stick my neck out. The judge is a lawyer and I'm satisfied that he's honest. No honest man could refuse you this writ."

Sam sat there, and I knew he was thinking about Ariane and Chip, now called Sam, Jr., and the world into which I would momentarily return.

"Look," I said, "if this judge doesn't act in your best interest, and

73

there's a way to do it, I'll do the rest of your time for you—I'm that sure."

"Okay," Sam said, "I'll hang on."

On March 17, we got lucky. I was at the Overseas Press Club in Manhattan for a panel discussion of attorney William Kunstler's book about the Hall-Mills murder case, *The Minister and the Choir Singer*. The panelists included Dorothy Kilgallen, who had covered Sam's trial for the *New York Journal-American*. During the discussion, Kunstler mentioned that the Hearst newspapers had been slapped with a successful lawsuit as a result of their coverage of the Hall-Mills trial. "In that case," said Dorothy, "Sam Sheppard should collect fifty million dollars because he had the worst trial I ever saw." She said it was to her that Judge Blythin, who had called her into his chambers for a chat just before the trial started, said that Sam was "guilty as hell."

Some days later, we obtained a deposition from Dorothy that was inserted into the petition submitted to Judge Weinman. It read in part:

He was very affable. He shook hands with me and said, "I am very glad to see you, Miss Kilgallen. I watch you on television very frequently and enjoy the program." And he said, "But what brings you to Cleveland?"

And I said, "Well your honor, this trial."

And he said, "But why come all the way from New York to Cleveland to cover this trial?"

And I said, "Well it has all the ingredients of what in the newspaper business we call a good murder. It has a very attractive victim, who was pregnant, and the accused is a very important member of the community, respectable, a very attractive man. Then, added to that, you have the fact that it is a mystery as to who did it."

And Judge Blythin said, "Mystery? It's an open and shut case."

I was a little taken aback because usually, I have talked to many judges in their chambers, but usually they don't give me an opinion on a case before it's over.

And so I said, "What do you mean, Judge Blythin?"

And he said, "Well, he is guilty as hell. There is no question about it."

By the end of May, all briefs had been filed. Along with Dorothy Kilgallen's statement, we submitted a statement from a court clerk, Edward T. Murray. He said that in July, 1954, he and three or four other people were chatting in a courtroom where vacationing judges could pick up their mail. They happened to be talking about the Sheppard case when Judge Blythin stopped by. They discussed the case further with him, and then the judge got his mail and left. As the judge was leaving, said Murray, "he made the remark that Sam Sheppard was as guilty as *he* was innocent."

As a result of the statements from Dorothy and Murray, a twenty third charge was added to our petition—that Judge Blythin (who had since died) had violated Sam's constitutional rights by failing to disqualify himself after making statements regarding Sam's guilt. Eventually, the twenty-three points were boiled down to nine stipulations. Judge Weinman consolidated these into four issues on which he said he would base his decision:

1. Was the newspaper publicity before trial and/or during trial such that it violated petitioner's constitutional rights?

2. Did the trial judge, by failing to disqualify himself after making certain statements regarding petitioner's guilt, violate petitioner's constitutional rights?

3. Did the trial judge, in permitting police officers to testify that petitioner had refused a lie detector test, and in permitting a witness named Houk to testify that he had taken a lie detector test, violate petitioner's constitutional rights?

4. Did the action of the bailiffs in permitting the jurors, during deliberations and without authority from the court, to hold telephone conversations with persons outside the jury room, violate petitioner's constitutional rights?

On July 15, 1964, Federal Judge Carl A. Weinman handed down his decision in the Sheppard case. His opinion filled eighty-six pages and opened a new, if short, chapter in Sam Sheppard's life by returning him to the world.

In discussing the press, Judge Weinman wrote in part: "Any one of the above mentioned factors, i.e., the insidious, prejudicial newspaper reporting, the refusal of the trial judge to question jurors regarding an alleged prejudicial radio broadcast and the carnival atmosphere which continued throughout the trial, would be sufficient to compel the conclusion that petitioner's constitutional rights were violated. But when they are cumulated, this Court cannot, unless it were to stretch its imagination to a point of fantasy, say the petitioner had a fair trial." He said that the "inflammatory and prejudicial reporting" continued throughout the trial. "If ever there was a trial by newspaper," Judge Weinman wrote, "this is a perfect example. And the most insidious violator was *The Cleveland Press*. . . . Freedom of the press is truly one of the great freedoms we cherish; but it cannot be permitted to overshadow the rights of an individual to a fair trial."

With regard to Judge Blythin's statements, Judge Weinman said: "It is not the purpose of this Court to condemn a man who has passed away and is unable to come to his own defense; however, the foregoing statements are part of the uncontroverted evidence in this case and must be accepted as being true. It must be recognized that judges are human and often hold some opinion as to the guilt or innocence of the person being tried before them. However, a judge must have no interest other than the

75

pursuit of justice and when he expresses in emphatic terms the opinion that the person before him is guilty, as was done here, the judge then has a personal interest in seeing that the defendant is convicted or the judge may well be embarrassed for having made such an emphatic statement of guilt."

In his conclusion, Judge Weinman said that the court found five separate violations of the petitioner's constitutional rights—failure to grant a change of venue or a continuance in view of the newspaper publicity before the trial, inability to maintain jurors' impartiality because of the publicity during trial, failure of the trial judge to disqualify himself although there was uncertainty as to his impartiality, improper introduction of lie detector testimony, and unauthorized communications to the jury during their deliberations. "Each of the aforementioned errors," he wrote, "is by itself sufficient to require a determination that petitioner was not afforded a fair trial as required by the due process clause of the Fourteenth Amendment. And when these errors are cumulated, the trial can only be viewed as a mockery of justice."

The judge did not rule on Sam's guilt or innocence; that was not the question before him. He ruled that Sam's conviction had been unconstitutionally obtained, and he threw it out. He gave either the state or Cuyahoga County sixty days in which to hold a new trial. And he ordered Sam's immediate release on $10,000 bond. For Dr. Samuel H. Sheppard, who at forty had spent one-fourth of his life in jail, the eighty-six-page ruling could be summed up in a single word: Freedom.

Sam first heard the news from a fellow convict, whose eyes were wet. "You made it," the convict said. "You made it."

"God damn," said Sam Sheppard.

Sam was released shortly before noon on July 16. As he walked across the prison yard, cheering and applause came from every section of the penitentiary. "Doc" was getting out; he should never have been in. Cons, after all, usually know when a man is innocent.

He was brought to the Federal Building in Columbus, where bail was posted and where we held a news conference. Sam answered questions forthrightly. He also enjoyed himself. What about the tan on his face and hands, someone asked. "We're told Dreyfus was in such shape when he left Devil's Island," said Sam.

From the Federal Building we drove to a motel in Columbus where Ariane, who was speeding in from Cleveland, was to join us. Sam was like a kid at his first circus; he wanted everything—little things that made you realize what it must be like to spend ten years in prison. The first thing he did when he got to the motel room was order two large glasses of fresh orange juice. Then he took his shoes and socks off and walked back and forth across the room so he could feel the carpeting beneath his bare feet. Then he took a shower. "How long can I stay in?" he asked me.

"Sam," I said, "you can stay in till you shrivel up."

He also wanted to take a swim in the pool with someone. I loaned him my bathing suit and my wife. Since Wicki is a blonde, onlookers assumed that Ariane had arrived and was swimming with Sam. The pool became a center of attention. When Ariane did arrive, she showed some annoyance over the mistake in identity. There was, she made clear, only one Ariane.

Sam had been free for about two hours when we were told that Federal Judge Lester Cecil of the Sixth Circuit in Cincinnati had stayed Judge Weinman's order pending a hearing. One rumor had it that bail had been revoked and that Sam had been ordered back to jail. I phoned Judge Cecil, and he said: "No, I didn't order him back to jail." But he had granted a stay.

Ariane's arrival presented us with another problem—one that was, to say the least, understandable. More than orange juice, showers, a swim, and the feel of a rug against his bare feet, Sam wanted Ariane. And who could blame him? She was a good-looking woman, he had been celibate for ten years, and he was very much in love with her.

Steve Sheppard and I opposed the idea of Sam's getting married the minute he got out of prison; we felt he needed time to take stock of himself and the world into which he had emerged. But we also knew that Sam's release had Louis Seltzer worried, and Louie had a lot of clout. I was afraid some people who wanted Sam back in jail might have him picked up for spitting on the sidewalk if they could. We couldn't risk a fornication charge, and so we went along with the idea of marriage.

The next day we drove from Columbus to Chicago. Sam was at the wheel, and Ariane and Wicki sat in the front seat with him. I sat in the back with Paul Holmes, who had arranged for Sam and Ariane to be married in Chicago by a magistrate. The *Chicago Tribune* was picking up the expenses in return for an exclusive, and we were trailed by several cars filled with reporters.

The wedding was held in the bridal suite of a Chicago hotel; I was best man and Wicki matron of honor. A television reporter spotted the newlyweds window-shopping that evening and took them out to supper. The following evening we were all guests of columnist Irv Kupcinet at the Pump Room. A few days later we flew to New York, where Sam met some of the reporters who had covered his first trial. After leaving New York we went to Cleveland for a late-night champagne party with Dorothy Kilgallen, whose deposition had meant so much to us.

Sam Sheppard's world had changed with a suddenness that had to shake him. And although the prison gates had opened in a wave of excitement, they were still there threatening to close him in again. On July 23, we were back in court.

5. *THE SUPREME COURT*

A week after Sam's release from jail, we appeared before a three-judge panel of the U.S. Court of Appeals in Akron, Ohio, on the state's attempt to put him back in. The issue was whether Sam should be permitted to remain free on bail while the state appealed Judge Weinman's reversal of his conviction.

The temperature in the steaming courtroom must have been over one hundred degrees that day. It was another mob scene, and federal marshals had to lock arms with Sam and Ariane to get them through the pushing crowd outside the court. The day's emotionalism typified much of what was left of Sam Sheppard's life—moments of high excitement peaking out of long periods of tension. And none of it strengthened his ability to survive.

The panel was made up of Chief Judge Weick and Judges Clifford O'Sullivan and Lester Cecil. The state was represented by John Corrigan and by Gertrude Bauer Mahon, who had been an assistant county prosecutor.

I cited Judge Weinman's decision. "This man," I said, "did ten years for what a federal judge says is a mockery of justice." I said we wanted to prove his innocence and added that he was not a professional criminal. "You don't think a $10,000 surety bond brought him here, do you? He came because he wanted to."

Corrigan argued that, over the years, a total of twenty judges had affirmed Sam's conviction. Mrs. Mahon's primary argument was summed up by what seemed to me an incredible statement: Weinman's decision wasn't based on the record of Sam's trial. "The entire records," she said, "show that Sam Sheppard's constitutional rights were protected."

Near the end of the hearing, Judge Cecil made a remark from the bench that showed the sort of resentment that existed toward Sam. "Mr. Bailey," he asked, "does he plan to settle down and not make a public spectacle of himself?"

78

I felt like saying it was none of the judge's damned business, that Sam was entitled to tell the world how he got shafted. I didn't, of course. "A spectacle was made of this case long before now," I said.

When the panel went out, Judge Weick said they would return with a verdict in ten minutes. They kept us waiting for more than two hours. Then Judge Weick announced that Judge Weinman's reversal was being stayed pending a hearing, but that, meanwhile, Sam would continue free on bail.

On October 8, 1964, we went before the Sixth Circuit Federal Court of Appeals in Cincinnati. This time the three-man panel was headed by Judge O'Sullivan, who, I thought, seemed antagonistic toward Sam. The other judges were George Edwards of Detroit, Michigan, and Harry Phillips of Nashville, Tennessee. The hearing lasted two hours, and we went home to wait. In the weeks that followed, Sam lived minute by minute, constantly fearful that he might have to return to prison. He had dreams about being back; he was alarmed each time the phone rang. Ariane got pregnant, but she miscarried on Christmas morning. Sam felt the accident had been brought on by the strain under which they were living.

By spring, I began to expect the worst. The decision was taking too long. As chief judge, Judge O'Sullivan had the right to decide how much time the panel should spend on the case, and I figured he and Judge Phillips would find against us. Sure enough, on May 5, 1965, with Judge Edwards dissenting, the panel ruled to upset the Weinman decision. Sam was ordered to return to the penitentiary within twenty days unless I could obtain a continuance.

When I asked for a rehearing before the entire six-judge court, the petition was denied. I appealed the case to the United States Supreme Court, getting permission from the Court of Appeals for Sam to stay out on bail in the meantime.

My greatest worry was my most immediate one: Would the nation's highest court hear the case? The nine justices would accept it only if they found the issues both great enough in depth and general enough in scope to justify their intervention.

In November, the Supreme Court announced that it would hear the Sheppard case.

The case, scheduled for February 24, was postponed to February 28. The 28th was a dreary day in Washington, marked by gray skies and a light rain. I hardly noticed the weather as I walked up the steps of the building with Wicki, Sam, Ariane, and Sam, Jr. I was about to argue a case before the U.S. Supreme Court for the first time. Outside, reporters and photographers were waiting for us. Inside, nine men whose decisions make history were waiting: Hugo L. Black, William O. Douglas, Tom C

79

Clark, John M. Harlan, William J. Brennan, Jr., Potter Stewart, Byron R. White, Abe Fortas, and Chief Justice Earl Warren.

The experience of appearing before the Supreme Court is one of the few experiences in the law that are as good as they're cracked up to be. The give and take, the strong personalities of the justices, the questions—these are all facets of what makes it so special.

Especially the questions. In the U.S. Supreme Court, you don't talk law. You talk reason and social order. And what is most important, you talk justice. They make the law, you don't have to tell them what law they made. They are not overwhelmed by anybody else's law. And the questions are marvelous.

As the petitioner, I argued first, but I reserved time to speak again after the state's turn. I began by describing the murder scene and Sam's story. When I mentioned the "form" that Sam saw in the bedroom, Chief Justice Warren interrupted with the court's first question: "Was there any question about whether this form was a human being?"

"Sheppard said he could not be sure," I said. "It had a white top. I think it was a human being, the question being whether it was a male or female."

Much of my presentation concerned the prejudicial publicity spearheaded by the *Cleveland Press,* but I made it plain that I was not trying to destroy freedom of the press, and that there had been other elements, such as the judge's bias, that resulted in Sam's being deprived of constitutional rights.

This brought a question from Justice Fortas. "Do you mean you are not pressing the point with respect to asserted excessive or prejudicial newspaper publicity?"

"No, your honor," I said. "What I mean is that although trial by newspaper represents a serious problem, we have sufficient remedies within law which were not exhausted in this case without coming to the question of what must be done to silence the press."

Judge Blythin's attitude toward Sam was a central issue. The Supreme Court had refused to hear the Sheppard case in 1956, and I was asked what new evidence I was presenting that had not been used then. I mentioned Dorothy Kilgallen's deposition. Ohio Attorney General William Saxbe, who was delivering the state's argument before the Supreme Court, complained that Dorothy Kilgallen's statement had not been taken under oath. This was true. When we had reached her apartment, the notary we'd called failed to show up. We decided to waive the oath and take her statement anyway, and Dave Kessler agreed. When I got back up before the court, I described the circumstances and said that the attorney general's office had consented to our taking the statement without a notary. I leaned over and said: "Is that true, Mr. Saxbe?"

Saxbe turned to Kessler and then said, "I'm afraid it's true." In his formal argument, Saxbe said the trial had been a good one. "To allow Sheppard to attack his conviction now with an emotional issue that obscures the overwhelming proof of guilt subverts the jury system," he said. John Corrigan, who appeared for Cuyahoga County, made a similar statement: "We have on trial the jury system of the United States."

To me, their arguments seemed weak. When we walked out, I was convinced that we would win, although I thought we might lose Justice Black on the issue of freedom of speech.

After the hearing there was a press conference, and a newsman asked Sam how he felt. "I can't afford to have too much emotion," he said. But he was tense. And as the months passed, the strain increased. He was free, but for how long? Among other things, he started drinking too much.

On June 6, 1966, I was defending an accused bank robber in Worcester, Massachusetts, when a bailiff brought a note to the bench. The judge read it, and stopped the trial. "Ladies and gentlemen, excuse me," he said, "but I want Mr. Bailey to know that he's won the Sheppard case."

The Supreme Court had voted eight to one (Black was the lone dissenter) to overturn Sam's conviction. In a twenty-nine-page decision written by Justice Tom Clark, the high court ruled that Sam had been deprived of a fair trial "because of the trial judge's failure to protect Sheppard sufficiently from the massive, pervasive, and prejudicial publicity that attended his prosecution."

Reaction to the decision was interesting, especially in Cleveland. Judge Blythin was dead, and Louis Seltzer had retired earlier that year. But in an editorial, the *Cleveland Press* tried to get off the hook by saying that its news coverage had reflected worldwide interest in the case, and that its editorials "were critical of police work which seemed, for a time, to be confused and inert." The *Press* added: "If there were excesses, as the court contends, they should be viewed against the circumstances of a case which, as the *Press* once said editorially, became 'too much a part of our lives.' " The *Cleveland Plain Dealer* was even less conciliatory. It said that in "zealously" guarding a defendant's right to a fair trial, the court "has narrowed the field open to the free press."

Elsewhere, editorials generally praised the decision as just, but were also defensive about it. The impression conveyed by most papers was that the court had pinned the bulk of the blame on the press, and that a new era of press restrictions would result. I think this feeling reflected the general defensiveness the nation's press had developed over the years about the Sheppard case. The news media were so ready to be slapped that they assumed they had been slapped. And this was not the case. Justice Clark had been very careful *not* to shackle the press. He advocated restraint, but he imposed no legal restrictions on the media.

Justice Clark went into detail about the publicity that marred the investigation and the trial, citing specific newspaper stories like a *Cleveland Press* classic published while the jury was being picked: "But Who Will Speak for Marilyn?" He also mentioned a radio broadcast in which Bob Considine had compared Sam to Alger Hiss, and a broadcast by Walter Winchell alleging with complete falsity that a New York woman was Sam's mistress and had given birth to his child.

But he reserved blame for the court, rather than the press. "The principle that justice cannot survive behind walls of silence," wrote Justice Clark, "has long been reflected in the Anglo-American distrust for secret trials. A responsible press has always been regarded as the handmaiden of effective judicial administration, especially in the criminal field. . . . The carnival atmosphere at the trial could easily have been avoided since the courtroom and courthouse premises are subject to the control of the court. . . . Bearing in mind the massive pre-trial publicity, the judge should have adopted stricter rules governing the use of the courtroom by newsmen, as Sheppard's counsel requested."

In another section of the opinion, Justice Clark wrote that "where there is a reasonable likelihood that prejudicial news prior to the trial will prevent a fair trial, the judge should continue the case until the threat abates, or transfer it to another county not so permeated with publicity." He said that if a fair trial is imperiled by publicity during the proceedings, a new trial should be ordered.

"The courts," he pointed out, "must take . . . steps . . . that will protect their processes from prejudicial outside interferences. Neither prosecutors, counsel for the defense, the accused, witnesses, court staff, nor enforcement officers coming under the jurisdiction of the court should be permitted to frustrate its function. Collaboration between counsel and the press as to information affecting the fairness of a criminal trial is not only subject to regulation, but is highly censurable and worthy of disciplinary measures.

"Since the state trial judge did not fulfill his duty to protect Sheppard from the inherently prejudicial publicity, . . . and to control disruptive influences in the courtroom," Justice Clark concluded, "we must reverse the denial of the habeas corpus petition."

As part of its decision, the Supreme Court ordered the issuance of the habeas corpus writ and the release from custody of Dr. Sheppard unless the state of Ohio retried him within a reasonable period. Sam was elated by the court's opinion, but nervous about the prospect of a second trial. Understandably, he had little faith in juries. "If we get the people on the jury who hate me, I can't win," he said.

"Everybody either loved you or hated you in 1954," I said. "This time, I'm going to get younger people on that jury, and they won't have those feelings. And they'll acquit you on the evidence—there's no question about it."

I felt there was a good chance the state would decide not to retry Sam, but I was wrong. At a televised press conference following the Supreme Court decision, John Corrigan made a statement: "I am mindful that this is a government of laws and not of men. In keeping with that principle, I have made a determination that society has been the victim of a most heinous crime and society demands redress. However, society also affords to an individual a fair, impartial and objective trial before a jury of his peers and so we will present this case to them for their consideration."

Sam and Ariane had watched Corrigan on television. Afterward, they walked to the door of their apartment, where reporters were waiting. In answer to a question, Sam said he was ready to go on trial right away. Then someone asked if he'd take the stand.

"You're damned right," he said.

Neither he nor I could have known that by the time the trial opened, I wouldn't dare take a chance on letting Sam Sheppard testify in his own defense.

6. WHEN SILENCE WAS STRATEGY

The second trial of Dr. Sam Sheppard was called for October 24, 1966 —exactly twelve years and six days after the first one had begun. For Sam, the gray building that housed the Cuyahoga County Criminal Court was hell revisited. The second-floor courtroom in which he had been sentenced to life imprisonment was across the hall from the one in which we would fight for his exoneration. He couldn't help remembering, he couldn't help being afraid. And nothing I said could make him trust the jury system.

"They put me away once before and I didn't do anything," he said right before the trial. "They put me away in the face of evidence that I had a fractured neck and broken teeth, which I couldn't have given myself—my God, Lee, how can you show me that they won't do it again?"

I gave him all the assurances I had given him before, but I couldn't give him an absolute guarantee. "In the unlikely event that they convict you," I said, "you're eligible for parole immediately. I expect they'd parole you rather than have you appeal." He nodded, but we both knew parole would now be a bitter substitute.

About this time, I had to face a depressing truth about Sam. He was losing his grip on life. Looking for crutches, he was finding booze and pills. I told him that I didn't want him to testify because he had already told his story over and over again, and because his appearance as a witness would do little except give the prosecution a chance to take pot shots at him. Both these arguments were legitimate, but the real reason was his condition. Hardly anybody knew it, but during the trial there were times when Sam was unaware of what was going on around him. I couldn't let him take the stand, and I couldn't let the prosecution know it. Instead, I led them to believe he was going to testify. I had a good reason for this—the prosecution was going to call up "Frenchy," a convict who had been in the Ohio Penitentiary with Sam. In return for clemency, according to my information, Frenchy would claim that Sam had conspired with him to kill Spencer Houk after forcing Houk to write a suicide note in which he would exonerate Sam and implicate himself in Marilyn's death.

I figured the opposition would hold Frenchy as a rebuttal witness, calling him after Sam had testified. So I played a game. "Obviously," I told people, "I'll have to put Sam on the stand." The prosecution bought it—they held Frenchy for rebuttal. Afterward, John Corrigan told me that I had surprised him by not calling Sam, that as a result, he'd lost the benefit of Frenchy's testimony. Since the trial, others have described my decision to keep Sam from testifying as a brilliant maneuver. The truth is that I had no choice. Sam simply was in no condition to testify.

I'll always believe that John Corrigan was troubled by the fact that he didn't believe his witness. Even without Sam's testifying, the judge might have allowed him to put Frenchy on the stand in rebuttal. Of course, if Frenchy had testified, I would have called a platoon of prisoners to testify that Sam had never had a private conversation with Frenchy. And I doubt that Frenchy would have lived very long after shafting Sam —his fellow convicts would never have put up with it.

At his first trial, Sam Sheppard spent three and a half days on the stand. At his second, he remained silent. And even if he'd been capable of taking the stand, it didn't matter. As things turned out, we didn't need him.

7. THE RETRIAL

The man who presided over Sam's retrial was Common Pleas Judge Francis J. Talty, a forty-six-year-old ex-trial lawyer. The book on him was that he was a no-nonsense judge who was determined to give the defendant a fair trial. I got my first close look at Judge Talty when we appeared before him to ask for a change of venue. He denied the request, but I had to respect his decision. In asking for a change, we were suggesting that even Judge Talty couldn't assure us a fair trial in Cleveland. In refusing the request, he was saying that he damn well could.

Judge Talty was tough on the press. He ordered all photographers and cameramen to remain outside the building, and he pretty much barred reporters from obtaining any information about the trial other than what happened in court. He assigned fourteen seats to the press, but only two of them to media representatives from outside Cleveland—one to the Associated Press wire service, and the other to United Press International. I objected. For one thing, I doubted that the residents of Cleveland would get a fair account of what happened. For another, I did not think the Supreme Court decision had been intended to give the courts this much power over the press. The objection was overruled, and the press did little by way of standing up for its rights.

It took over a week to select the jury—seven men and five women, most of them relatively young. I was especially pleased with the naming of Ralph Vichell, a quality control engineer, as the foreman. He was my age, thirty-three, and he was well qualified to understand the new scientific evidence. Once the jury was picked, Judge Talty ordered that it be sequestered at a hotel for the duration of the trial. It turned out to be the hotel at which I was staying, and I immediately moved to another.

The real weakness of the defense in Sam's first trial had been his attorneys' inability to gather evidence. This time, we had the testimony of Dr. Paul Leland Kirk, the criminologist who had examined Dr. Sheppard's bedroom. Also, Andy Tuney had started working with me, and we had found and interviewed witnesses all over the country who appeared for Sam in 1954.

The state presented its witnesses first. Most of them had testified in 1954; this time, they didn't come off so well. There was officer Robert

Schottke, a homicide detective for the Cleveland Police Department at the time of the murder and a star for the prosecution at the first trial. Schottke had interrogated Sam in a hospital room only hours after the murder and accused him of committing it; he had been hailed at the time as a combination Dick Tracy-Sergeant Friday who stood firm against the Sheppard power and pinpointed the murderer. In my cross-examination, I first established that Schottke had been present when the Houks' teenage son found a boat tool bag containing Sam's bloodstained watch, his key chain, and a fraternity ring.

"Did you realize that Marilyn's killer had probably left prints on those items of jewelry, Mr. Schottke?" I asked.

He conceded this might have been the case.

"And did you think it important to ascertain just what prints were there before accusing anyone of this murder?"

Schottke hesitated, and then nodded. I asked if there was any reason why he hadn't checked for prints before accusing Sam, and he couldn't give me one.

"Officer Schottke," I said, "you knew Sam was in bed with possibly serious injuries. You know that his neck had been X-rayed. Did you make inquiry as to just how badly he had been hurt?"

He admitted that he had not.

"You knew, did you not," I said, "that if these injuries were serious beyond the point where they might have been self-inflicted, then Sam could not be guilty?"

Schottke agreed that this was the case.

"Then it appears, does it not," I said, "that you accused the doctor without troubling yourself to determine whether or not he *could* be the guilty one?"

Schottke nodded. Now a sergeant, he was no longer in the homicide bureau. And when he left the stand, he was no longer Dick Tracy.

Spencer and Esther Houk also testified again for the prosecution. I asked the ex-mayor, now divorced from Esther and remarried, why he hadn't immediately phoned the police when Sam called him for help. Why hadn't Houk brought a weapon with him? And when they arrived at the Sheppard house, how had Esther known that Marilyn was in the bedroom? For the most part their responses were vague, their general line being that they had not given these things much thought at the time.

Then there was Dr. Samuel Gerber, the state's number one witness at the first trial, the white-haired coroner who had leapt into action with an inquest at the snap of a *Cleveland Press* editorial. To put it mildly, I was waiting for Dr. Gerber.

At the first trial, Dr. Gerber had gotten a lot of mileage out of the bloodstains on Marilyn's pillow, testifying that in one bloodstain he could make out the impression of a surgical instrument. He never specified the instrument, but described the imprint as being that of two three-inch blades, with indentations at the end of each blade as if they had teeth.

But in the affidavit submitted after his study of the murder room, Dr. Kirk had said: "The pillow from the victim's bed indicates far more than was stated or implied in the testimony regarding it. Solid regions of blood-stain are present on both sides of the pillowcase. . . . Blood spatter from the blows themselves shows that the side opposite of the alleged instrument mark was upward during the beating. . . . It is certain that the pillow was either used to prevent outcry earlier, or that the victim attempted to shield herself by holding the pillow on her face or head. In either case the pillow had to be moved at a subsequent time, and was probably doubled down on itself and folded in such a manner as to produce a mirror-image blood impression later interpreted as an 'instrument impression.' "

Corrigan avoided the surgical-instrument theory in Gerber's direct examination. The coroner, when shown the pillow, simply said the impression was that of some "object." Evidently Corrigan realized the surgical-instrument gambit wouldn't work this time. But I figured that Gerber still supported it, and on cross I pushed for what he'd actually seen in the imprint. He didn't disappoint me. "It looked like a surgical instrument to me," he said.

"Well, now, Dr. Gerber," I said, "just what kind of surgical instrument do you see here?"

"I'm not sure," he said.

"Would it be an instrument you yourself have handled?"

"I don't know if I've handled one or not."

"Of course," I said, "you have been a surgeon, have you, doctor?"

The doctor admitted he hadn't.

"Do you have such an instrument back at your office?"

He shook his head.

"Have you ever seen such an instrument in any hospital, or medical supply catalogue, or anywhere else, Dr. Gerber?"

"No, not that I can remember."

"Tell the jury, doctor, where you have searched for the instrument during the last twelve years."

I couldn't have asked for a better answer. "Oh," said Gerber, "I have looked all over the United States."

"My goodness," I said, "then, please, by all means, tell us what you found."

"I didn't find one."

"Now, doctor," I said, "you know that Sam Sheppard was and is a surgeon, don't you?"

The coroner nodded.

"And you didn't describe this phantom impression as a surgical instrument just to hurt Sam Sheppard's case, did you, doctor? You wouldn't do that, would you?"

"Oh no," said the man who had done his best to nail down Sam Sheppard's conviction twelve years before. "Oh no."

I had a few other questions

"Did you, Coroner Gerber, tell a young intern about a month before Marilyn Sheppard was murdered that you intended someday to 'get' the Sheppards?"

"Any man who says that is a liar!" Gerber yelled.

"On the day of the murder, didn't Dr. Charles Elkins, a prominent neurologist, tell you that Sam was badly hurt?"

"No, he didn't."

"Didn't you permit several children to go through the house on the morning of the murder?"

"No," said Gerber. He had the same answer to the next question, which was whether he'd told a reporter during the week following the crime that he thought the murderer was a woman.

When the defense's turn came, we produced two witnesses who contradicted him on each point. Each was a reputable citizen. Each stated that Gerber had done or said what he denied.

Gerber's assistant, Mary Cowan, also testified for the prosecution. In cross-examination, I discussed the blood pattern in the murder room with her, going over photographs that Dr. Kirk had taken. She said there was no way to determine whether the killer had delivered the death blows with his left or right hand. I got her to agree first that the killer must have stood at the foot of Marilyn's bed as he swung the murder weapon; then, that blood spots on a closet door near the bed had resulted from the back swing of the weapon.

"Does it not appear, Miss Cowan," I asked, "that this weapon was swung in a left-handed arc?"

"It would seem so," she said.

When the state rested, I moved that the case be dismissed for lack of evidence. Judge Talty rejected the motion, and we started calling our witnesses. Our star was Dr. Kirk, whose background and credentials took about half an hour to present. Among them were his years of specializing in using such sciences as physics and chemistry in the examination and interpretation of physical evidence, and his appearance as an expert witness in federal and state courts throughout the country.

Working with Dr. Kirk was a pleasure; we were like a pair of basketball guards so keyed to each other's moves that it was almost impossible to miss a pass. Dr. Kirk presented his findings smoothly and clearly, and with impressive details. First, he gave a lecture on blood—grouping, typing, the manner in which it flows and dries, and what can be learned from its spatter. Then he went into the evidence he'd found at the murder scene.

By diagramming the room and then drawing lines from the outer limits of a bloodless area to the center of Marilyn's bed, Dr. Kirk pinpointed the attacker to the east side of the bed near its foot.

Careful investigation of the spots on the east wall had enabled him to determine which had spurted from Marilyn's wounds and which had been thrown off by the murder weapon. He had also computed the weapon's arc, and concluded from the attacker's position in the room and the pattern of the blood spots that the killer had swung the weapon with his left hand. Finally, he was able to establish that a large blood spot on the closet door had been left by someone other than the Sheppards.

When Dr. Kirk finished his direct testimony, I had no worries about cross-examination. John Corrigan was too good a lawyer not to know that there was nothing to be gained by extensive questioning. I was not surprised when he confined himself to fewer than a dozen questions.

Others called by the defense included the witnesses who refuted Gerber, a witness whose testimony pointed in the direction of a possible suspect other than Sam, and two witnesses who attested to the serious injuries Sam had suffered the night of the murder. One was Sam's dentist, Dr. Richard Koch, who testified that two of Sam's teeth had been broken, and his mouth badly cut. Sam, he said, could not have caused the damage himself.

The other was Dr. Elkins, an osteopath who testified that his examination of Sam two days after the crime had revealed a fracture of the third cervical vertebra and a bruise of the spinal cord. I asked if Sam could have inflicted the wound himself. Only if he had dived out a second-story window, said Dr. Elkins.

The prosecution called a few rebuttal witnesses, who tried to minimize Dr. Kirk's testimony. Among them was Dr. Roger Marsters, who had filed in 1955 an affidavit attacking Dr. Kirk's contention that the large spot on the closet door came from someone other than Sam or Marilyn.

"You have some substantial experience with grouping whole blood, Dr. Marsters, have you not?" I asked him on cross.

"Yes, I do."

"And prior to your participation in this case in 1955, had you ever tried to group dried blood, doctor?"

"As a matter of fact," he said, "no."

"Dr. Marsters," I said, "there has been evidence that the blood spots that Dr. Kirk grouped were at one time dusted with fingerprint powder. Do you have an opinion as to whether or not this might interfere with later attempts to group the blood?"

89

"Oh yes," said the witness. "I think it might substantially interfere with or contaminate the blood."

"You are firm in this opinion, Dr. Marsters?"

"Oh yes," he said, "definitely."

I pulled some papers out of my pocket. "Did you, Dr. Marsters, by chance write an article about the deterioration of dried blood?"

Yes, he said, he had written an article for a scientific journal.

"And did you, Dr. Marsters, report in that writing some tests which you made, in depth, in order to determine whether the presence of fingerprint powder would contaminate dried blood?"

"Yes," he said, "I think I did make tests like that."

"And did you not report, Dr. Marsters, that fingerprint powder does not contaminate dried blood?"

Yes, he said, he had.

In my closing statement, I compared the state of Ohio to a woman who was poking around in the gutter beneath a street light. When a passerby asked what she was doing, she said she was looking for a dollar bill she had dropped fifty feet away.

"Then why aren't you looking over there?" asked the passerby.

"Because," she replied, "the light is better over here."

The jury went out on November 16. As the hours passed, I began to sweat. I still felt we would win, and a friend who phoned during the afternoon told me the bookies in Las Vegas were giving twenty to one on acquittal. The bookies in Cleveland were only giving six to five, and that worried me. This was Cleveland, I thought, and when it comes to Sam Sheppard, anything can happen.

We had lunch and dinner at my hotel. Afterward, Sam and Ariane went upstairs to my room with Russ Sherman to wait. I stayed at the hotel bar. At 9:30 P.M., Judge Talty phoned to tell me that the jury had not yet reached a verdict, and that he was sending them to their hotel for the night. I called Russ Sherman, and told him to bring Sam to the lobby. We had to be at the courthouse when the judge sent the jury to bed.

When we got there, the judge had a surprise for us. While we were on our way over, the jury had reached a verdict. It was 10:20 P.M. when they entered the room. As the jurors filed in, one of the men winked at me. I leaned over to my client. "Sam," I said, "We made it." I could tell he didn't believe me.

"We have a verdict," said Ralph Vichell, the foreman.

"Do you have that verdict?"

Vichell handed the paper on which the verdict was written to a bailiff, who gave it to Judge Talty. The judge unfolded the paper, and read it. "We find the defendant not guilty," he said.

Bang! Sam Sheppard's big hand slammed the table in front of us. "It's about time!" he said.

"Hold on Sam," I told him. "This is still an open court."

But I sure as hell couldn't blame him.

8. EPILOGUE

It had taken me a long time to realize it, but when Sam Sheppard got out of jail, he was a condemned man. Nothing could put him back into a personality that would last. He won his freedom, and he won exoneration. But he couldn't win back his life.

He couldn't get it back professionally, and he couldn't get it back personally. Ten years of jail, two years of strain and tension. Booze and pills, and the end of a man. In 1967, the Ohio Medical Board gave him back his license to practice. As was the case with most of the amends society made to Sam Sheppard, it came too late. The following year he joined the staff of a hospital in Youngstown, Ohio. Within months, he was sued for malpractice in the death of a patient. He quit his job, and a day later there was another parting. The storybook romance of Ariane Tebbenjohanns and Sam Sheppard ended as Ariane filed for divorce.

Sam moved to Columbus, where he tried without much success to make a go of private practice. Finally, he made a pathetic attempt to cash in on his name by becoming a small-time professional wrestler. In October, 1969, he married Coleen Strickland, his manager's twenty-year-old daughter.

A few months later, just before Christmas, I had dinner with Sam. There was very little left of the man I had met eight years before in the visiting room of a prison. That man had impressed me with his spirit and his condition; I never saw the erosion that was already wearing him down. But now it was in the way he looked, the things he said. During dinner, he told me that he wanted to die. "I doubt that I'll be alive six months from now," he said.

He was right. On April 6, 1970, Samuel H. Sheppard was found dead in his home. His new wife said that he had been violently ill the previous night, that he thought he had the flu. But the cause of death was found to be an overdose of pills. And there was evidence that he had been drinking as much as two fifths of liquor a day. He was forty-six years old.

I was a pallbearer at Sam's funeral. I remember that Sam's manager was wearing a sport coat, a plaid shirt, and a tie with a Hawaiian dancing girl on it. Richard Sheppard was there, but Steve and Sam, Jr., were traveling in Europe and unable to get back in time. The mourners included a group of young hot-rodders with whom Sam had become friendly. And then, of course, there were the newspaper and television people.

Sam's casket was lowered into the grave and covered with dirt. As I walked away, the last thing I could see was the cameras. They were still grinding.

III

The Grandest
Haul
of All

CAST OF CHARACTERS

PATRICK SCHENA— He was driving the money truck when a car swung across the road.

WILLIAM BARRETT— "Open up," the man with the tommy gun told him, "or I'll blow your head off."

F. LEE BAILEY— The learned counsel. He flew to Montreal with a mysterious cardboard box.

INSPECTOR DUNNE— He didn't always use a search warrant—nor did he find anything.

THOMAS R. RICHARDS— He had a new concrete patio until the government tore it up.

JOHN J. KELLEY— The smiling Irishman.

GEORGE W. AGIASOTELIS— Better known as Billy A., he carried a bug in a shoulder holster.

JOSEPH TRIPOLI— The postal inspectors put his name on a flyer. He knew John J. Kelley.

RICHARD CHICOFSKY— The feds wanted him to mastermind a kidnapping.

PATRICIA DIAFARIO— The angry defendant. She wanted to sue somebody right away.

PAUL MARKHAM— He had the misfortune of having to handle the government's case.

JUDGE CHARLES E. WYZANSKI— At one point, even his honor nearly broke up.

HERBERT A. PERRY— An observant airline pilot. He was out driving when he spotted a large bosom.

ROGER DAILY— He never noticed the obvious.

WILLIAM FITZGERALD— He remembered a nose that resembled the prosecutor's. Or did it?

95

FRANCES KISSELL—	Not all lawyers make good witnesses.
DR. JOSEPH FREEMAN—	His cross-examination was classic.
VARIOUS POSTAL INSPECTORS—	The Keystone Kops.

1. *THE HEIST*

As usual in the summer, Cape Cod was a gold mine. More money was being spent than the local banks could hold. And so, at regular intervals, huge sums of cash were stuffed into canvas bags and sent to the Federal Reserve Bank in Boston—by ordinary mail truck.

For a while, state police rode shotgun for the truck on the seventy-five-mile run from the Cape hub of Hyannis up Route 3 to Boston. But in July of that summer in 1962, the U.S. Post Office notified the state police that an armed escort was no longer necessary. The reasons for this decision were never fully explained, but as everyone knows, neither snow, nor rain, nor heat, nor gloom of night deters a mailman from his appointed rounds, so why should robbery? Besides, there were two mailmen on the truck, a driver and a guard, each of whom carried a .38.

On the evening of August 14, driver Patrick Schena and guard William Barrett boarded the truck in Hyannis for the trip back to Boston. It was a pleasant night, and Schena and Barrett had no special worries; certainly not the locked canvas sacks in the back of their truck that contained over a million and a half dollars in small bills.

The sky was clear and the roads were dry as the truck left the Cape and moved north up the southern coast of Massachusetts Bay on Route 3. The first big town they would pass would be Plymouth. As it goes through Plymouth, Route 3 winds over hilly terrain. Along one stretch, the northbound and southbound lanes of the superhighway are a hundred yards apart. In some places, the center island climbs to as much as forty feet, so that one lane is not visible from the other.

The truck approached Plymouth and reached the Clark Road exit at the southern edge of town. As it went by the exit, two Oldsmobiles shot by in the passing lane. Neither Schena nor Barrett saw anything to get nervous about. But when they passed the Clark Road exit they looked back and saw detour signs spread across Route 3 behind them, funneling all northbound traffic off the highway. Similar signs blocked the Clark Road entrance, preventing cars from getting onto the highway. The mail truck was isolated.

The Oldsmobiles stopped on the right side of the road about two miles beyond the exit, where the southbound and northbound lanes were obscured from each other. As the truck came within two hundred feet, one of the cars suddenly swung out and blocked the road. Schena braked to a stop; both he and Barrett were still unaware of what was happening. They found out quickly when a man in a policeman's uniform hurried over to the passenger side of the truck and stuck a tommy gun in Barrett's face. "Open up," he said, "or I'll blow your head off." The next instant, a smaller man was at the driver's side with a duplicate message for Schena.

Before you could say "the mail always goes through," Barrett and Schena were being hustled into the back of the truck. The bandits tied their hands and feet and told them to lie flat on the floor. The phony cop, a big man whom his associate called "Tony," kept them company with his tommy gun. "Do as you're told," he said in classic robber tradition, "and you won't get hurt." The smaller man, who was called "Buster," got behind the wheel and moved out.

Within minutes the victims felt that they were riding on narrow, bumpy roads. Two or three times the truck stopped and money bags were unloaded. It stopped a last time, and the robbers got out. "Stay still for fifteen minutes," said one of them, "because we may be back." Five minutes later, Schena tried to free himself only to find that someone had come back. There was another warning. This time, both he and Barrett remained still.

Just how long they stayed that way is unclear, but they finally freed themselves and climbed out of the truck. Barrett looked at his watch. It was 9:35 P.M. The truck was parked in the breakdown lane of Route 128, a superhighway that circumscribes Boston and connects with Route 3. They were south of the city, about forty miles northwest of the point where the truck had first been stopped. Barrett and Schena were still dazed, and with reason. Tony and Buster and their confederates were $1,551,277 richer. The truck was empty.

The two victims tried to flag down passing cars and finally stopped a young man on a motor scooter. He was a foreign student with a faulty command of English, but Barrett and Schena eventually were able to make themselves understood. They had been robbed, they needed help— they needed police. The student put-putted off to find a real cop. . . .

About thirty miles north of the spot where Barrett and Schena had clambered out of their truck, I was sitting on the patio at the house of some close friends and clients, Ted and Jane Pitman, enjoying the fine summer night and talking about the Sheppard case. One of the Pitmans' children was listening to music on a transistor radio, and we all paid attention when an announcer interrupted with a news bulletin:

". . . authorities say that the million and a half dollars consisted mostly of small, worn bills, none of which are marked. Meanwhile, the FBI, state and local police, the postal inspection service, and the Coast Guard are cooperating in the greatest manhunt in the history of New England to find the robbers. . . ."

Ted Pitman grinned at me over his glass of Scotch. "Now there," he said, "are some people you ought to represent. With the retainer they could pay, you might be able to handle the Sheppard case the way you'd like to."

"Good clients, indeed," I said. "I bet the tongue of every lawyer in New England is hanging clear to his knees right now. A million and a half bucks. That's more than the Brink's bandits got."

That was about as far as my conjectures went. Whatever suspects might be accused of the million and-a-half-dollar mail robbery, they would want a more experienced lawyer than Lee Bailey. As far as I was concerned, the grandest haul of all was another case I would have to read about in the papers.

2. THE SUSPECTS

Almost immediately, the holdup that made history was immortalized by the press as the "Great Plymouth Mail Robbery." And indeed, it was an impressive undertaking. As befits a project of such scope, the robbery had been beautifully planned and executed. The only phase of the case that didn't live up to the crime was the investigation. From the very beginning, it was a disaster.

In the immediate wake of the holdup, investigators of various agencies spread through New England like the flu. Rewards were offered in amounts reminiscent of the Irish Sweepstakes; one offered ten percent of the money recovered, while another posted $50,000 for information leading to the arrest and conviction of the culprits. Would-be stool pigeons implicated everyone whose name they had ever heard. Hundreds of post office employees underwent lie detector tests. And *Life* magazine ran a picture story on the robbery.

Then the U.S. Post Office's own investigative arm, the postal inspection service, took over the operation. The postals did everything but hit each other in the face with custard pies; the Keystone Kops never looked sillier. The only difference was that the Keystone Kops were lovable.

In October a chief inspector named Raymond J. Dunne filed an affidavit before a U.S. commissioner in which he claimed that a Weymouth, Massachusetts, electrician identified as Thomas R. Richards had admitted socking away a million dollars' worth of the loot in his house. Dunne obtained a warrant to search for the money. To paraphrase Sherlock Holmes, the game was underfoot.

A couple of days after Dunne got the warrant, federal agents marched on the Richards home in Weymouth, armed with jackhammer, crowbars, and a power hoe. The feds attacked the house like giant termites, and they did that kind of damage.

The event attracted a nice-sized crowd. Reporters took notes, TV men took pictures, and the United States government took a private home apart. Concessionaires moved through the mass of onlookers, hawking popcorn, ice cream, hot dogs, and coffee while everybody waited for clouds of money to come billowing out of some secret cache.

They waited in vain. All the money the searchers found was $330 stowed in the rafters of Richards's basement. The money couldn't be traced to any source, and Richards had an explanation: he'd won the $330 in a poker game and was hiding it from his wife, who handled the family finances.

By the end of the day, the federals had demolished a man's home and uncovered his poker winnings. But U.S. Attorney Arthur W. Garrity, who would become a federal judge, left with his troops as though they had actually done something constructive. He announced that the search was a "qualified success," but failed to spell out the qualifications. He also announced that the government had no intention of repairing the damage at 90 Regatta Road.

Along with a mess, the search left two big questions. One was how Chief Inspector Dunne had wound up with a sworn affidavit attesting to something that wasn't true. The other was even more basic: How in the hell could the government get away with that kind of nonsense?

There would have been more questions if the public had been aware of a government search for a few days before in Watertown, a Boston suburb about seventeen miles north of Weymouth. The target was the home of John J. Kelley, a man who would come to dominate the Great Plymouth Mail Robbery case the way Casey dominated Mudville.

The search at Kelley's place couldn't approach the Richards hunt in terms of destruction, but it outclassed it in illegality. There was no "sworn affidavit" in this one; the searchers didn't even have a warrant.

Once again, the man behind the search was Chief Inspector Dunne. Dunne & Co. knew they had no basis for getting a warrant, so they decided to hit the Kelley apartment at 360 School Street when Mrs. Kelley was home alone. They would make a quick search and take off with whatever incriminating material they turned up. If Mrs. Kelley objected, they could always claim later on that she had consented to the search.

One element was necessary for success—they had to be sure Jack Kelley wasn't home. The day before the search, they asked the police chief of Watertown to arrest Jack on a phony charge and hold him for as long as it took them to go through his quarters. The chief refused.

On the day scheduled for the search, Kelley left home early in the morning. Postal inspectors kept him under surveillance as he drove to Lawrence, about thirty miles away. When they were sure he couldn't interfere, they called Dunne.

There are conflicting versions as to what happened next. Mrs. Kelley's version was found credible by a federal judge, and I happen to believe it myself.

Mrs. Kelley opened her door to an imposing sight—Chief Inspector Dunne, a large man, and Inspector McNabb, even larger. Dunne spoke first. "We have a warrant for the arrest of John J. Kelley for a bank robbery in Ohio."

Before Mrs. Kelley could say "let me see it," McNabb bumped her aside with his belly, and the postals tromped up the stairs to the Kelleys' second-floor apartment.

Mrs. Kelley, a devoutly religious woman, said she wanted to call her minister. "Absolutely not," said Dunne and McNabb. Then they started fine-combing the apartment. They found a locked closet, and Mrs. Kelley said she didn't know where the key was. Dunne sent an aide out to get a master key. When he returned, the closet had been forced open. Inside it were two money bags (the type used by merchants, not mail trucks), a length of clothesline rope, $235 in cash, and some shotgun shells.

The inspectors took everything. About this time, Jack Kelley called home. He was in Lawrence, visiting an old friend, Joseph Tripoli. Between sobs, his wife told him what was happening. Jack told her to put Chief Inspector Dunne on the phone. Dunne offered to meet him at his office in downtown Boston, but Jack had a better idea. "You wait right where you are," he said.

When Jack arrived at the apartment, he showed more-than-admirable restraint. He didn't hit anybody. He did ask the postals to show him the warrant for his arrest. In response to his next question they admitted that they didn't have a search warrant either. To top it off, they no longer had the money they had taken out of the closet.

Dunne said the cash had been sent to a laboratory for examination. But he said he had replaced it with $235 from his own pocket, and he pointed to a pile of currency on the sitting-room table.

That did it for Kelley. He picked up the pile, threw it in Dunne's face, and ordered the chief inspector out of his home. "Don't try to plant any money on me!" Dunne & Co. left promptly.

The next development (after the fiasco at Richard's's) was the issuance of a post office flyer naming four men as suspects in the Plymouth mail robbery. The flyer contained each man's picture, name, and address, as well as the make, model, and license number of his car. It urged postal employes to be on the loockout for the men and their autos, and to report all sightings.

The four men were John J. Kelley, Thomas R. Richards, Joseph Tripoli, and George William Agiasotelis.

It is a day in 1954. Jack Kelley is enjoying the races at Suffolk Downs in Revere, Massachusetts. With him is a long-time friend, George William Agiasotelis, better known as "Billy A." Billy, a gunner on a B–17 during World War II, has never completely adapted to civilian life—there are still moments when he needs to feel a machine gun in his hands. When these moments come, he keeps busy by robbing banks, trucks, supermarkets, and whatever else is available.

Billy is standing next to Kelley when he spots some men approaching. They look like cops. Billy pulls a wad of sixteen one-dollar bills out of his pocket and hands it to Kelley. "Say you won this gambling."

The men, state police officers, frisk Billy A. and Kelley. Billy A. is clean, but the sixteen one-dollar bills are Jack's undoing. Their serial numbers are on record at the Harvard Trust Company in Belmont, Massachusetts, robbed a few months before.

When he hears where the money comes from, Jack Kelley realizes that Billy A. has been busy again. But Jack has a wife and stepchildren whom he adores, and he is not about to endanger them by crossing up a machine-gun buff like Billy. He tells the police he won the money gambling.

Kelley is tried for receiving stolen goods. The trial ends in a hung jury. He is retried, and this time, he's accused of robbing the band *and* of receiving the money. It is legally impossible to be guilty of both offenses, but the state wants to get him on something. As it turns out, he is acquitted of the robbery but convicted of receiving money he knew was stolen. He gets the maximum sentence of five years in prison. And his conviction is affirmed by the Massachusetts Supreme Court.

Jack, an exemplary prisoner, is paroled after twenty-two months and spends the last part of his stretch as a chaplain's assistant in the Plymouth area at one of the so-called "camps" that are adjuncts to the Massachusetts prison system.

Soon after Jack Kelley goes to jail, Billy A.'s mother dies. On the day of her funeral, Billy robs a bank in Quincy, Massachusetts, and is chased by police to a golf course. Billy A. hops aboard a power mower and tries to escape across the course. But the power mower only does eight miles an hour. The police start shooting, and Billy A. is hit in the back.

End of chase, but not of Billy A. He survives, stands trial, and is convicted. He gets a thirteen-to-fifteen-year sentence, and is paroled in the spring of 1962—just in time to be at large for the Great Plymouth Mail Robbery. Billy A.'s face wins a place on the post office flyer.

On December 10, not quite four months after the heist, William F. White, Boston's chief postal inspector, issued a public statement to the effect that the Great Plymouth Mail Robbery had been solved. The guilty parties were known and would be arrested before the year's end. In the meantime, they were being allowed to run loose in the hope that they might lead investigators to the money.

If White was serious, his statement has to be one of the most moronic moves ever made in the name of criminal investigation. You didn't have to be Ellery Queen to deduce that the four men on the flyer were the suspects White intended to arrest.

When the phone rang on the evening of December 11, I was in Columbus, Ohio, preparing to plead before the Ohio Supreme Court Sam Sheppard's right to prove his innocence by submitting to polygraph tests.

Billy Norton, a top reporter for the *Boston Traveler,* was calling to ask whether I would be willing to supervise some polygraph tests for suspects in the Great Plymouth Mail Robbery. They were sick and tired of being persecuted by the postals. They wanted to be cleared, and would take any tests that I thought fair.

We made an appointment to meet in my Boston office.

3. THE BUG

Billy Norton came into my office on December 12, 1962, with Jack Kelley and Joe Tripoli. Physically, the two friends and fellow suspects couldn't have been more different. Kelley was over six feet tall, weighed more than two hundred pounds, and had a prominent nose, deep wrinkles, a thinning shock of graying red hair, and bright blue eyes. Tripoli was about five feet six and stockily built with graying black hair, a widow's peak, and a friendly dark-eyed smile that was showing strain around the edges.

Their mutual objective was to get out from under federal harassment. They wanted me to represent them. The postals had asked them to take polygraph tests, but they had refused because they didn't trust their would-be testers. They wanted to take tests, but they wanted to be sure the tests were impartially administered.

"That's all very well," I said, "but there's one thing you'd better understand. If you know anything at all about the robbery, you're going to flunk the test. Don't think you're going to fool the examiner."

I would start with Joe Tripoli. First, I sent a letter to Chief Postal Inspector White, telling him that I expected to give Joe a test, and inviting him to attend with his own expert. I said the test would be fair and that if Joe flunked, I'd hand him over on a silver platter. But if Joe passed the test, the postal inspector service would have to stop persecuting him, and his name would have to be eliminated from the flyer. White said no twice, telling newsmen that he had no interest in any Bailey-run test, and refusing to confirm that Kelley and Tripoli were suspects.

At that first meeting, Kelley and Tripoli also discussed their finances. They said they would have to borrow the $200 necessary for the testing. "If you think we've got the money from the robbery, guess again," Kelley told me. "Trip runs a bar, and the place is so overrun with postals that nobody wants to drink there and he's going bankrupt. I try to make a living selling real estate, but with the postals keeping me under surveillance all the time, I can't even approach a customer."

When Joe Tripoli showed up at Charlie Zimmerman's office for a test the next day, the place was overrun with newsmen. After an hour Charlie told me Joe "reacts to everything from the mail robbery to Santa Claus.

Let him cool down, and we'll try again. And it would help if there weren't so many people around."

I announced to the reporters that the test was incomplete and was being halted for the day. Billy Norton reacted by rushing into print with a front-page story claiming that Joe Tripoli had flunked a lie detector exam.

The next day Kelley, Tripoli, and I met with Charlie in a suite at Boston's venerable Parker House Hotel. As we got ready to retest Tripoli, Thomas R. Richards appeared. Since he was associated with Jack and Trip on the post office flyer, he'd decided he might as well join them with regard to counsel. Then Billy A. phoned to say that he too wished to be represented.

By the time Billy appeared, Charlie had finished testing Joe Tripoli. Trip, he said, was clean. He knew nothing about the persons involved in the robbery, or about its planning or execution.

I looked at my four new clients. "I'm going to announce the results of Joe's test to the post office," I said. "If they are now willing to have the rest of you tested on the grounds that they'll leave you alone if you pass, so be it. Until I find that out, there's no point in running tests for the rest of you because this would give their examiner grounds to claim that subsequent tests might be less valid."

But there was another matter. "Representing multiple suspects in the same case is a delicate business," I said. "If any of you have inconsistent interests, it would be both unethical and improper for me to advise all of you. Therefore, since we're all here and Charlie has the instrument ready to go, I'm going to ask that you take a test—for my edification only—as to whether or not you know of any conflict of interests between you."

They agreed, and thirty minutes later, Charlie took me aside. "Kelley and Richards are okay," he said, "but Billy is just about to blow up the machine. It looks to me as though he's got something against the other three." One look at the chart told me Charlie was right.

I told Charlie I would handle Billy A. Then I went back into the other room and told the four suspects that they had all passed. We made an appointment to meet the next day.

Almost every day for the next two weeks we held conferences to discuss the postal harassment and our own strategy. Billy's attention never wavered. I was ready to make my move but first I let Kelley in on the secret.

"Do you think Billy might be a spy for the post office?" I asked.

"Anything's possible," said Kelley, "but it seems funny that they'd put him on the flyer if he wasn't a real suspect."

"That could just be a cover," I said. "Billy flunked the lie test cold."

"You didn't tell me that before," he said. "You mean the bastard's against us?"

"Could be," I said. "But if he is, we might be able to work it to our advantage. Let me try something."

I reassembled the full group. "Gentlemen," I said, "I want all of you to be extremely careful not to get so provoked at these post-office clowns that you get into any physical fights with them. That would be very bad. They carry guns, and you might get hurt. I am going to give each of you a cheap and very simple camera. Any time you see a postal inspector near you, take his picture and keep snapping until he leaves. This may give you some peace, and give us enough evidence to get an injunction against the sons of bitches. Just bring all the film to me.

"I repeat: don't get provoked into fights. Any of you could get shot at any time." I turned to Billy A. "Especially you."

"Whaddya mean?" he said. "Why me?"

I pulled out a copy of the poster that offered $50,000 reward for the arrest and conviction of the robbers. "There is a phrase in this reward offer that provides that any robber who is killed while resisting arrest will be 'deemed convicted' for the purposes of the reward. In other words, the easiest way to get the money is to kill you. This cuts out waiting for the trial or risking the possibility of acquittal.

"You, Billy, are an especially likely target. You have a record for armed robbery, and have carried a gun in the past. So whereas the others are not considered dangerous, you are. Anyone could gun you down and then claim that he thought you were about to shoot him."

When I got to my office the next morning, Billy was waiting at the door. "I've got something to tell you," he said as we walked into my office. "I been working with the postal people, steering them on Tommy and Kelley and Trip and some other guys. They been paying me every week. Seventy-five bucks. And they said I'd get a big reward if anything broke."

I lit a cigarette and took a puff. "Let's start at the beginning," I suggested.

Billy A. unbuttoned his jacket, loosened his tie, and began. "A few days after the robbery," he said, "some postal inspectors came to me and said I could help them. They said I was a convicted bank robber, and probably could give them some leads on who might of done the Plymouth job. I told them I wasn't interested in being an informer even if I knew something, which I didn't. They told me they could go to my parole board and get me violated so I would have to go back in the can. But if I cooperated, I could get some cash, maybe a whole lot of it. All I had to do was give them some names.

"I didn't want to go back to the can, so I agreed. I figured I'd give them some bullshit, and when they didn't get nowhere, they'd leave me alone.

"They asked me to take a lie detector test so they'd know I wasn't involved myself. I took it, and they said I passed and gave me fifty bucks. Then they asked me if John Kelley might have been in on the job. I said sure, he could of done it, he's smart enough. So they asked me if Kelley knew anyone who didn't have a record and could hold the money without being suspected.

"I had once met this guy Richards with Kelley, except that at the time, his name was Bagdalian. He had a steady job as far as I knew, and no record. So I gave them his name. I also mentioned Tripoli, who used to be in business with Kelley selling used cars. They put taps on all their phones. They would play the tapes for me to see if I could tell who was on the other end of the line.

"Anyway, on the same day they busted into Kelley's apartment, they talked to Richards in a post office in Fall River. He denied knowing anything, but they thought he acted suspicious. When they told me that, I egged them on. I said he probably had the money buried somewhere near his house.

"Then they found out that he put in a new cement patio right after the robbery. They were sure that was the spot. Dunne saw Richards the next day, but couldn't get anything out of him. They wanted me to help them break into the house some night when no one was home and make sure the money was around, and then they would get a warrant. They even gave me money for some rubber gloves so we wouldn't leave any fingerprints.

"But that never worked out because when Tom and his wife went out they always left a babysitter. Finally, they said they were positive Tom was the right guy, and they were going to get a warrant anyway. They said they could file a statement saying Tom admitted having the money, and that would be enough. I said how the hell could you do that if Tom said he didn't know nothing about the money? They said it would be Tom's word against Dunne's, and any federal commissioner would take the word of an inspector against the word of a slob like Tom.

"So they got the warrant and ripped up the house and they didn't find a goddamned thing."

I tried for an icy stare. "If Kelley and Tom and Trip were the guys who pulled the robbery," I said, "they would also be the kind of guys who might get wise to you and buy you some cement shoes. Did you ever think of that?"

"Of course," said Billy. "I had some other names I could have given, but those names have guns. Kelley and the others are just clowns, I knew they wouldn't do anything."

"If you're not afraid of them," I said, "why did you decide to tell me all this?"

"It's the goddamned poster," Billy said. "I could get shot in the face on account of that thing. The postals are so goddamned stupid. You have no idea how stupid they are. You know, one time they told me they didn't know nothing about robbery cases, and I was running their investigation because I was an expert. How do you like that? Me, the expert of the investigation."

"That's all very interesting, Billy, but I had you figured for a stoolie. You didn't do too well on that lie test we gave you. Now tell me something I don't know, because I'm very busy and so far you've wasted a lot of my time."

Billy's expression went from angry to pouting. "I can tell you something else," he said. "They wanted me to name Tommy on the Quincy job."

"What do you mean?"

"There were three men on that job. They only caught one—me. The postals said that if I claimed Tommy was one of the others, they could have him arrested and then, when he was in the can, they could make him talk. If he wouldn't talk, they would get some of the other inmates to help him want to talk. You know what I mean?"

"I know what you mean, Billy. But what were you going to get out of this? I mean for implicating Tommy?"

Billy grinned. "They were going to give me a hundred grand."

"And just where would that kind of money come from?" I said. "I know the feds have a slush fund for stoolies, but not that kind of money."

"You may not believe this," said Billy, "but it's true, so help me. They were going to collect a hundred bucks from each postal inspector in the country. Anyone who wouldn't kick in would be transferred to Boston. They all hate Boston and so all of them would pay. I swear to God."

"Billy," I said as gravely as possible, "you have done your friends a great injustice. I think you should do all you can to repair the damage."

"Yeah," said Billy. "Sure. What do you want me to do?"

"You have spied on us," I said, trying for a pontifical manner, "and that was a grave transgression." I'm not sure he knew what a "transgression" was, but he nodded. "I think the only fair way you can repair the damage you've done is to do a little counterspying."

"You mean I should keep working for the postals, but really be working for you, right?"

"Exactly, Billy. It's the only way to square things. Okay?"

Billy agreed. He said the postal inspectors would never catch on. "They're too goddamned stupid."

Later that day I equipped Billy with a Minifon wire recorder, which fits under the arm in a shoulder holster and can be connected to a tie-clip or wristwratch microphone. The recorder runs for hours, certainly enough time to pick up a few words from one of the postal inspectors. "By the way," I said, "where do you meet these guys?"

"I don't have to go very far,' he said. "The postals bought the house next door to me and have a guy named Earl Wheeler living there. I have a direct phone line to his basement, but I usually just walk over."

The postals certainly had gone to a lot of trouble. I asked Billy why.

"I dunno," he said. "All I can tell you is what they told me. They said they had the word from the attorney general, Robert Kennedy. He said this was the biggest robbery ever, and he wanted it solved one way or another. They figure that means they can do anything they want, that they can throw out all the rules."

"Okay," I said. "Oh, one other thing, Billy—what would you do to me if this was the other way around? Suppose I took a counterspy assignment for you, and then crossed you up?"

"I'd blow your head off," Billy said.

"Do you think Kelley or Richards or Trip would do that to you if you pull something on us?"

"Nah. They ain't got the guts."

"Do you think I would?"

For five or ten seconds we stared at each other. Finally, Billy answered. "You might," he said. "I don't think you would, but you just might."

"Billy," I said, "I think we have a deal. Be square with me, and I'll do the same with you. I want that recorder to tell me that the postals have offered you $100,000 to frame Tom Richards, and I'll figure you've done your bit. Also, every dime you get paid, I want the money. I'll give you dollar for dollar, but I want what you get. A deal?"

Billy stuck out his hand. "Deal."

Each night, Billy would crunch across the packed snow to the back door of the house next door. There would be the sound of barking, and Earl Wheeler's voice silencing a dog. Then Billy and Wheeler would talk. Within five conversations, I had recorded evidence of the plan to break into Richards's home, the mention of a $100,000 payoff for implicating Richards in the Quincy bank robbery, and several other interesting items.

While this was going on, Bob Leary, a reporter for the *Boston Globe*, called to say he had discovered that Billy A.'s next door neighbor was a postal inspector, and he was about to publish the story. He had called me for a comment. I asked him to hold off. "I've got something going out there," I said. "Your story could interrupt it, and it's important."

Leary said he'd hold his story if I promised him an exclusive on whatever was happening. Giving an exclusive is no way to endear yourself to the press in general, but Leary had me over a barrel. "You're a competitive guy," he said. "What would you do if you were in my place?"

I let him listen to the tapes we'd already collected; then I decided that one radio station and one television station should also be informed. I called in Jim Jensen from WBZ-TV and Dick Levitan from WBZ radio. Both agreed to sit tight.

On January 10, 1963, after Billy A. had been playing counterspy for two weeks, I called in Kelley, Richards, and Trip, who voted to light the fuse. The *Boston Globe* ran its exposé, and WBZ gave the story the works. The next day my office was a city room as reporters from other papers and stations tried to catch up on the story.

Billy wrote and signed a long affidavit detailing his dealings with the postal inspectors, and we corroborated much of it with recorded conversations. The most dramatic item was Wheeler's voice agreeing that Billy would be paid $100,000 for implicating Tom in the bank job, the money to be raised by collecting one hundred dollars from each of the nation's postal inspectors.

News film showed us ceremoniously unearthing the special telephone line that ran from Billy's house to Wheeler's residence. I took the yellow handset that the postals had installed in Billy's cellar to my office, and announced that its real owner could claim it there. For some reason, no one ever showed up.

For three days, the tale of Billy A.'s double agentry dominated the front pages of Boston's newspapers. Through all the furor, the postals kept silent.

Public reaction to the story could be summed up in a single word—indignation. The disclosure of the government's dealings with Billy probably prevented an unjust indictment and possible convictions. Where corrupt public officials are willing to suborn perjury and manufacture evidence, wrongful convictions are easily obtained. Public officials respond to the one power they fear most—not prosecution for their wrongs, for they are the prosecutors and they do not prosecute themselves, but to the power of a free press.

4. THE HARASSING

"I'll be ready to move some of the stuff tomorow," I told Jack Kelley on the phone. "I'm going to rent a Cessna and fly to Canada." In a sense, it was an open invitation. I knew the postals were listening.

They were also watching and following. The Plymouth mail robbery probe was not so much an investigation as it was a harassment campaign.

As the federals bugged and bumbled, I figured the least we could do was help them along. Especially when it came to phone taps. It was during this period that I answered my phone, "Hello, bug." Every now and then, I would call one of the suspects and say in my most conspiratorial manner that I needed "another chunk of green." I'd designate a meeting place, and say we would go from there to the "cache." When the meeting took place, a couple of postal inspectors would be around trying to look inconspicuous. All they could do was watch while we had coffee, made small talk, and then went our separate ways.

The call to Kelley represented another effort to keep the postals on the go. Except that in this case, they would have to go a little farther than usual. One day in 1963, I decided an overnight trip to Montreal would be a pleasant break for Wicki and me. (We had been married since July of 1962.)

I invited one of my investigators to come along, and then remembered that one post-office theory was that some of the loot might have been spirited away to Canada. A made-to-order situation. First, I invited a close friend of Kelley's to come along. Then I rang Jack about moving "the stuff," without saying where in Canada I was going.

Early the next morning we met at Beverly Airport, a municipal field north of Boston. We put our luggage on the plane, and then Jack Kelley backed his car up to the cargo door. As conspicuously as possible, we took a large cardboard carton out of the car's trunk and loaded it into the Cessna. Needless to say, we did our best not to obstruct the view of the men in the two post-office cars parked at the edge of the field.

I waved good-bye to Kelley and took off abruptly. I had deliberately neglected to file a flight plan or mention my destination to the man from whom I'd rented the plane. I headed east and flew low over the water so that no radar could track us. After following the coast to the Maine border, I turned northwest to Burlington, Vermont.

In good weather, it's perfectly legal to fly all over the U.S. without filing a flight plan or notifying the FAA. But leaving the country is another matter, so as we passed over Burlington, I called the Flight Service Station and filed for Montreal. But I baited the hook by deliberately estimating my flying time at double what the trip was likely to take. Then I throttled back until the plane was crawling through the air. As we flew north, I stayed too low for continuous radar coverage.

When we were halfway to Montreal, I knew the postals had taken the bait. Unless an emergency exists, there is no reason for the tower of a large municipal airport to call a private plane. But the Montreal tower was calling me by aircraft number. I was pretty sure my excessive time estimate had led somebody up there to suspect that we planned to set down in a meadow as soon as we crossed the border, unload the carton, and take off again. If I did land somewhere, I'd be unable to hear the tower's call and respond.

I disappointed whoever it was by answering that call and several others on the way to Montreal. At the airport, customs officials showed little interest in our personal luggage, but seemed surprised when I told them there was a large carton in the plane that would be left on board. Before leaving for town, I locked the aircraft and pasted two small strips of Scotch tape across the bottom of both doors. The cardboard carton could be seen through the plane's windows.

When we returned to the field the next morning to fly home, the doors were still locked, but the tape on the pilot's side had been broken. The box was intact and as empty as it had been when we loaded it on the plane.

The cardboard caper was one of dozens of incidents in the black comedy we played out with the postals. I had explained to my three clients at the start of 1963 that notwithstanding the Billy A. exposé, their troubles were far from over. The postals were too committed to them as suspects to give them up. This is not to say that other people weren't being investigated; during the next few years, about fifteen different "suspects" appeared in my office. But they were suspect as henchmen of the original three, not as substitutes.

We fought nonviolently on several fronts. The place we were least successful was the courts. Both Richards and Kelley sued the government for slander. Tom also sued for damages to his house, and Kelley asked for his $235 back. Both actions were dismissed on the ground that federal investigators were immune from suit no matter what wrongs might have been committed. I brought appeals in which I contended that there had to be limits to official immunity, and won reversals of both decisions. But

Kelley subsequently lost his suit in a jury trial, and Richards's case was never tried.

We tried five times to bring complaints against postal inspectors for harassment. In four cases, we were turned down by local magistrates. In the fifth, we had photographic evidence. Tom Richards, walking up to the front door of his home one Sunday afternoon, had been serenaded by the catcalls of two postals. When he ignored them, one of the inspectors rushed at him swinging a fist. Tom, who had his camera with him, got some excellent shots of Inspector J. Donahue, his face twisted in anger, his arm coming around. We showed the pictures to a local district court judge, who issued an assault complaint against Inspector Donahue. But Donahue's attorney succeeded in having the matter transferred to a federal court, and it never came to trial.

We were more successful at counter-harassment, particularly in mixing up the phone-tappers and confusing the car-tailers. When it came to cars, Jack Kelley was our expert. His favorite strategem was to accelerate gradually until the inspector tailing him was too busy driving to know where he was going. Kelley would turn up a dead-end street. As the inspector wrestled his car to a stop, Kelley would make a power-skidded left turn, wheel around behind the postal's car, and block the road. Then he would walk over to his tail and ask what the inspector happened to be doing in the neighborhood.

And ten there was the Richard Chicofsky affair. In April, 1964, I got a call from Bob Barton, a lawyer with whom I shared space. "Lee," he told me, "I've got a guy here with some information that's absolutely crazy, but I believe him."

A few hours later, Richard Chicofsky was telling me his story.

Chicofsky had a prison record, but he was not popular with other ex-cons. He had once set up some defendants for the narcotics bureau, and had been a prosecution witness at the trial. Narco agents had given his name to the postals, who approached him with a job offer.

"They wanted me to kidnap Richards," said Chicofsky. "Beat the shit out of him. Make him tell where the bread is hid. They told me to get whoever I needed to make him talk."

"How would that help the postals? Why would guys tough enough to make Tom Richards talk ever let the government see the money?"

"That's part of the deal. I'd have to tell the postals where they took Richards. They'd be nearby while he was getting worked over. If these guys tried a double cross, they'd get arrested for assaulting Richards, and I'd disappear. But if they played ball, they'd get some of the money and immunity to spend it."

"So why come to me?"

"I got something I want," Chicofsky said.

"What's that?"

He smiled. "Don't worry, it ain't bread. What I want is a way to square things a little before these guys I put away hit the street. I got squeezed into stooling against them, but I ain't no stool pigeon. I figure if I help you, you can reach the right people and let them know I helped somebody. Maybe they'd relax a little if they heard I did a good thing for some other guys."

"Okay," I said. "I can't promise it'd do much good, but I'll do what I can. Meanwhile, you play along with the postals and see how far they'll go. Set the plan up in detail, and keep in touch with me. I'd sure like to know just how they'd try to get Tom Richards to talk."

"I know that already," said Chicofsky. "They told me to get a glass tube—like the ones expensive cigars come in—and a little white mouse. You put the mouse in the tube, and hold the open end against the guy's bare chest. Then you light a match under the other end, and the mouse wants out. Only way he can get out is to eat away at the chest. One of the postals had a friend in the O.S.S. during the war who knew this trick. Said it worked every time. It would work on me, all right. You too."

The next day I put Chicofsky's story on sound film, with Bob Barton doing the questioning. For the next several days, I guided Chicofsky through a series of meetings with postal inspectors, which at least established that he was having business of some sort with them. I was afraid to take a chance with bugging devices; the postals' experience with Billy A. had left them wary, and they often frisked Chicofsky before talking to him.

At my suggestion, Chicofsky stalled them by asking for a $5,000 down payment. Although they said the money was no problem, they didn't seem able to come up with it. Finally, it was arranged that Chicofsky would meet with a senior inspector in the parking lot of Faulkner Hospital in South Boston. I wanted like hell to get a corroborative proof of their conversation, but I was afraid to wire Chicofsky, and using a third party as a witness was even riskier. Ironically, this was one of the few occasions on which he he wasn't frisked.

The postals promised Chicofsky his money in a week. But someone must have gotten wise. In the next few days, the negotiations ground to a halt.

I knew that it would be impossible to get federal officers prosecuted on little more than the word of an ex-convict, so I turned again to the news media. Although the story wasn't as big as the Billy A. blast, it did make enough noise to cause the postals to hole up for a few days.

When the inspectors returned to action, they added Chicofsky to their list of harassment targets.

5. *THE VANISHED*

As the investigation dragged on, the postals lost interest in Joe Tripoli as a suspect. Other faces came into the picture. In the fall of 1965, Santo and Patricia Diafario came into my office; they were being harassed so much that Mrs. Diafario was on the verge of a breakdown.

Santo, who was called Sonny, and his striking young wife said that their friends and relatives were undergoing steady questioning by postal officers. Some of them had been told that the Diafarios were prime suspects in the mail robbery. Pat's anxiety was compounded by the fact that she was pregnant. She had suffered two miscarriages and feared that she would have a third unless the postals stopped hounding her.

"It's crazy," Pat said when I asked why the postals had picked on her and Sonny. "The only thing we can figure is that they're after us because Sonny was in the detention camp down at Plymouth once with that Mr. Kelley. I never even met him."

"There were lots of guys at the Plymouth camp with Jack Kelley," I said, turning to Sonny. "Have you been friendly with him since you got out?"

Sonny shook his head. "I've seen him maybe one or two times for coffee, nothing else. These fools seem to think I'm his partner or something. They're telling a lot of people I'm going to jail. I can take it, but I'm worried about Pat."

I arranged a meeting for myself and the Diafarios with Stanley Suchecki, an assistant U.S. attorney who had been among those in charge of the case in its early stages. In his office, I outlined the Diafarios' complaints. "These men have a right to investigate," I said, "but there are reasonable limits. Mrs. Diafario says that their tactics are upsetting her greatly. If a miscarriage should result, the finger is going to be pointed at the postal inspectors."

"I suppose we can do without that kind of publicity," Suchecki said. I'll see what I can do."

The pressure let up, and the next spring Pat had her baby without any complications. But the Diafarios continued to figure in the case.

Then one day in November, 1966, Billy A. came to my office, looking as if he had just been sentenced to prison. "They're going to violate me," he said. "I got the word."

"What for, Billy?"

"I dunno exactly. Being seen with Kelley, I guess. Anyway, the word is I'm going back, no matter what you do. I even heard they ain't going to let you come to the hearing."

"We'll see about that. How much time have you got left on your sentence?"

"Ten months."

"That's about the amount of time the postals have left to solve the robbery before the federal statute of limitations runs out," I said.

"These guys probably figure that if they can get me in the can, I'll cooperate. They sure don't want me testifying against them."

I agreed. "Without your testimony, I can't prove they put a spy in my office, and I can't get those recorded conversations with Earl Wheeler before a jury. I'll call the parole board and see about a hearing."

My call to the parole board confirmed Billy's information. He would not be permitted to have a lawyer at his revocation hearing. I immediately filed suit in Massachusetts Supreme Court to prevent the exclusion of counsel from a hearing that might cost a man his liberty. The U.S. Supreme Court has since ruled that anyone in such circumstances is entitled to counsel, and they presumably would have made the same decision in Billy's case.

But Billy A. didn't wait around to find out. He didn't show up for his parole board hearing, and his suit was dismissed. I have never seen him since. To this day, I have no idea whether Billy A. is alive or dead.

By the summer of 1967, the postals were faced with a do-or-die situation. The federal statute of limitations ran out that August 14. If there were no indictment by then, the state would have until 1972 to act. But it seemed unlikely that state authorities would want to pick up the mess left by the postals.

In July, it was announced that a grand jury was hearing evidence on the Great Plymouth Mail Robbery. Kelley, Richards, and the Diafarios asked me what I thought would happen. It seemed to me that the government was simply going through the motions. An announcement would be made that the grand jury had decided not to indict because the investigation was incomplete. But the announcement would also say that federal officials would work closely with state authorities over the next five years to bring in the guilty parties. That would ease the postals off the hook, and the case would die a natural death.

I was wrong.

On July 30, I heard that Kelley, Richards, and Diafario were indicted

I hurried to my office, announced night duty for everyone, and asked someone to find Joe Balliro for me.

A former public defender, and one of the state's finest criminal lawyers, Balliro would be representing Sonny Diafario.

When we reached him at a nearby restaurant, he agreed to meet me and come to the arraignment. I called Charlie Baker, a bail bondsman, picked up Balliro and took off for Lynn. "Tell Sonny and Kelley to call me at the commissioner's office," I said.

"It isn't Sonny you want," said Bernie Kunsky, one of my associates, "it's Pat."

"You're kidding!"

"No, it's been on the radio several times. Jack Kelley, Tom Richards, and Mrs. Patricia Diafario. Sonny wasn't indicted."

At Commissioner Farrell's office, I asked Paul Markham, who would prosecute the case, how he felt about bail.

"I figure $25,000 each for the men, and $5,000 for Mrs. Diafario."

That was low for such a big robbery. Possibly Markham feared he would have to expose his case in a bail reduction hearing. Or perhaps he realized that since Kelley and Richards had stayed around for five years, it would be hard to convince a judge that they would run now.

Within two hours, Kelley and Pat showed up, and their bail was posted. Kelley was good-natured, but lost no time kidding me about my opinion that there would never be an indictment. Pat was in tears. "This is crazy," she sobbed. "My God, what will I tell my children? Can't we sue someone right away?"

Unfortunately, there was nothing she could do but defend herself. Whoever had accused her was immune from suit, and so was the grand jury that had indicted her. The most she could hope for was an acquittal. The damage had been done—arrest is all it takes for that to happen.

On the way back to my office that night, Jack Kelley asked me what I thought would happen now.

"I think," I said, "that I would be wise to keep my opinions to myself. I didn't do so well the last time."

"Well," Kelley said, "you're just a young fellow, and you'll make mistakes from time to time. Stick with me, though, and I'll make a good lawyer out of you yet."

Judge Charles E. Wyzanski's half-rim spectacles were clues to his rulings. As he sat at the bench you could anticipate what he was going to say by the way he gazed through—or in most cases just over—the lenses. Judge Wyzanski, by length of service the chief of Boston's Federal Court Judges, was assigned to the Great Plymouth Mail Robbery case. It was our good fortune; he is the kind of trial judge whose mold should be saved.

At the arraignment, Joe Balliro and I moved for dismissal of the indictment on the ground that the government had deliberately and unconscionably delayed in obtaining it. Judge Wyzanski ruled that he would wait until trial, when the government had put forward its case, before deciding. But he gave the defense a rare opportunity that should be commonplace: he ordered Paul Markham to give us a copy of the grand jury testimony so that we could investigate the causes for the delay.

We then moved, almost reluctantly, for a change of venue. Much of what had happened over the past five years had produced a public antipathy toward the postals, but publicity had linked Kelley and Richards to the robbery. The safest bet was to ask for another site for the trial.

Judge Wyzanski glanced at the news clippings we submitted, and ruled quickly. "The court is not unaware that there has been vast publicity," he said. "One would really have to be a Rip Van Winkle or his heir not to know that over television, over radio, through the newspapers and through other media, this community has been flooded with stories—not only at the time the mail robbery occurred, but indeed since this indictment has been sought before the grand jury and thereafter. I grant the motion for change of venue, and hereby transfer this case to San Francisco in the Northern District of California."

It would be the longest change of venue in the history of American jurisprudence.

Although the hearings were closed, the press knew about the change even before we left the courtroom. In response to reporters' questions, Jack Kelley observed at some point that although he would be delighted to visit California, he didn't know how he'd be able to finance the trip for himself and his witnesses.

The next day Judge Wyzanski heard about Kelley's remark, and called us back. He said he had considered the matter of expense, and was willing to move the trial to the New York metropolitan area. Joe and I agreed, but had a reservation. "The defendants consent," I said, "assuming that your honor will preside in New York."

The next day, we were back once more. "For reasons not clear to me," said Judge Wyzanski, "it appears that another judge will be assigned to hear this case if it is tried in New York. I mention this because of counsel's reservation yesterday. The next move is up to the defendants. I will hear from you on Monday."

Joe and I felt we had a case that should be dismissed without risking a jury decision. We felt that if Judge Wyzanski thought this was warranted, he would have the courage to throw the case out. Another judge might not be so strong.

I filed a long statement withdrawing under protest our motion for a change of venue. In effect, I said that we had a right to continue with one judge until the matter was concluded. In taking certain steps, we had been relying on the knowledge that Judge Wyzanski would preside. Matters that we were content to hold in abeyance might have been pressed had we known that another jurist would handle the trial. While we did not wish to forfeit our change of venue, we regarded its loss as the lesser of two evils.

Before it had even begun, the trial of the Great Plymouth Mail Robbry had boomeranged across the continent. It had wound up back in Boston.

Tom Richards was a good client. He did as he was told, he didn't bug me with trivial phone calls, and he never acted as if his case were the only important one in the office.

Tom was outraged by his indictment, and seemed sure that he would be cleared at the trial. I only wish that I could have had the chance to defend him.

Several days before the trial was to open, I got a call from Tom's wife, who wanted to know if I had seen him.

"Not for a couple of days," I said. "Where is he?"

"I don't know," she said, obviously worried. "He left work in the afternoon the day before yesterday, and no one has heard from him since. Nobody knows where he is."

"I hope to hell he hasn't taken off," I said. "As far as I can tell, he's been very confident. Has he seemed jittery around the house?"

"Oh, no. He thinks the whole trial is a waste of time. The only thing he's been grumbling about is that he's going to lose two weeks from work."

I told her I'd ask around, and to call me if she heard anything. I also told her to keep Tom's disappearance quiet; press reports that he was missing could hurt his chances for a fair trial.

Jack Kelley got busy trying to find Tom, and I tapped a few special sources of my own, but all we came up with were some theories. If he hadn't taken off on his own, like Billy A., he might have been seized by federal underlings nervous about a shaky case, or by hoods who thought he could tell them where the loot was. And if he had been abducted, he was very likely a dead man—there was no way his captors could let him go without risking prosecution.

In January, 1968, Tom's car was found in the parking lot of a suburban motel. No one seemed to know how long it had been there. Neither Tom's wife Sylvia nor anyone else I know has ever seen him since the day he left work.

And if anybody knows what happened to him, they're not talking.

6. *THE FIRST WITNESSES*

On the morning of the trial, I reported Tom Richards' disappearance. Paul Markham wanted a delay while an investigation was made, and I agreed. But Joe Balliro felt that Pat Diafario had suffered long enough. The judge felt the same way, and the trial opened.

In less than an hour, we had impaneled a jury. Even though in most cases Massachusetts jurors are picked without screening by counsel, Judge Wyzanski helped us by summarily dismissing all those who had the slightest degree of prejudice or personal interest in the case.

When the jury had been sworn, the judge suggested a ten-minute recess. When we returned, the government made its opening statement.

The prosecution's case depended on eyewitness testimony, which, Paul Markham said, would tie the defendants to the crime. Joe Balliro and I had been able to study the testimony given to the grand jury, but under a crippling federal law known as "Section 3500" we had not been able to go over the statements made by witnesses immediately after the crime had taken place. We would not be permitted to see these statements until each witness's direct examination had ended and cross-examination was about to begin.

Both Joe and I felt we might well win or lose on our cross-examination of prosecution witnesses. Jack Kelley and Pat Diafario had the most common kind of alibi—Kelley was at a movie in Boston with his wife on the night of the robbery, and Pat was at home watching television. Unless we could catch each witness in definite contradictions, we would have trouble.

Markham's first witness was Patrick Schena, the driver of the robbed truck. During his direct testimony, Joe and I listened carefully for his description of the man who stayed in the rear of the truck with the victims, and the precise time that Schena freed himself and emerged from the truck.

"Mr. Schena," I asked on cross, "did you not six days after the robbery tell Captain McCarthy of the Massachusetts State Police that you would not know the robber 'Tony' if you ever saw him again?"

I held up a transcript of Schena's interrogation in my hand, and showed it to him. A good witness would have said "yes" right away. A bad witness would have said "no." Schena said, "I don't recall."

"Did you tell investigators right after the robbery that 'Tony,' the policeman, was in the back of the truck with you and Barrett from the time it started to move until it was abandoned by the robbers?"

"Yes," said Schena.

We know that on the way to Hyannis to pick up the cash, he and the guard had stopped for a brief visit with a friend who lived along the way.

"You told the postal inspectors that you went directly from Boston to Hyannis?" I said.

"Yes, sir."

"That wasn't true, was it?"

"No, sir."

"Why did you make a false statement to the inspectors under oath?"

"Because I thought if I told them I would lose my job."

Schena had told the grand jury that when he got out of the truck on Route 128, it was 9:35 P.M. Now he claimed the time was between 9:35 and 9:45.

As we recessed for lunch, the prosecution had produced one witness. He could not know it, but he had seriously undermined four future witnesses who would try to link the defendants to the crime.

The afternoon's first witness was postal guard William Barrett. His direct testimony echoed Schena's. He said that after the "policeman" had forced him to the back of the truck, he had not seen him again. But he said he had looked at his watch when he left the truck and it was 9:35 P.M.

Markham asked Barrett to identify the man who had been dressed as a police officer. The guard pointed at John J. Kelley. He said he had first come to this realization while observing Kelley at a Watertown diner in June, 1964—nearly two years after the robbery.

Markham gave us Barrett's pretrial statements and sat down. Although I couldn't study them I asked for a minute to scan them. Partly because of Schena's statements, I knew where to look for some of what I wanted. While I was still reading, I began the cross-examination.

I first established that both on the day after the robbery, and five days later, he had lied to authorities about the stop he and Schena made on the way to Hyannis.

"Did you know when you gave a statement under oath, knowing it to be false, that it was a criminal offense?"

Markham was on his feet objecting, claiming that whether or not the lie was a criminal offense was irrelevant. Judge Wyzanski peered down over his glasses at both Markham and the witness. "It has a great deal to do with the gravity of the false statement whether one knows one is committing an offense or whether one thinks one is merely telling a lie to a friend."

Barrett said he did not know that the lie was a crime. He and Schena had agreed to cover each other, he said, to preserve their jobs—jobs that they still held.

"And did you tell the officials who interviewed you any other falsities?"

Barrett swore that he had not. I then showed him two statements in which he had said that "Tony" had never left the back of the truck while it was in motion. He admitted the statements were his. When Schena testified, he had ascribed a New York accent to "Tony." By this he said he meant an accent similar to that of Sergeant Bilko, a television character played for some years by comedian Phil Silvers. Now, Barrett said his original statements about "Tony's" whereabouts were based on hearing the Bilko voice near him, feeling a gun pressed against him, and on other indications. He said his eyes had been shut tight the entire time.

When, I asked, had Barrett decided to change his position on where "Tony" had been during the ride? He hedged, and finally remembered that in 1964, a postal inspector had suggested to him that he really couldn't be *sure* where the "policeman" was. He had agreed.

This sequence is a classic example of something that infuriates me. In the initial investigation of a crime, authorities want detailed, accurate statements as to what happened. At this point, there is no one to build a case against, and the witness's memory is fresh. Consequently these statements are probably the most truthful accounts recorded in the case. But when a suspect has been targeted and trial evidence is being assembled, discrepancies that can hurt the case often crop up in the stories of various witnesses. In such circumstances, investigators frequently take the easy way out by getting the witnesses to change the stories just enough to make them dovetail. One way to do this is to "suggest" possible mistakes. The other is to assure the witness that "independent evidence" available only to officials supports him on such shaky points as recognition of the defendants. The prospective witness is led to believe that he is helping justice by shading his testimony. Some law enforcement people regard this technique as integral to the business of getting convictions. But this kind of perjury has been responsible for the imprisonment of one hell of a lot of innocent men.

In the case of Barrett's identification of Kelley as the "policeman," my cross-examination was based upon the assumption that Barrett could not possibly have recognized either of the men who had robbed him. The men who pulled the Plymouth job were obviously professionals, and professionals don't show their faces in robberies in which the victims are left alive.

I outlined the chain of circumstances by which Barrett's identification of Kelley had been procured. In his initial description, Barrett said the "policeman" had a dark complexion, dark hair, and markedly protruding eyes whose color he didn't see. He had gotten only a quick look, and he wasn't certain he could recognize the man if he saw him again. He didn't mention Kelley's most obvious feature—a hawk-like nose. He helped two different police artists draw sketches, and thought they were good likenesses, except that the eyes didn't protrude enough.

A month after the robbery, he had been shown pictures of possible suspects, among them one of John J. Kelley. Barrett didn't recognize it.

Five months later, the Billy A. story broke, and Kelley's picture was in newspapers and on television. Barrett didn't recognize him.

In April, 1963, he had seen Kelley's picture in the *Saturday Evening Post* in connection with a story on the robbery. Still no recognition.

In October, 1963, Barrett was taken to a courthouse where Kelley was appearing as a defendant. The lighting was good, and Barrett viewed Kelley in a corridor and a waiting room. He could not make an identification. There were similarities, but there were also differences.

Eight months after that, in June, 1964, he was taken to the diner in Watertown. Kelley entered, wearing sunglasses. At that moment, said Barrett, he recognized him.

I asked Barrett if Kelley's eyes were anything like the protruding eyes of the man called Tony. He said they weren't.

In view of all these discrepancies, I asked Barrett to explain just what his basis for recognition was.

"There is something in my mind," he said, "that nothing can explain."

"We want it out of your mind," I said, "and into the jury's mind. Now will you help us?"

Barrett shook his head. "I can't do it."

When he left the stand, Judge Wyzanski called a recess and we went for coffee and a smoke. Eddie Corsetti of the *Record-American* was among the reporters covering the trial. "So far the defense has two good witnesses," he said. "When does the prosecution start?"

7. *THE LIGHTEST MOMENTS*

The outstanding feature of the blonde staring at the side of the road, said Herbert A. Perry, was her large bust. He couldn't be mistaken about a thing like that.

Perry was one of several witnesses who relieved the monotony of prosecution testimony, the bulk of which followed the pattern set by Barrett. Most witnesses had come forward within forty-eight hours of the robbery. Subsequently they had seen Kelley's and Richard's faces splashed across the media without reacting. Then they had been led down the identification aisle by postal inspectators, some within a year of the robbery, some as late as three years after.

But a few of the witnesses brought a little individuality to the stand, like Captain Perry, who described himself as a qualified aircraft commander and flight instructor for Northeast Airlines. About a half hour before the holdup, Perry had been driving north on Route 3 toward Logan International Airport. Half a mile beyond the Clark Road exit, he saw two cars pulled over on the grass on the right side of the road. As he sped by, he noticed a blond woman talking to a police officer. The woman, he claimed, was Pat Diafario.

The postals who first interviewed Perry decided that he saw a motorist talking to a legitimate cop. But in its inexorable way, time brought changes to the official posture. In January, 1965, Perry was shown some movies of Pat but couldn't identify her. The postals were undaunted. In August, 1965, Perry was taking to a motel where the Diafarios were vacationing. After watching Pat at the swimming pool for a while, he said yes, she was the one.

The two most important elements of Perry's testimony from our point of view were: 1) he had only a two-second glimpse of the woman as he drove by, and 2) he told the inspectors she had a large bosom. When Joe Balliro got up to cross-examine, he rose to the occasion. Pat Diafario is a very attractive woman, but there is nothing out of the ordinary about her bosom. Confronted with her chest in the courtroom, Captain Perry said that perhaps her blouse was tailored so as to deemphasize her bust. We had Pat leave the courtroom, remove her bra, and put on a sweater. Then we invited Perry to take another look.

The captain faced the truth. Pat's bosom was not the same as the one he had seen in 1962. How then, asked Joe, could he account for the discrepancy? Herbert A. Perry thought for a moment. "It could," he said hopefully, "have been padding."

After the captain had taken off, the prosecution called a friendly Texan named Roger Daily, one of the postal inspectors imported for the investigation. Daily had produced the movies of Pat that were shown to Perry. He was a first-timer at both armed-robbery probes and movie making, and his direct testimony was bland. But on cross-examination, Joe quickly established that Inspector Daily had also been assigned to watch Pat from September, 1965, through April, 1966. "Did you notice anything unusual about her during that time?" he asked.

"No," said Daily.

Joe turned to the jury and raised his eyebrows. "You saw her in September, did you not?"

Daily, who never stopped smiling, nodded.

"And when you saw her in October, did you notice anything different about her?" Joe thrust his belly forward and put his hand on it.

"No," said Daily. "I didn't."

"Was her appearance different in December?"

"No, I don't think so."

"How about January, or February, or March?" By now, Joe had clasped both hands together and was running them up and down his stomach. Daily began to hedge a little. He said he had lost the "trail" in April. When another inspector picked it up, Pat was in a maternity ward. Daily had never noticed that she was pregnant.

Another government witness, William Fitzgerald, an investigator for the U.S. Civil Service Commission, claimed to have passed the moving mail truck after it had been commandeered. As he went by the truck, Fitzgerald glanced at the driver.

Fitzgerald's testimony during direct examination focused on a description of the driver. When the prosecution had trouble getting responsive answers, Judge Wyzanski tried to help. Fitzgerald said the most distinctive feature he recalled was a large nose, and the judge asked him to describe it. When there was no definite answer, Wyzanski asked him to draw it on a blackboard. Fitzgerald tried but wasn't much of an artist. Finally, the judge suggested that he try to find a comparable nose in the courtroom.

Fitzgerald's gaze paused briefly on several people including Kelley, and finally stopped. "Mr. Markham," he said. "The nose looked like Mr. Markham's!"

Soon after, when we recessed for the day, I noticed Fitzgerald writing on a piece of paper, which he put in his pocket as he left the stand.

The next morning Fitzgerald continued his direct testimony. Despite the fact that he was a federal investigator in his own right, he had made no report in the immediate wake of the robbery. But a few days later, he was in an elevator in the Federal Building when a man entered from the fifth floor, where postal inspectors had their offices. Fitzgerald ascertained that the man was an inspector, gave his name, and said he was a witness to the Plymouth mail robbery. He was told he would be contacted.

Almost two years passed. In June, 1964, he happened to be in the postal inspection service office and once again mentioned that he had seen part of the robbery. Shortly thereafter, he identified Kelley as the driver of the truck.

Now, when Fitzgerald pointed at Jack and said, "That's the man I saw driving," I couldn't wait to start cross-examining.

First I asked him why he hadn't reported his information immediately. He said he was too busy working on an investigation of his own.

"I wonder," I said, "if you could describe for the jury the case that you had to investigate on your own, whose priority was such that in your own mind it supervened the importance of the largest cash robbery in the history of the United States of America."

Fitzgerald said he had been making a background investigation of a woman who had applied for the Peace Corps.

Next I asked him if he had been jotting down notes the day before. He nodded.

"Let me see the notes, please."

Fitzgerald pulled a slip of paper out of his pocket, glanced at it, and started to put it back. "I tore up yesterday's notes," he said. "These are some I made last night." Politely, I snatched them out of his hands.

"I see that at the top of this sheet you have noted the names and dates of birth of your daughters. Is that correct?"

He nodded.

"I take it that as you sat at home last night, you considered the possibility that I might cross-examine you this morning?"

"I knew you would."

"And you felt that as part of that cross-examination, I might try to demonstrate defects in your memory, right?"

Yes, he said, the thought had crossed his mind.

"And in order to guard against such a demonstration you put to paper here the names of your own daughters, in order to have a reminder in the event you should forget those names while being questioned? Is that correct?"

Unhappily, Fitzgerald said that it was. The gallery began to giggle.

"And here further down on the sheet I see you have suggested to yourself, 'Always say, "to the best of my recollection." ' Did you write that?"

"Oh yes, but that was because the judge here pressed me very hard when he was questioning me yesterday and I said some things I didn't really mean to say."

"I see. You were 'pressed.' Do you usually make notes to yourself under circumstances such as these?"

"Yes," he said enthusiastically. "I think it's always better to write things down."

"Indeed. I shall ask you at the conclusion of this cross-examination if you are still of the same mind."

Fitzgerald stared at the sheet of paper, and then at me. "I'm already sorry," he said. He was a man you had to like.

Nodding toward the chief prosecutor, I said, "Mr. Markham, before

I put the next question, I wonder if you would be good enough to stand for a moment here before the witness box?"

Paul complied, and I went on. "Now then, would Inspector Luther Finerfrock come forward and stand next to Mr. Markham?" Postal Inspector Finerfrock stepped up. He was a tall, gaunt, red-haired man with a generous nose.

"Now then, Mr. Fitzgerald," I said, "I seem to recall that yesterday when asked by Judge Wyzanski to point to a nose in the courtroom similar to the one you had seen on the night of the robbery, you pointed to Mr. Markham. Isn't that true?"

Fitzgerald agreed.

"And didn't you last night," I thundered, "didn't you last night write a note here, on this very piece of paper, which reads, 'Change the nose to Luther?' "

Under normal circumstances, Judge Wyzanski would never have countenanced the riot of laughter that roared back and forth across that room. But these were not normal circumstances. Judge Wyzanski had all he could do to keep from laughing himself.

I wasn't as successful as the judge.

8. *THE WORST OF ALL*

If Captain Perry, Inspector Daily, and William Fitzgerald left us laughing, there were other witnesses who left us disgusted. Certainly Mrs. Frances Kissell, a lawyer, and Joseph Freeman, a dentist, fell into that category.

I think the reason Mrs. Kissell bothered me so much was because she was a lawyer, from whom as such we should be able to expect high standards of accuracy and consistency. Mrs. Kissell was employed by the government as counsel for the Small Business Administration. And at the time of the robbery, she had been an assistant U.S. attorney. She had appeared in Judge Wyzanski's court on several occasions, and when she took the stand, he gave her a nod of recognition.

Mrs. Kissell testified that on the night of the robbery, she left her home in the Dorchester section of Boston to join her family in Cape Cod. As she left the house, she noticed the time on a grandfather clock in the hallway: 9:25 P.M. On Route 128, she saw a mail truck stopped by the side of the road. A man was standing in front of it with his thumbs hooked in his belt. In court, she looked directly at Jack Kelley. "That is the man I saw," she said.

Joe Balliro and I had seen her grand jury testimony, and we were sure the man she had seen was Schena. She had told her story to an FBI agent a day or so after the robbery, and he'd come to the same conclusion. Not until 1965 had she identified Kelley. I started the cross, holding the original statement she had given the FBI agent—in which she indicated she had only gotten a quick look at the man, and could offer no real description of him.

After discussing the contradictions in her description, we turned to the details of her trip to Cape Cod. Andy Tuney, to whom by now I had sold my investigative service, had reconstructed Mrs. Kissell's route. The distance from her home to the point where the truck was found was about eleven miles, three of them along municipal approach streets.

Mrs. Kissell stuck to her original departure time of 9:25. But while she had told the FBI agent she spotted the truck at 9:45, she told the court it had been 9:30. She could have driven the eleven miles in twenty minutes, but not in five. When I asked if she realized that this would have required a driving speed of 135 miles per hour, her answer was a sour "no." She had never checked the mileage between the two points, nor could she explain why she had changed the time she originally gave the FBI.

The last identifying witness was Dr. Joseph Freeman, whose performance made Mrs. Kissell look like St. Joan. In terms of courtroom drama, his turn on the stand was the high point of the trial.

Dr. Freeman was in his middle forties, stocky, round-faced, balding, and antagonistic. He told the court that on the night of the holdup, he had left his home in North Randolph, Massachusetts, with his wife (now his ex-wife) and her thirteen-year-old brother-in-law to get ice cream cones. Returning home on Route 128, Freeman spotted a mail truck stopped in the far right lane. He saw a man standing beside the truck. The man wore a short-sleeved, open-collared blue shirt, and had sparse brownish-gray hair, prominent cheek bones, a prominent nose and a jutting chin. The man's nose, he said, was identical to Jack Kelley's.

At this point, the judge asked him to see if anyone else in the courtroom had a similar nose. After walking about the room, the dentist picked out a spectator. Judge Wyzanski motioned to the man. "Will the gentleman stand up, please, and step forward in front of the jury?" he said. "It is a very small price to pay for being a spectator."

The spectator rose. "I'm innocent," he declared.

Later, the dentist described his trip down the identification trail. A month after the robbery, his wife called the postal authorities, and an inspector named Walter J. Zygmunt came to the house and interviewed the Freemans for about half an hour. The postals didn't look up Freeman again until January, 1965. Then, Inspectors Sullivan and Finerfrock came to his home with twenty photographs and two reels of film, one in color and the other in black and white. The subject of both the stills and the cinéma vérité, of course, was John J. Kelley.

Freeman picked three photos as "just like" the man by the truck. He said the protagonist of the movies also looked "just like" the man, but that "there were differences" and an in-person glimpse would be helpful. On March 4, 1965, an Inspector Ross took the dentist to a Boston apartment building, where he saw Kelley. He made a positive identification. At the end of his testimony, Freeman pointed to Kelley and said he was the man. "Your witness," said Ed Lee.

Joe and I figured that Freeman had passed the truck, but had seen Schena. I went over what Freeman had done that night, and checked on how much time he had spent at each stop. The time elements were essential: if Freeman passed the truck from 9:35 on, he would have had to have seen Schena, who by his own testimony was standing outside the vehicle then. When he had talked to Zygmunt, Freeman said he arrived home (his house was about two minutes from the spot) between 9:30 and 9:45. Now he was saying between 9:20 and 9:30.

Under cross-examination, Freeman conceded that he left the house at 9:00 P.M., and that the whole trip took about half an hour.

"Then why did you say between 9:20 and 9:30 instead of 9:30?" I asked.

"You are trying to trap me into a time limit," he complained.

A few questions later, his resentment and evasiveness increased.

A. You are trying to lead me into making an error in time which I don't think is important to my testimony.

Q. You don't think the time is important?

A. Yes.

Q. Have you been placed in charge of this case?

A. No. Have you?

Q. For the defense, yes. I think it is very important, as you well know. You know that the time of your arrival at that position is critical, don't you?

A. I did not look at a watch.

Q. You know that the time at which you arrived is critical—Yes or No

A. I said I did not time myself.

THE COURT: No, no. The question is whether you are aware that the time that you gave as the time of your arrival is a critical matter. Are you aware of that?

THE WITNESS: I am aware of that.

Q. Are you aware more specifically, Doctor, that if you arrived after 9:35, all of your observations are probably meaningless?

A. I did not say I arrived after 9:35.

THE COURT: No, no. I am afraid you didn't get the point of the question. Mr. Bailey asked you whether you have some information which leads you to realize that if you place the time of your arrival after 9:35, in Mr. Bailey's view your observations would be meaningless.

THE WITNESS: I did not place my time of arrival at 9:35.

THE COURT: We understand that. Would you read the question again. (Question read)

THE WITNESS: I am aware of that.

Freeman denied that anyone had ever told him the time was critical. We discussed the fact that his wife was the one who went to the postals and he conceded that it was not his idea to become a witness.

"Was there any particular reason why you, as a citizen, did not see fit to put in the hands of those charged with the solution of this most heinous robbery such information as was then at your disposal?" I asked.

"I thought the man I saw standing outside of the truck was a driver who had released himself and was waiting for some help," said Freeman. "I never dreamed a suspect would stand out in full view to be observed by hundreds of passing motorists, and I thought the information I had was worthless."

In this opening encounter, Freeman had said and indicated a number of things helpful to the defense. For one thing, he had made it plain that he was afraid of being "trapped." Every witness should be aware that the cross-examiner may try to get him in a corner, but single-minded concentration on not being "trapped" is a good way to ensure that you will be trapped, retrapped, and trapped again.

And in trying to defend his failure to come forward with what he had seen, Freeman had stated precisely what we wanted the jury to believe—that he had probably seen the driver of the truck, not one of the robbers.

His testimony had also given the defense the opportunity to use Inspector Zygmunt's report of their half-hour conversation a month after the robbery. In contrast to Freeman's later accounts, the report made no mention of cheekbones, noses, jaws, or shoulders; and Freeman had told the inspector that he had arrived home between 9:30 and 9:45.

I confronted Freeman with the report, and asked him about the description. First he equivocated, then he said that Zygmunt had omitted these details from his report. This put us in a position where we could impeach a government witness with the testimony of a government investigator. (Zygmunt testified that he recalled no such omissions.)

Next I asked about the time conflict. Again Freeman accused the postal inspector of handing in an inaccurate report. As he said this, I looked at the jurors. I could tell they didn't believe him.

When we resumed after lunch we discussed the precise moment at which Freeman had passed the stopped truck. According to one of Zygmunt's reports, Mrs. Freeman said the dentist had veered out to go by the truck. He testified to the contrary, and went on to say that he wasn't close enough to the man standing by the truck to be in any danger of hitting him.

When questioned, he said that he traveled about thirty feet while he was looking at the man, and that he was driving about thirty-five miles an hour. When I asked how much time this gave him for observation, he admitted that traveling thirty feet at that speed would have given him "less than a second."

"Now, I asked, "what fractional part of a second was it that comprised your total observations that night?"

"Let's not minimize a second for the benefit of the courtroom," said Dr. Freeman. "That's what you are trying to do."

It was a frightening exchange. Joseph Freeman was willing to help send a man to prison on the basis of his fraction-of-a-second view of a stranger, more than two years before his identification of that stranger.

Knowing that the postals had never confronted the dentist with Schena, I arranged to have him brought back to the courtroom and asked Freeman to look around and see if he could recognize anyone. He walked past the rail Schena was standing outside and identified Inspector Finerfrock. Did he know anyone else, I asked. He walked past Schena, and I stopped him. "Since you walked directly by this gentleman in the greenish blue sport coat and gave no indication of recognition," I said, "I take it that you do not recognize him."

I had moved Schena up to the front of the witness box, thinking my point made. But Freeman was still worrying about being trapped. "I do recognize him," he said quickly.

Freeman said I hadn't given him enough time to indicate he knew the man, and that he didn't know what I meant by "the rail" when I told him to look around. I assumed at this point that he knew the man was Schena—either because he now recognized his face from newspaper photos or because he had figured out that the driver was most likely to be the person I would single out. Still, I decided to make the most of the fact that he hadn't recognized Schena instantly. I didn't know how much help I'd get from the dentist:

Q. All right. After you returned to the stand and I pointed out to you that you indicated no recognition and designated the man in question, you now say you recognized him?

A. Yes.

Q. Who is he?

A. Mr. Zygmunt.

Q. Mr. Zygmunt? Are you sure of that?

A. Quite sure.

Q. This is the man who interviewed you and took the statement from you?

A. Yes.

Q. And the man whose report you say is incomplete based on what you think you told him?

A. Yes.

Q. Will you give us a description now, without looking at him, and just to test your powers of recognition of Mr. Zygmunt as you remember him on September 11?

THE COURT: Please turn this way.

THE WITNESS: I am not looking at him. He is about five feet ten, dark hair, roundish face, straight nose, medium build.

Q. Anything else? What about his hair?

A. Dark.

Q. Brownish?

A. No.

Q. Darker than brown?

A. Yes.

Q. All right. Without looking back, will you describe the man that you just examined?

A. Describe what?

Q. The man that you walked by, did not indicate recognition of, and then came back to the stand and said you knew—describe him; he is standing right there.

A. I just described him.

Q. You say that the description indicates one and the same man?

A. Yes.

Q. Now I take it that you are satisfied that you have correctly identified Mr. Zygmunt, right?

A. Yes.

Q. And are you as sure that this is Mr. Zygmunt—

THE COURT: The answer is "yes," is it not?

Q. Are you as certain that this is Mr. Zygmunt as that the man you saw for less than a second on August 14, 1962, was this John Kelley?

A. I am not that sure.

Q. You are not as sure?

A. No.

Q. But you are pretty sure?

THE COURT: You have to say it for the record.

THE WITNESS: I am not sure.

THE COURT: Well, weren't you a moment ago satisfied that the man was Mr. Zygmunt?

THE WITNESS: It looks like him.

THE COURT: Didn't you say just a moment ago that you were satisfied that it was Mr. Zygmunt? There is a great difference between "identical" and "similarity." In fact, it is a basic problem throughout this case. Did you not earlier say that you were satisfied that that man was Mr. Zygmunt?

THE WITNESS: I am not sure.

MR. BAILEY: Now will you come forward, sir, and stand right here?

Q. Now, I want you to take as long as you think you need, and to direct this man to turn himself in any way that will be helpful to you, and then tell the jury whether or not you recognize him as Mr. Zygmunt?

THE WITNESS: Will you turn around please? I cannot be sure.

THE COURT: Are you mindful that you testified you were for a half hour with Mr. Zygmunt?

THE WITNESS: That is correct.

THE COURT: And are you telling us that following a half hour of what undoubtedly must have struck you as a very important conversation, you cannot tell us whether this is the man with whom you talked for half an hour about the greatest mail robbery in history the first time you ever contemplated being a witness?

THE WITNESS: I am not sure.

Q. Now, when you talked with Mr. Zygmunt, you knew it was a moment of importance, did you not?

A. I didn't realize it.

THE COURT: What? Didn't you realize that you were being asked about a million-and-a-half-dollar robbery that might involve the liberty of human beings?

THE WITNESS: Yes.

THE COURT: Have you been in anything more important in your life?

THE WITNESS: I would say "no."

After an afternoon recess, I got Freeman to concede that Zygmunt and Schena didn't look anything alike, and that his mistake in confusing them was considerable. Then I put this question to him:

"Now, doctor, with all of the caution that you have said you have been using in your process of identification, and having in mind your very bad performance in making a mistake of that gross nature, do you think there is any possibility that you might be mistaken in your identification of Mr. Kelley?"

"No," said Freeman.

"You have, no doubt, given him the benefit of every doubt?"

"Yes."

"And used all of your human generosity?"

"Well," Judge Wyzanski interrupted, "he need not use generosity."

"No, that was a bad word, your honor," I said. "I am sorry."

The judge turned to Freeman. "He has used the test that Cromwell used: 'In the bowels of Christ, do you think it possible you may be mistaken?' "

"I do not think I am mistaken," said Freeman.

There was no reason to show the dentist any mercy. During the recess, I had asked that Zygmunt be brought to the courtroom. The inspector looked nothing like Schena, and I wanted to face Freeman with the extent of his mistake. Even if he recognized Zygmunt, he was still in trouble.

As the cross-examination continued, Freeman admitted that the description he gave of Zygmunt had actually been a description of Schena, the man he had been asked to identify. He denied that this was a deliberate falsehood, but called it a "mistake." Or, as he elaborated: "I thought that this man in an instant was Mr. Zygmunt, and then I tried to describe this man, and as I described him I realized that it was not."

With the inspector in the wings, I finally asked Freeman to tell me what Zygmunt looked like:

A. I cannot give you a description of him.

Q. Do you have any recollection whatsoever of the inspector named Zygmunt?

A. Yes.

Q. Is he a male or a female?

A. Male.

Q. That's a beginning. How tall was he?

A. About five-feet-eight or so.

Q. Do you stand on that recollection, five-eight?

A. Five-eight or nine.

THE COURT: I beg your pardon?

THE WITNESS: Five-eight or nine, I would say, not very tall.

Q. Would you say he was about my height? Yes?

A. About.

Q. Would you say he is considerably shorter than Mr. Schena?

A. Yes.

Q. Whom you estimated at five-eleven, right?

THE DEFENSE NEVER RESTS

A. Yes.

Q. What about his face? Was it round or square or pointed?

A. Round.

Q. And did it have a nose?

A. Yes.

Q. Describe it.

A. There was nothing distinctive about the nose that I can remember.

Q. It was neither large nor small?

A. I can't remember.

Q. You can't remember. What about his eyes? He had eyes?

A. I think he wears glasses.

Q. Well, you could see through them, couldn't you, to see that he did have eyes? Yes?

A. Yes.

Q. What color were his eyes?

A. I don't remember.

Q. What color were the eyes of the man you saw standing by the side of the road?

A. I don't know.

Q. How do you know they weren't brown?

A. I don't know.

Q. Do you realize that if they were brown you have made a mistake in picking Mr. Kelley, who had blue eyes, don't you?

A. I did not say they were brown.

THE COURT: No, no. That isn't the question. The question is if the eyes of the man who was beside the mail truck were in fact brown eyes, then Mr. Kelley was not the man, was he?

THE WITNESS: If his eyes were brown, if the man standing beside the—

THE COURT: Well, the question has in it the hypothesis.

THE WITNESS: If the man's eyes were brown, and Mr. Kelley does not have brown eyes, then it couldn't be Mr. Kelley.

Q. You do not know the color of the eyes of the man you saw?

A. No.

Q. All right. Is there anything else at all about Brother Zygmunt that your recollection is able to dredge up?

A. He was wearing a light suit.

THE COURT: Well, now, you are not really being asked that. You said earlier, in response to a question from me, that you realized that this was the most important single event in which you had ever participated? You told me and the jury that for half an hour, in close quarters, you talked with this man. And you are now being asked to describe this man with whom you were having a conversation about the most important matter that you have ever been concerned with in your life. And the object, obviously, of putting this question to you is to see whether you can be believed in connection with an identification you have made based upon a one-second glance at a person who had no special significance to you at the time you glanced at him, a man you glanced at on a public road, in the dark, even if it were lighted by passing lights. . . .

Q. Now have you completed your description?

A. Yes, I have.

THE COURT: You can't do any better?

THE WITNESS: I had no reason to remember the details of Mr. Zygmunt.

THE COURT: You certainly had no reason to remember the passing individual whom you saw as you went by? It had no importance at that moment, did it?

THE WITNESS: Well—

THE COURT: Did it?

THE WITNESS: Not at that moment.

Q. Dr. Freeman, if you were to see the inspector again, could you recognize him?

A. I might.

Q. What?

A. I might be able to.

Q. Well, having in mind the fact that you have already demonstrated that there are very few details of his appearance that you are able to recall, would you nonetheless be willing to identify him?

A. I could try.

(A pause—an unidentified man steps in front of the witness box.)

Q. Take a look, Doctor.

A. No.

Q. That's not the man, is it?

A. No.

Q. And are you as certain of that as you are about the rest of your testimony?

A. Yes.

Q. All right.

MR. BAILEY: May I have your identification please?

(Document handed to Mr. Bailey by unidentified man.)

Q. Now, Doctor, you have just told this jury under oath that this is not the man that interviewed you and that you are as certain of that as you are of the rest of your testimony and I have just taken his identification card from his pocket and I invite you to read it and weep.

A. I don't remember—

Q. Walter J. Zygmunt.

135

MR. BAILEY: May the record show that the witness is now confronted at a distance of ten feet with Postal Inspector Walter Zygmunt?

Q. Now, having been aided by his identification badge and a direct statement of your error, do you recognize him?

A. No, I do not.

THE COURT: I am going to take an adjournment and I am going to suggest that you give prayerful thought about what you should say the first thing tomorrow morning when I ask you if you want to change any of your testimony. You are under oath.

THE WITNESS: I realize.

THE COURT: I am sending you home to reflect until ten o'clock tomorrow morning.

The next day, Dr. Joseph Freeman rejected Judge Wyzanski's invitation to modify his testimony.

Before I could continue questioning the doctor, Markham asked for a conference at the bench. He said the dentist's ex-wife (whom we had been unable to find) had called his office to say she could no longer permit Freeman to give the kind of testimony she had been reading about in the papers. She not only remembered the night in question, she recalled certain aspects of the doctor's condition that tended to preclude accurate observations on his part. Markham said she was being brought to his office for a fuller discussion.

A half hour later, Markham called Joe Balliro and me into his conference room. He said that in view of what the doctor's ex-wife had to say, he would move to strike Freeman's testimony. We had no objection, and when court resumed, he told the judge.

With Freeman still in the box, Judge Wyzanski turned to the jury. "This morning," he said, "word reached the United States Attorney with respect to the testimony of Dr. Joseph Freeman. It would not be just for me to now recite in public what that information was. All I am going to say is that the government, acting on its own initiative, has determined that it ought to move to strike the testimony of Dr. Freeman. There is no objection to that motion, and I am granting it. You are to disregard entirely everything that was said, either on direct or cross-examination, by Dr. Freeman. The United States Attorney is considering whether to draw the matter to the attention of the grand jury."

He turned to the witness. "Dr. Freeman," he said, "you are excused."

9. *THE VERDICT*

The end of Dr. Freeman was pretty much the end of the government's case. After calling a few witnesses to identify bits of evidence that were not tied to either defendant, the prosecution rested.

Joe and I quickly presented several motions that could have ended the trial right there, but the judge had other ideas. "I could rule on those motions now," he said, "but I think it better for both sides to have a jury decide this case. I take it the defendants rest?"

"We do, your honor."

My closing statement was short and harsh. I felt the prosecution had been so decimated as to absolutely compel acquittal. Joe Balliro was equally aggresive. Paul Markham mistook our assault for a personal attack, and told the jury with some emotion that he had neither falsified nor twisted any evidence. It was unnecessary; neither Joe nor I had meant to imply that Markham was anything but an honest lawyer whose honesty had not prevented some lesser government official from stooping to subterfuge.

Judge Wyzanski's charge to the jury relieved us of our only fear— that the jury might have been influenced by what lawyers call "stacking." This occurs when the prosecution produces no single piece of evidence that provides a believable tie between the defendants and the crime, but does offer separate fragments that seem significant if added together. Even if no one eyewitness is sufficiently credible to justify conviction, laymen may succumb to reverse reasoning and think, "Well, they can't all be wrong."

Judge Wyzanski told the jurors to imagine themselves on one side of a ten-foot-wide chasm. Conviction, he said, was on the other side. In order to cross the chasm, they would need a board longer than ten feet. If any one witness had been sufficiently credible to represent a plank of that length, then conviction was in order. But if no one witness-plank was that long, then there was no way across the chasm. There was, he said, no legitimate means in a case of this sort to hook any two or more boards together.

The judge also said in his fifty-eight-minute charge that the thirteen prosecution witnesses might have been "led down the path of identification" of Kelley or Pat Diafario. How far, he asked, either through stupidity or intent, did they (the postals) narrow down the field of suspects?

"You have been told by the government that these were disinterested witnesses," the judge went on. "Do you really believe there were disinterested witnesses? Many of them knew there were rewards of up to $150,000 offered for a solution of the case. Is this not a situation in which motive must be weighed?"

The jurors conferred for less than an hour. Their verdict of "not guilty" came as no surprise.

10. EPILOGUE

In his own way, Jack Kelley was a complicated man—or, at least, a man with contrasting sides to his character. There was the time he was taking a walk with Charlie Zimmerman and they passed a Brink's truck. "Now if I was going to knock off a truck," Kelley said, "I wouldn't hit that one. They got one guy with the gun and the other guy with the money bag. Psychologically, the guy with the gun is free to make a decision. Now if he had the gun in his left hand and a money bag in his right hand, that would be different. He wouldn't know what comes first, the money bag or the gun." He was smiling as he said it, but anybody listening would have had to wonder.

On the other side, there was the night he called my office all upset over a story he'd read in the evening paper. "This woman who lives in Dorchester, she was going to visit her husband at the V.A. hospital," Kelley reported. "He's dying. Well, some kids knocked her down, broke her glasses, and stole her pocketbook. Terrible!"

"It is terrible," I said, "but why are you so upset about it?"

"Those kids ought to get the chair," he said. "Look, you got somebody there with you?"

"Sure. Kurt's sitting right here."

"Good. Now this woman, they took thirty-eight bucks from her. I'll give you her name and address. Tell Kurt to give her fifty dollars. You give it to him, and I'll pay you back tomorrow. And I'll give you the name of my optometrist. Tell her to go to him, and he'll fix the glasses on me. Can Kurt do that right away?"

A year and a half later, the law grabbed Jack Kelley. This time, it was for the robbery of a Brink's truck. They apparently had him cold, and Jack turned state's witness in the case. He also sang about some other matters of which he had knowledge.

But Kelley has never made any official admission about the mail robbery. On the basis of what the government presented at the trial, he deserved to be acquitted. The postals did a lot of persecuting, but they didn't come up with any evidence. And no one has ever found the money. For the record, the Great Plymouth Mail Robbery remains unsolved.

IV

The Man Who
Did
The Stranglings

1. "IF A MAN WAS THE STRANGLER . . ."

"If a man was the strangler," George Nassar said, "the guy who killed all those women, would it be possible for him to publish his story and make some money with it?"

"We were in the prisoners' waiting room at Essex County Superior Court, where a motion had just been granted to continue Nasser's period of observation at Bridgewater State Hospital. Before answering the question, I looked at Nassar, a tall, lithe man I was representing in a murder case. "You mean before or after this man is tried for the crimes?"

"Before," said Nassar.

I had to smile. "It's perfectly possible to publish," I said, "but I wouldn't advise it. I suspect that a confession in book form would be judged completely voluntary and totally admissible. I also suspect that it would provide the means by which the author would put himself in the electric chair."

"I'll pass on the information," said Nassar. "I promised this guy at Bridgewater I'd ask you. He's been after me to have you come in and talk to him, but I know you're pretty busy."

I was vaguely curious. "What's the guy's name?"

"Albert DeSalvo," Nassar said.

Shortly before 4:00 P.M. on September 29, 1964, a tall, dark-haired man in a tan trench coat plunged a knife into the back of a gas station attendant named Irvin Hilton in Andover, Massachusetts. Hilton fell to his knees and turned, facing his attacker. If he was begging for what was left of his life, he never had a chance. The man in the trench coat pulled out a .22 automatic and fired six shots into his kneeling victim.

As the killer started to fire, Mrs. Rita Buote and her fourteen-year-old daughter, Diane, drove into the station. They were halfway from the street to the pumps when they saw the shooting take place. Mrs. Buote braked but had the sense to lock the doors from the inside. The killer spotted her and Diane, and walked to their car. Finding the door locked, he stared at Mrs. Buote through the closed window on the driver's side, pointed the gun at her, and pulled the trigger. Two clicks. The trench-coated killer banged on the window. Then, as matter-of-factly as it had begun, the terror ended. The man glanced at the street, walked to a dark sedan parked near the pumps, and drove off.

The crime seemed as senseless as it was brutal. The cash register had not been disturbed, and Hilton's wallet was still in his pocket. There were few leads other than the recollections of Mrs. Buote and her daughter. After searching unsuccessfully through mug shots, Mrs. Buote described the killer to a police artist, and a rough sketch was published in newspapers throughout the greater Boston area. Two days after the slaying, a patrolman in a Lawrence station house was comparing police photos with the sketch when he came to the face of a man he knew. Yes, he thought, there was a definite resemblance. The patrolman was staring at the photo of a onetime classmate, George Nassar.

Nassar's picture was not in the files for some petty crime. In 1948, when he was fifteen years old, he had shot a grocery store proprietor to death during a holdup. Because of his age he was allowed to plead guilty to second-degree murder, which calls for a life sentence with a chance for parole after fifteen years. Nassar's intelligence (his I.Q. was over 150) and willingness to rehabilitate himself impressed several ministers and other persons interested in the welfare of prisoners. With their help, Nassar successfully petitioned the parole board and the governor to commute his sentence to thirty-years-to-life.

In 1962, Nassar was released. Although he was unemployed at the time of the Hilton slaying, he had been studying Russian and was planning to attend classes at Northeastern University. He'd held several jobs, including those of newspaper reporter and hospital attendant. He'd taught Sunday school, and, a couple of times, had taken over the pulpit for one of his minister friends.

Now, a resemblance between his mug shot and a rough sketch was about to cut off his freedom. The patrolman and an officer who was working with him felt the resemblance was worth following up. The other cop was a sergeant named Keenan; sixteen years before, he had arrested George Nassar for the grocery killing. The two officers went to the Buote home with a single photo—a head-and-shoulders shot of Nassar. Both Mrs. Buote and her daughter made a "positive" identification, and George Nassar was seized at his apartment in Boston's South End.

When he was arrested, Nassar turned down the chance to call a lawyer. He didn't need one, he said, because he hadn't done anything. A police lineup? Sure. On the way to Lawrence, Nassar made a bet with Sergeant Keenan that he'd be released as soon as the witnesses got a look at him. To his amazement, both mother and daughter said he was the killer who had stared through their car window. That was the only evidence that would ever link Nassar to the crime, but it was enough. He was charged with first-degree murder.

I was asked to defend George Nassar by Francis Touchet, a social worker who had come to know Nassar while he was in the prison at Walpole, Masachusetts. He and several other substantial citizens had come to Nassar's aid and wanted me to take the case. It was obvious from the little I had read that Nassar was not about to get the benefit of any presumption of innocence, and I was glad to represent him.

I had hardly begun working on the case when Nassar spoke to me on behalf of the man who claimed to be the Boston Strangler.

"He's been committed for some sex crimes," George said. "He hasn't been tried yet because they think he's too screwy, but I think he's playing it shrewd. Anyway, he's given me some strong arguments for believing that he's the guy who did the stranglings."

"Come on, George," I said, "you're not really going to tell me you're all excited about the story of some nut in Bridgewater, are you?"

"I don't think this guy's a nut at all," Nassar said. "I've talked to him a lot, and he's told me some things about the stranglings that would be pretty hard to make up. If you're down at Bridgewater one day, it might be worthwhile for you to see him."

"You really think this guy looks genuine?"

"Yes," Nassar said.

Half an hour later, I was having lunch with Dr. Ames Robey, the chief psychiatrist at Bridgewater. When I asked if he knew an inmate named DeSalvo, he laughed. "I know Albert very well," he said. "If you believe one-tenth of what he says, he has the strongest sexual drive in the history of the United States. But I'm afraid most of it is fantasy."

"Do you think this fellow could be homicidal?"

"I don't think Albert could kill anybody if his mother's life depended on it. But now that you mention him, he's been bothering me about wanting to see you. I haven't said anything because we have a lot of inmates who say they want to see you, and I know you haven't got time to commute to Bridgewater for every little case."

When Joseph DeSalvo called our office a week or so later, to report that his brother Albert, an inmate at Bridgewater, wanted to see me, I made a mental note to look in on him the next time I was there. Knowing I would need some guidelines to help me determine whether I was listening to a lot of nonsense or not, I called Lieutenant John Donovan, the homicide chief of the Boston Police Department. I told him I might be talking to a man who was likely to claim he had committed some of the stranglings. I needed a few clues—things known to police but not the general public—that would help me judge the man's validity. Donovan sent his chief assistant Lieutenant Edward Sherry to my office, and Sherry gave me a few leads.

On March 4, 1965, I went to Bridgewater to see a client named Alan Blumenthal. While there, I added two more names to my visiting list. One was George Nassar.

I had trouble remembering the other name. A check of the records at Bridgewater State Hospital will show that on March 4, 1965, I asked in writing to see an inmate named "DeSilva."

2. *THE GREEN MAN*

When Albert DeSalvo was seven years old, he saw his father knock most of his mother's teeth out and break every one of her fingers. His mother, a police lieutenant's daughter who had married at fifteen, was never able to cope with her husband's rages. Neither were Albert's three brothers and two sisters. As for Albert, he would run away from their apartment in Chelsea, a lower-middle-class suburb of Boston, when the beatings got too bad and hide out for days under the docks in East Boston. When Albert was eight his father abandoned the family, but he returned every now and then to terrorize them. Most of the time they were on welfare, and Mrs. DeSalvo took in sewing. In 1944, she finally got divorced.

Crime began early. By the time Albert was five, his father—who shuttled in and out of court on wife-beating and breaking-and-entering charges—had taught him the rudiments of shoplifting. At twelve, Albert was arrested for helping a friend beat up a newsboy and steal $2.85. His sentence was suspended. But five years later, he and his buddy were arrested for a housebreak that netted them twenty-seven dollars' worth of jewelry. This time, Albert spent ten months in a correctional school.

Sex also came early. A twelve-year-old girl taught Albert what fellatio was all about when he was nine. By fifteen, he was getting advanced sex lessons from a thirty-five-year-old woman who had a son his own age. His father had always carried on openly with prostitutes, and when he was a little kid he'd watch people having sex on a couch on the roof of his apartment building. The summer he graduated from junior high school, he worked as a dishwasher in a Cape Cod motel, where he got his kicks masturbating on a roof while he watched guests in the rooms below.

Albert graduated from junior high school at sixteen, and joined the army less than two weeks after his seventeenth birthday. He stayed in the service for eight and a half years, spending five of them in Germany, where he helped keep the peace as an M.P., rose to sergeant, won the middle-weight boxing championship of his outfit, and met and married his wife, Irmgard.

Back in civilian life, he was arrested on breaking-and-entering charges in 1958 and 1959. In March, 1961, he was arrested at gunpoint by police as he ran across a yard after trying to break into a building in Cambridge. Under questioning, he admitted to an unusual series of acts that had upset housewives in the area. He was the "Measuring Man," a fast talker who had been bothering women living around Harvard Square. He would knock on an apartment door, and if a young woman answered he would tell her that he was from a model agency and that she could make as much as forty dollars an hour posing in gowns and bathing suits. But, of course, he needed her measurements—at which point he'd pull out a tape measure and start taking her supposedly vital statistics. Some of the women complained to police and brought charges after DeSalvo was arrested. Years later, DeSalvo would boast to his wardmates at Bridgewater that some other women had no complaints at all, that one girl stripped to the buff so that he could take more accurate measurements and a few wound up in bed with him.

The Measuring Man spent eleven months in jail, getting out in April, 1962. In October of 1969, he was in trouble again—a newly married twenty-year-old Boston University co-ed identified him as a man who had entered her Cambridge apartment one morning, held a knife at her throat, and told her: "Don't make a sound or I'll have to kill you." Whereupon he stuffed her panties into her mouth, tied her hands and feet to the bedposts with her husband's pajamas and some of her clothing, and kept her that way for an hour while he abused her sexually.

DeSalvo denied the attack and was released on bail. But his picture, sent out over a police teletype, had drawn the attention of Connecticut detectives. They believed DeSalvo was the "Green Man" who had been molesting women throughout the state. In each case, he first tied up the victim on her bed. His nickname came from the green workman's clothes he usually wore.

This time several women identified DeSalvo, and he started talking. He had committed more than four hundred housebreaks in the Cambridge area. And as the Green Man, he had attacked at least three hundred women in Massachusetts, Connecticut, Rhode Island, and New Hampshire. At one point, a police sergeant asked him about one of the stranglings, but he denied having anything to do with it.

DeSalvo was put under observation at Bridgewater, where Ames

Robey's staff found that he had a "sociopathic personality disorder marked by sexual deviation, with prominent schizoid features and depressive trends." But they said he was competent to stand trial. Back in the Cambridge jail, he became despondent. He was returned to Bridgewater for more tests. Now, the doctors said that Albert's problems had increased to the point where he was no longer competent to undergo a trial. On February 4, 1965, a judge committed him to Bridgewater as mentally ill.

On March 5, 1965, Detective Phil DiNatale showed up at Bridgewater to obtain the palm print of an inmate named Albert Henry DeSalvo. A Boston homicide detective who had been probing the stranglings almost since their inception, DiNatale had been assigned to the special investigative bureau that was set up by the state Attorney General's office in the wake of eleven stranglings that had terrorized Boston from June, 1962, to January, 1964. Previously, DeSalvo had been passed over as a possible suspect because of an error in his prison records, which indicated that he was locked up during the first six homicides. But now, the "Strangler Bureau" felt he was worth taking a look at. For one thing, a man in a green outfit had been seen near the home of one of the victims on the day she was murdered. Then there was DeSalvo's record as a sex offender. And there was his *modus operandi* as both the Measuring Man and the Green Man, indicating an ability to talk his way into homes without having to resort to forcible entry. In none of the stranglings was there evidence that the killer had broken into the apartment, despite the near hysteria that the killings had provoked among women throughout the Boston area: the Strangler had to be a con artist.

DiNatale obtained a copy of DeSalvo's print and decided he might as well speak to him while he was there. Routinely, he asked if DeSalvo had a lawyer. Yes, he was told, F. Lee Bailey had signed in to see him the day before. Immediately DiNatale gave up any idea of questioning DeSalvo—he knew it would be against a suspect's constitutional rights to talk to him unless his lawyer were present.

If an interrogation had been held, I think DeSalvo might have talked. He had reached a point where he was bursting to confess. He had almost let go on two prior occasions—once to a Cambridge police sergeant, and once to a psychiatrist assigned to the Attorney General's Strangler staff. And DiNatale is a first-rate officer with a teddy-bear appearance that helps elicit confessions. If DeSalvo had talked, authorities would have been able to undertake the most notorious murder prosecution in the history of the United States.

There was just one hitch. DiNatale was a day too late.

3. *A GENTLE MURDERER*

After knowing Albert DeSalvo for half an hour, the average person would feel perfectly comfortable about inviting him home for dinner to meet the family. That was one of the pieces that fell into place in the puzzle of the Boston Strangler. It helped explain why he had been able to evade detection despite more than two and a half years of investigation. DeSalvo was Dr. Jekyll; the police had been looking for Mr. Hyde.

One of the things that struck me about DeSalvo at our first meeting was his courteous, even gentle manner. I stared at him, seriously considering the possibility that he might be the Strangler, and I felt something that verged on awe. As for DeSalvo, his gaze dropped from time to time in what appeared to be embarrassment.

George Nassar introduced me to DeSalvo in one of the small, bare rooms at Bridgewater that are reserved for the use of attorneys and their clients. DeSalvo was thirty-three at the time, about five-nine with broad shoulders and an extremely muscular build. His brown hair was combed back in an exaggerated pompadour. His nose was very large, and his easy smile was emphasized by even white teeth.

DeSalvo's I.Q. consistently tested out as slightly below normal. But I found him quick to understand what was being explained. We began carefully, never using the word "stranglings." I said I understood he had a matter of some importance to discuss with me, and he nodded his head. I warned him that because George was in the room he could not enjoy the attorney-client privilege—he should avoid any direct statements as to any acts he might have performed that could be regarded as criminal.

"Specifically," I asked, "what do you want me to do for you?"

DeSalvo kept his answer hypothetical. "If a man had done some terrible things, and if he were sick and wanted to make those things known so that he could get better help and maybe be some good to society, could a lawyer help him do that?"

"Yes," I said, "but it might be a ticklish business."

"Well, that's really what I want," DeSalvo said. "That's why I asked George to see if you'd come down and talk to me. These are some pretty big things that I need to tell about."

I asked why he was finally coming forward. He said it was because of his wife and children—he had a two-year-old son and a seven-year-old daughter. "I know I'm going to have to spend the rest of my life locked up somewhere," he said. "I just hope it's a hospital, and not a hole like this. But if I could tell my story to somebody who could write it, maybe I could make some money for my family."

I explained about the problem of confessing to a crime in print in a case where no trial has ever been held. Nevertheless, I said, "there must be a way somehow to get your story told without causing your execution."

Finally, I tried DeSalvo out on some of the clues the Boston police had given me. Although I had no real way of determining the validity of his answers, I was impressed by the speed with which he responded. The entire interview lasted a little over half an hour. On my way back to Boston, I called Lieutenant Sherry and suggested that he meet me later in my office.

My first job as DeSalvo's counsel was to determine whether he was a killer, a man who imagined he was a killer, or a liar who for some reason wanted to be known as a killer. I could only find that out with police help. In so doing, I was not putting my client in jeopardy—he had made no waiver of his right not to incriminate himself, and the police had asked for none.

Lieutenant Donovan came along to my office with Sherry. As I went over DeSalvo's answers, I could see the interest of both men intensify. "Based on this material," Donovan said when we were done, "I can't rule him out. I can't rule him out at all. If you're going back to see him again soon, we could give you some more questions that would put us in a hell of a lot better position to decide whether or not this guy is for real."

"I can go back and see this man the day after tomorrow," I said. "This time, I could record some of the conversation and then let you listen to it. But there would have to be some conditions. This would be strictly for the purpose of helping ascertain this man's identity, and nothing said on the recording could be used against him. I don't intend to ask him for any kind of waiver, and since he's presently judged incompetent to stand trial I doubt that he could make a valid waiver anyway. In addition, I'll vary the playback speed so that no person listening to the recording could legitimately claim to recognize my voice or that of my client. Is that agreeable?"

Donovan looked at Sherry. "I guess we don't have any choice," he said. "If this is our guy, I suppose our first job is to make sure he stays off the street permanently, even if we can't get his statements into evidence." They gave me some additional information on the stranglings and left the office.

On Saturday, March 6, I arrived at Bridgewater with a dictaphone and paid my second visit to Albert DeSalvo. There was a trace of nervousness in his voice, but his general manner was unchanged; he was still a man you would bring home to dinner.

Before we began, DeSalvo told me that his palm print had been taken the previous day. I asked if he might have left prints in any incriminating places, and he shook his head. "They're wasting their time," he said.

Then we started recording, and I became certain that the man sitting in that dimly lit room with me was the Boston Strangler. The face was still Dr. Jekyll's, but the memories were Mr. Hyde's. Not only did he admit the eleven killings that police believed to be the work of the Strangler, he added two others to the list. He said he had murdered sixty-nine-year-old Mary Brown, beaten and stabbed in her Lawrence apartment on March 9, 1963. And he was responsible, he said, for the death of eighty-five-year-old Mary Mullen of Boston, who apparently had suffered a fatal heart attack as his arm went around her neck.

Anyone experienced in interrogation learns to recognize the difference between a man speaking from life and a man telling a story that he either has made up or has gotten from another person. DeSalvo gave every indication that he was speaking from life. He wasn't trying to recall words; he was recalling scenes he had actually experienced.

He could bring back even the most inconsequential details. Or, at least, details that would have been inconsequential at the time—the color of a rug, the content of a photograph, the condition of a piece of furniture. When a fact didn't come quickly enough, he would press the thumb and middle finger of his right hand against the corners of his eyes next to his nose, and close his eyes. Then, as if he were watching a videotape replay, he would describe what had happened, usually as unemotionally as if he were describing a trip to the supermarket.

For example, there is his description of his attack on his fourth victim, Ida Irga, seventy-five, of Boston, on August 19, 1962:

"I said I wanted to do some work in the apartment and she didn't trust me because of the things that were going on and she had a suspicion of letting, allowing anybody into the apartment without knowing definitely who they were. And I talked to her very briefly and told her not to worry, I'd just as soon come back tomorrow rather than—in other words, if you don't trust me, I'll come back tomorrow then. And I started to walk downstairs and she said, 'Well, come on in.' And we went into the bedroom where I was supposed to look at a leak there at the window and when she turned, and I put my arms around her back. . . ."

"Where was the bedroom from the front door? How did you get there?"

"All the way—I think it went through a . . . a parlor as you walked in, and a dining room and a bedroom. Oh, before the bedroom was a kitchen, and the bedroom was way back. The bed was white. It wasn't made, either. . . . She was in the midst, probably, of making the bed up. And there was an old dresser there and I opened the drawers up and there was nothing in them, nothing at all. They were empty. And, uh, when I did get her by the neck and strangle her . . ."

"From behind?"

"Yes. Manually. I noted blood coming out of her ear—very dark."

"Which ear?"

"Yes, uh, to my right, the right ear. I remember that, and then I think there was the dining room set in there, a very dark one, and there was brown chairs around it, and I recall putting her legs up on her two chairs in a wide position—one leg in each chair—and . . ."

Before we finished discussing the killing of Mrs. Irga, I tried to find out why he would pick a seventy-five-year-old woman for a sex attack.

"Attractiveness had nothing to do with it," he said.

"It didn't have anything to do with it?"

"No."

"She was a woman?"

"Yes."

Then there was Sophie Clark, a twenty-year-old black student at the Carnegie Institute of Medical Technology, who became victim number six on December 5, 1962, in her Back Bay apartment.

"She was wearing a very light, flimsy housecoat, and she was very tall, well built, about 36–22–37. Very beautiful. . . ."

"Describe her apartment. What kind of door did it have?"

"It was a yellowish door, a faded yellow door. . . . And she didn't want to let me in, period. Because her roommates weren't in there at the time . . . and I told her I would set her up in modeling and photography work, and I would give her anywhere from twenty dollars to thirty-five dollars an hour for this type of modeling."

A few questions later, I asked him about the furnishings in the apartment.

"Well," he said, "there was a place where there would be a . . . what do you call a flat bed, where you put a—something over it, but you take it off, you can use it to sit on, like a couch? It had fancy little pillows on it, colorful ones, purple ones. It looked like a purple or black cover."

The details of all these cases were bricks adding up to a wall of truth. DeSalvo knew, for instance, that there was a picture of Helen Blake's (victim number three) niece atop her radio. He said he had a cup of coffee with twenty-three-year-old Patricia Bissette, victim number seven. Only the police knew that a half-full cup of coffee had been found in the living room of her Back Bay apartment. He recalled the design of the headboard against which he had placed the body of nineteen-year-old Mary Sullivan. He had to be the Strangler, I thought. He knew too much not to be.

Later, Sherry and Donovan listened to the playback at my office. Frequently one man or the other, or both, nodded at something that was being said. When DeSalvo came to Sophie Clark, Lieutenant Sherry leaned over the machine.

First, DeSalvo said that when he attempted intercourse with Sophie he discovered she was menstruating. He described the napkin he removed from between her legs, and the chair he had thrown it behind. Second, he said that as he was going through Sophie's bureau looking for a stocking to knot about her neck, he knocked a pack of cigarettes to the floor. He named the brand and described the place on the floor where he left them. At this, Sherry grabbed his briefcase and pulled out a photo showing a bureau and a pack of cigarettes just as Albert had described them. On the back of the photo there was an inscription "Homicide—Clark, Sophie—December 5, 1962."

"John, this guy has got to be it," said Sherry. "The odds against some nut making up a story and getting in details like the napkin and the cigarettes are impossible."

Donovan agreed. "You listen to the rest of this, Ed," he said. "I think it's time to get hold of the commissioner."

Boston Police Commissioner Edmund McNamara agreed to come to my office at once. As Donovan left to pick him up, I called Dr. Ames Robey and asked him to come over from Bridgewater.

When we were all together I played the recording again. From time to time the police officials conferred in muted tones. Occasionally, Sherry referred to a document or a photograph. When the blue plastic belt stopped turning, McNamara lit a large cigar and peered at his homicide team.

"Well, gentlemen," he said, "what do you recommend?"

"I think we ought to follow up in every way," said John Donovan. "More questions, more details, more everything. Things he says that aren't in the files or that some detective doesn't remember, we can go back and check. Also, if counsel will permit it I think we ought to have a lie detector test as soon as possible. If he's a phony, a good examiner should be able to tell us right away."

"Why, lieutenant," I said, "*of course* we can give him a polygraph test. I'm pleased to see that you belong to the modern school of scientific crime detection. And in any event, there'll be no risk to Albert—the results are wholly inadmissible in court."

Donovan took my sarcasm with a smile, but before he could answer, Dr. Robey jumped in.

"I think you fellows are overlooking some things," he said. "You may recall that some months ago, *I* declared this man as incompetent to stand trial. As long as he's my patient, there can be no lie detector tests or any

153

other tests unless I reexamine him and find him competent for whatever particular test you have in mind."

I glanced at Donovan, who inclined his head slightly. Dr. Robey would have to get a piece of the action.

"For chrissakes, Ames," I said, "you must know that the man has a pulse and blood pressure and breathes normally. That and the ability to comprehend articulated questions are all it takes to submit to a lie test."

Commissioner McNamara stared at Robey. "Of course we'll be guided by the doctor's medical judgment," he said. "I'm sure DeSalvo can be reexamined tomorrow, if necessary. I'm also sure, doctor, you understand that this matter may be of tremendous importance to every person in this commonwealth. I *know* that you're anxious to cooperate with us as best you can—and that's all we ask."

Certainly, said Robey, the commissioner could count on his cooperation. "I'll have a look at DeSalvo tomorrow, even though it's Sunday."

The next morning, I met Donovan and Sherry at Bridgewater. First I talked to DeSalvo and told him what was happening. He agreed immediately to the polygraph test but wanted nothing to do with Robey, whom he disliked. Finally he agreed to a limited examination.

"Dammit," I warned him, "don't give this man a hard time, or I may have to get another psychiatrist and a court order before we can go ahead. At the moment, I would very much prefer that neither the courts nor the newspapers hear anything about you for a while."

DeSalvo reacted like an artist who had just been asked to demonstrate his talent. I had broken through to the con man.

"Don't worry about Robey," he said. "I can handle him. I'll convince him that today I'm fine."

Fifteen minutes later, Robey came out of the consultation room to report that DeSalvo was in satisfactory condition for a polygraph test. His only request was that he be present when it was given. Donovan, Sherry, and I agreed, and decided we'd try to get Charlie Zimmerman to run the test the following morning. Charlie was familiar with the stranglings, having tested other suspects for police.

It was a smooth beginning. Looking back, I'd have to describe it as ominously smooth.

4. WHEELINGS AND DEALINGS

"I suppose I better give John Bottomly a call and bring him up to date," John Donovan said as we left Bridgewater.

Bottomly was the lawyer Massachusetts Attorney General Edward Brooke had named to head the Strangler Bureau.

"You do that, John," I said. "And while you're at it, ask my esteemed colleague Mr. Bottomly to think up some way to give Albert immunity. After that, you can all question him to your heart's content. Right now I've got to go to Springfield to give a speech. See you."

When I got back to Boston late that afternoon, the apartment phone was ringing.

"He gave me all the details," said Bottomly. "It's a funny thing, you know, we were right on the edge of zeroing in on this man ourselves. We had his palm print taken a couple of days ago."

"The palm print won't win you much," I said, "but I think we can work things out. So long as Massachusetts has the death penalty on the books, permitting any formal confessions is going to be a little sticky from a defense point of view. But there are still some useful things we could accomplish. If you people can establish to your own satisfaction that DeSalvo did the stranglings, you'll halt an expensive investigation, clear the other suspects, and permit large numbers of female citizens to sleep a little more soundly. Albert doesn't expect ever to be released, and certainly there are a lot of good reasons why he shouldn't be."

Yes indeed, said Bottomly, these were all points worth considering, and we would have to discuss them at length. I told him about our plans for a polygraph test. He said it was a fine idea, Zimmerman was a good man. He insisted that state police lieutenant Andy Tuney, a member of the Strangler Bureau, be present; he agreed somewhat reluctantly to allow John Donovan's presence as well.

The next morning I arrived at Bridgewater with a polygraph machine and Charlie Zimmerman. When I signed in, I was told to go at once to the office of Superintendent Charles Gaughan.

"I have orders from the Attorney General personally," Gaughan said. "Personally. You are not allowed to see Albert DeSalvo or George Nassar. Those are my orders."

Obviously, I'd miscalculated John Bottomly's determination to remain kingpin of the Strangler investigation.

"Mr. Gaughan," I said, "I don't give a damn what the Attorney General said or just how personal his request was. The United States Constitution gives both these men the absolute right to consult with counsel of their choice whether that choice suits the Attorney General or not. I'm the attorney for both of them. These are normal working hours when visits with counsel are ordinarily conducted, and I demand to see DeSalvo and Nassar at once!"

"You will not see them!" Gaughan shouted. "I'm running this institution, and I take my legal advice from the Attorney General, not the Constitution."

"Perhaps a civil rights suit in federal court will clear your thinking," I said. "George Nassar is going on trial for his life soon, as you well know. You can explain to a federal judge why you saw fit to interfere with his right to counsel at this time. I'm sure the Attorney General would agree. Do you mind if I call him?"

I picked up Gaughan's phone and put in a call to Edward W. Brooke. After being transferred from one secretary to another, I was told that the Attorney General was too busy to talk to me. I finally got the chief of his criminal division, Walter Jay Skinner, whom I had known for several years. I demanded both a confrontation with Brooke and the right to see my clients. Jay said I might be able to see Brooke the following day. In the meantime, the Attorney General's order would stand.

There was nothing more I could do at Bridgewater, and I hurried back to Boston. On the way, I thought about the pressures that were making a pawn out of Albert DeSalvo. On one side, there was the resentment of the police toward Bottomly, who had never handled a substantial criminal case before. On the other, there was Bottomly's insistence on retaining control of the investigation. And there were, perhaps, other pressures. Republican Senator Leverett Saltonstall was seventy-two years old, and there were indications that he planned to retire. The contenders for his seat were expected to include Republican Edward W. Brooke, the first black Attorney General in the country's history, and Democrat John F. Collins, the Mayor of Boston, who had appointed Police Commissioner Edward McNamara. The man whose office could claim credit for ending the terror of the Boston Strangler would make an attractive candidate.

As far as I was concerned, Bottomly had double-crossed me and I had no intention of letting him get away with it.

I filed a petition for a writ of mandamus to obtain a court order that would overrule the Attorney General and direct Gaughan to refrain from interfering with George Nassar's right to see a lawyer. I drew up a similar petition with regard to DeSalvo but didn't file it. When it came to Nasser, the opposition didn't stand a chance. But DeSalvo had been found incompetent to stand trial, and there might be some question about his competence to choose a lawyer—not a strong argument, but one they might reach for.

I also sent a telegram to DeSalvo, informing him of what was going on. I assured him I was fighting for his rights, and warned him not to let anyone interview him by subterfuge.

I stayed late in my office that Sunday night, mulling over the case that had produced so many complications in just a few days. Through a curious turn of events, DeSalvo had found counsel before the police had found him. No responsible lawyer could advise him to openly confess what he claimed to have done—to do so would be to invite his own execution. But advising him to keep his mouth shut permanently was no answer either. That would force the continuation of an expensive investigation, cause further misery for other suspects, and perpetuate the fear that gripped the city. There was only one line of reasoning that made sense: if DeSalvo was to make a confession, it had to be with immunity.

There was a meeting in Brooke's office the next afternoon. Participating were Jon Asgeirsson, the attorney who had represented DeSalvo as the Green Man; Jay Skinner; the Attorney General; and myself. I had sent Brooke a telegram the night before, suggesting that his illegal orders with respect to DeSalvo and Nasser were politically motivated. He assured me I was wrong. He insisted that he was concerned that the rights of DeSalvo not be jeopardized. He said a temporary injunction had been issued restraining *Life* magazine, Charlie Zimmerman, and others including Asgeirsson and myself from mentioning anything about DeSalvo to the news media. The petition also called for the appointment of a guardian to represent DeSalvo, who—as I had expected—was judged incompetent to select his own counsel.

Skinner conceded that I had every right to see George Nassar, and that the order prohibiting me from talking to him had been revoked. I told Brooke that his refusal to see me had prompted my actions, and that neither I nor any of the other persons named in his petition had any plans to give the story to the news media. "Had you gone over the demands of this petition with me before filing it," I said, "I think we might have agreed upon every point except the question of 'competence to choose counsel.' I doubt that there is such a thing in our jurisprudence. If that were the case, the chief law enforcement officer in the state could control the appearance of defense counsel for every defendant who suffered from mental disease. Surely that would destroy our adversary system."

"I agree there's a conflict there," Brooke said. "However, I think I have a duty to prevent a mental patient in custody in a state institution from being exploited. I admit that I may have to prosecute that same man. I think the matter ought to be presented to a court for decision."

I agreed. Brooke and I shook hands. "This meeting was much more successful than I anticipated," he said. "I hope things work out."

In order to make the temporary injunction Brooke had mentioned valid, I was supposed to be served by telegram immediately. But on Tuesday night the telegram still had not come. I was brooding over being sued for something I would have agreed to in advance. I had serious doubts about the power of any court to impose a sweeping injunction against free speech on the news media. And I was annoyed by the attempt to use guardianship as a device to oust me as counsel. By 9:30, I suspected that no temporary injunction had been issued (which proved to be the case). I called Jay Skinner and told him that since no telegram had arrived I didn't consider myself enjoined, that my silence was voluntary. I also told him I'd contest the Attorney General's right to intrude upon the relationship between a defendant and a licensed lawyer.

Along about midnight, I remembered the old saying that "a man who represents himself in court has a fool for a client." I needed a lawyer. Despite the hour, I called Paul T. Smith, a justly famous criminal lawyer practicing in New England. The previous year, Paul and I had defended attorney Joseph Sax, tried in federal court in New York as a narcotics conspirator. Paul told me to come to his house, and met me in his bathrobe. We conferred over coffee, and he said he would take the case. "Give them nothing," he said. "This is an old play, a steamroller job. When the prosecutor starts picking out the defense lawyers an accused can have, we might as well all start turning in our tickets."

Word of a possible break in the Strangler case had leaked out, and the Suffolk County Courthouse was filled with newsmen as I picked my way over cables and past cameras to the courtroom door. Behind me, Paul Smith paused just long enough to proclaim the Attorney General's petition a damnable outrage and an affront to the United States Constitution.

Presiding for the Supreme Judicial Court was Associate Justice Arthur E. Whittemore, a man before whom I remembered having argued a mock case when I was a senior in law school. Now, that seemed a lifetime ago.

At no time in the proceedings did anyone use the word "strangler." I assured the court that neither I nor Jon Asgeirsson nor any of the other defendants, to our knowledge, had any intention of giving out stories. So far as that went, the principal source of information thus far was the lawsuit filed by the Attorney General. As for the guardianship plea, I thought it wrong that a man who might have to prosecute DeSalvo on a capital charge have anything to do with selecting his lawyer.

Justice Whittemore dismissed the petition. "Based on the assurance of counsel that there is no plan to publicize this matter," he said. "I see no reason for injunctive relief if any were appropriate. I should, however, like to have a mental examination for the benefit of the court, and I shall appoint psychiatrists for that purpose. The inmate, DeSalvo, is of course entitled to have examination made by doctors of his own selection."

A few minutes later, in his chambers, the judge suggested a procedure that Skinner, Asgeirsson, and all I found acceptable. The psychiatric report would be impounded as soon as he received it. We would be able to inspect it in his office. "Whether there is to be a further proceeding on the question of guardianship can best be decided when the doctors' reports are available," Justice Whittemore said.

Two state-employed psychiatrists were appointed to examine DeSalvo. Their report delicately skirted the central issue—whether he was incompetent to select an attorney—and the matter of guardianship remained unsettled for a couple of months.

Meanwhile, I made phone calls. One was to Dr. Robert Mezer, who agreed to give DeSalvo an intensive examination. Next I called my colleague Melvin Belli. In defending Jack Ruby for the murder of Lee Harvey Oswald, Belli had done a great deal of research into the psychiatric aspects of homicide, and he was able to give me some very helpful information.

Finally I called Dr. William J. Bryan, the most knowledgeable man I knew on the subject of hypnosis.

5. "I HAD TO HURT TO HELP"

The two hypnotic sessions conducted at Bridgewater by Dr. William J. Bryan were among the most intense experiences I've ever had. They were also the closest look I ever got at what made Albert DeSalvo kill.

I had first met Bryan in 1961, shortly before attending a special hypnosis seminar for trial lawyers run by him and Melvin Belli. There was some skepticism about hypnosis at that seminar, until Bryan performed a small experiment. He called me and two other attorneys to seats in the front of the room, and asked each of us to close his eyes and raise his right hand. "Thank you," he said. "You may notice that as you hold your right hand high, your arm is becoming very stiff and rigid. Becoming numb, very numb." He kept repeating the words in an insistent monotone. Occasionally I felt him lightly rub my right hand, which was supposed to be getting numb. As far as I was concerned, all I was getting was impatient.

"All right, gentlemen," Bryan said. "Open your eyes, please." We did. Each of us had a hypodermic needle sticking through his hand.

"What you have observed," said Bryan, "is the elementary use of hypnosis as anesthesia. It has several advantages, including reduced bleeding. You may note that the punctures I have made have not caused bleeding. As I speak, you will observe a slight drip of blood commence in response to my suggestion." Insult added to injury: we started to bleed. At which point, Bryan removed the needles and resumed his lecture.

Now, four years later, I felt that Bryan could make a valuable contribution to the study of the Strangler. I remembered a California case he had worked on a few years before. The defendant, Harvey Bush, had strangled three older women, and his attorney, Al Mathews of Los Angeles, had decided that his only defense was insanity. The psychiatrists who examined Bush offered no interpretations as to *why* he had murdered, and Mathews called Bryan in to see what he could learn through hypnoanalysis.

Bryan, through a study of the crimes and the defendant's background, decided that mother-hatred might be the key to the killings. He and Mathews visited Bush in jail. Through hypnosis, Bryan created a scene that he felt would trigger the killer in Bush. He used Mathews as the mother figure. Just as Mathews provided the last essential condition by turning his back on Bush, the prisoner let out a scream and attacked him. If Bryan hadn't been there to grab Bush and bring him out of his trance, Attorney Mathews could have become victim number four.

On March 20, 1965, I picked Bryan up at Logan Airport and drove him to Bridgewater. During the forty-minute ride, I told him as much as I could of DeSalvo's story. At the hospital, he met the other doctors who would observe the session, and then DeSalvo. He spent close to two hours digging into DeSalvo's background; particularly his relationship with his wife, his mother, and his daughter, Judy.

He also determined the prisoner's susceptibility to hypnosis. DeSalvo was an excellent subject. Within minutes, Bryan had him in a deep trance and had slowly pushed a needle through the fleshy part of DeSalvo's arm. "You will feel pressure," he repeated, "but no pain, no pain at all, no pain at all. . . ." When the point was all the way through, he told DeSalvo to open his eyes and look at his arm. He then removed the needle. DeSalvo's arm dropped limply to his side.

Now, Bryan moved his chair close to DeSalvo's. Speaking in a low voice and almost talking into his ear, Bryan started taking him back through the preceding days, months and years. "The top page of the calendar shows the date, March 20, 1965, today. Now you tear off that sheet, and you see March 19. You tear that off and you do it with each sheet, back, back farther and farther. . . ." He took DeSalvo back to September 8, 1963, the day Evelyn Corbin, victim number nine, a fifty-eight-year-old divorcee, was killed in her Salem apartment.

"Now, Albert," Bryan said, "tell me what's happening. It's all right. You can tell me. What's happening?"

DeSalvo was reliving it. He had walked into the building through the front door and gone to her apartment. When she opened her door, he told her he had come to fix the bathroom. Talking in the present tense, DeSalvo described the scene. His voice was an imitation of a woman's: "Who sent you? Who sent you?" Then he was himself: "The superintendent. There's something wrong with your bathroom. I've got to check it out."

He put a knife to her neck. "You're not the Strangler, are you?" she asked him. DeSalvo assured her that he wasn't. As he took her to the bed, she told him that she couldn't have intercourse. "She says she can't do nothing, the doctor told her no. She says, 'Don't hurt me, please.' I told her I won't hurt her."

At this point, DeSalvo blocked out what was happening. Bryan's voice became louder, more insistent. Now, DeSalvo was holding his hands out in front of him, twisting his wrists, manipulating his fingers. Earlier, while giving Bryan his history, DeSalvo had used similar gestures. . . . His daughter had been born with a leg defect, and that was the way he had been instructed to massage her.

"Her thighs," yelled Bryan, "you're doing something to her thighs. Tell me, it's all right, you can tell me. Tell me what you're doing to her thighs. . . ." DeSalvo screamed—a shrill, piercing sound that brought us straight up against the back of our chairs.

"Relax," Bryan commanded. "Deep, deep, deep, deeper relaxed, deeper relaxed. There, that's better. Now, what were you doing? It was good. You can tell me. What was it?"

DeSalvo groaned: his words were unintelligible. Then, without warning—"Judy!"

Bryan was pressing. "What did you do with Judy?"

"I massaged her."

"You massaged her. That's right. With your thumbs. And what happened?"

"She got well."

"That's right. You massaged her right on the thighs. Now, isn't that what you did with every other victim, too?"

"Yes."

Bryan was pushing, trying to find out *why* DeSalvo wanted to make his victims "well." He brought DeSalvo back to Judy. He was massaging her; she was crying. "She thinks I'm hurting her," DeSalvo said. "I don't mean to hurt her, I want to help her. She doesn't understand. She's a child. I'm trying to help her and I must hurt her to help her."

"If you want to help them, you have to hurt them," said Bryan. "Isn't that the idea? If you're going to help a woman, you have to hurt her. . . ."

In a few seconds, Bryan brought DeSalvo awake. But first he instructed him to dream about the Evelyn Corbin encounter that night, to recall all his thoughts and feelings at the time, and then to wake up and write down what he had dreamed.

As Bryan and I drove back to Boston, he said: "We're close, very close, I'm sure of it. The daughter is the key. She's got to be. It's not just a mother-figure hatred, or there wouldn't have been those young girls, those young victims. The dream may tell us. He'll have the dream all right, you can be sure of it. He'll have it and he'll write it down. All I hope is that I find what I'm looking for."

"So do I. But just what the hell is it?"

Bryan told me that evening. His description of significant incidentals from the past and his interpretation of them made sense:

When Judy was born, Irmgard, who elected to have natural childbirth, had suffered great pain. She said she didn't want to become pregnant again, and swore she wouldn't have intercourse. To make matters worse, Judy was born with a serious leg defect. This was at Fort Dix, New Jersey, and the army doctors said the child might be permanently handicapped. They prescribed a "frog cast"—a harness that surrounded her hips and upper legs, and had to be laced into place. The bow-like knot that DeSalvo tied around the necks of his victims was the same knot he had tied on his daughter's harness.

The doctors also prescribed physical therapy. The DeSalvos were told to manipulate Judy's leg each day, even though she cried. Most of the time, the chore fell to Albert. He would place Judy on her back, and slowly and evenly move her thighs open and closed like a bellows. Often she cried in pain, and Albert would be near tears himself. She was his child, and he loved her. She was only a baby, she couldn't understand, but he would tell her that in order to help her, he had to hurt her.

When she was two, Judy was still crawling. Then, one day, she pulled herself up to the knobs of a television set. Without knowing what would happen, she twisted the volume control. A blast of sound frightened her so that she jumped up and ran to her mother's arms. From then on, her leg was normal.

"What did Albert do," Bryan asked, "when I lost him this afternoon just as he was about to describe the sex act between himself and Evelyn Corbin? What did he *do?*"

"He held his hands out, and began to move them apart and then together again."

"Exactly!" Bryan said. "He was doing what he did when he manipulated his daughter's thighs. It was the communication he went to when his voice failed him, when he should have been talking about intercourse and stranglings—things he couldn't describe because they were too horrible to him. He skipped over them to the last thing he did before leaving the murder scene. He had to hurt people in order to help them. I think Albert always wanted to help people, which is why his personality is so pleasant most of the time. He wants to be thought of as kind; he wants to be loved and popular and admired. But all this runs up against hostilities that have been built into his psyche almost since the day he was born. And these are precisely the ingredients that could produce a strangler who would be hard to catch—he never struck at anyone he knew or had feelings for; he only struck at images, at total strangers.

"Somewhere in the motivations that took Albert down strange streets at times he couldn't anticipate, we'll find the women he knew in his life. His mother, whom he loved and hated. His wife, whom he loved almost desperately, but who was physically cold to him. And his daughter, whom he loved very deeply and yet resented because, in a sense, she cost him his wife's affections. I don't know if we'll ever get the images sorted out, but I do know they're all there."

I have heard a lot of theorizing about DeSalvo's compulsions, but I don't think I have ever heard anybody make more sense than Bill Bryan did that night.

The next day, a Sunday, we were back at Bridgewater. Before the session started, DeSalvo took me aside. "They had two women in here this morning," he said. "They brought me out to talk to Dr. Allen, and there were these two women sitting opposite a couple of inmates at the visiting table. Only these inmates are too screwy to have any visitors. The women looked at me, but I don't think they recognized me. I recognized them right away, though. One was that German girl I ran away from, and the other was that colored woman I talked to who lived in the same building as that colored girl, the pretty one, her name was Clark. I'll bet they were in here trying to pick me out."

He was right. The "visitors" were Gertrude Gruen and Mrs. Marcella Lullka. Miss Gruen was a German waitress who had fought off a strangling attempt on February 18, 1963. Mrs. Lullka had spoken to DeSalvo only minutes before he killed Sophie Clark. He said he left her apartment without touching her because she had a small child. The two women had been brought to Bridgewater to look at both DeSalvo and George Nasser. Ironically, neither of them had recognized DeSalvo, but both thought there was something familiar about Nasser. Because I'd met DeSalvo through Nasser, some people—including Bottomly, Ames Robey, and Robey's assistant, Dr. Samuel Allen—thought DeSalvo might be a decoy, that the real Strangler was George Nasser. The theory was as naive as it was preposterous: the most any lawyer could win by pulling that kind of stunt would be disbarment. As for the women feeling that they might have seen George before, I wouldn't have been surprised to learn that somewhere along the line they had been given some advance hints.

A few minutes later, when we were in the examining room waiting to begin, I leaned over to Dr. Allen and said that I didn't know he played detective on the side. "The German girl and Mrs. Lullka," I said, "they were in here this morning pretending to be visitors. They couldn't recognize Albert, but he recognized them. How do you explain that, doctor?"

Allen mumbled something about not knowing what I was talking about. "Dr. Allen," I said in my best courtroom manner, "I assume you had some purpose in interviewing my client this morning—in the visiting room, of all places. Since he didn't ask for you, and since no court appointed you, and since the substance of your interview was not especially psychiatric, you must have had some purpose. Were you conspiring to aid detectives for the commonwealth? You should be able to answer that, it's a simple enough question. After all, there were witnesses who saw you talking to Albert."

"I can't discuss it," he said. It was a pleasant moment. My only regret was that I couldn't be present when the conversation was reported to John Bottomly.

Bill Bryan started questioning DeSalvo. Sure enough, he had got up during the night and written about a dream on the pad next to his bed. When he woke in the morning, he thought the writing had been part of the dream. Then he saw the pad:

"I went to the apartment, rang the door bell. The door buzzer rang. I opened the door. . . . E.C. was at the door. I said, 'Hi . . . The superintendent sent me to check the leak in the bathroom.' She and I went into the bathroom. She said, 'I don't see any leak.' Her back was turned to me. I put a knife to her neck and told her, 'Don't scream and I don't hurt you.' She said, 'O.K.' She said, 'You're not the Strangler, are you?' I said, 'No, I just want to make love to you.' I took her into the bedroom. She said, 'I can't have intercourse. I'm not well.' I said, 'O.K. Will you blow me?' She said, 'Yes, but please don't hurt me.' I said, 'O.K.' I took a pillow from the bed, put her on her knees at the foot of the bed. I sat on the edge while she blew me. Before I came, she reached over and got white Kleenex tissue and finished it with her hand. After that, she got up and I told her to lie on the bed and she did, so I could tie her hands up in front of her. Then I got on top of her and put my hands on her neck and pressed very firmly and then I have to spread her legs apart and pre—" The last word was unfinished.

Bryan read what DeSalvo had written. Then he sat next to him as he had the day before, put him into a trance, and took him back, back to the day Evelyn Corbin was murdered.

"Now, Albert," he said, "that word you failed to finish, that word was p-r-e-s-s-e-d, wasn't it? That's where you couldn't write any more, isn't it? That's because you began to see Judy in your dream, isn't it? It was Judy whose thighs you were opening and closing, pressing and pressing. It was Judy, isn't that so, Al—Judy!"

DeSalvo kept shaking his head, mumbling, sounding confused. From time to time, his body quivered. But Bryan kept pounding at him with the child's name. Weren't each of Albert's victims identified with Judy? Wasn't each strangling a re-creation of his effort to cure Judy? Wasn't it Judy he was after?

Now Bryan leaned in closer. "You were killing her. Killing your own daughter. Killing Judy because she came between you and Irmgard and took Irmgard's love from you." Then, his voice dropping to a whisper, his mouth almost touching Albert's ear, he repeated over and over: "You were killing Judy, each time you killed someone it was Judy, it was Judy, Judy. . . ."

Suddenly, the hands of the Boston Strangler flashed up from his lap and shot out at Bryan's throat. "You're a liar!" Bryan parried the thrust, and slammed back into the wall. At the same time he brought his hands down hard on DeSalvo and yelled "Sleep!" DeSalvo relaxed.

Then Bryan started probing DeSalvo's feelings about Irmgard. "Were you attacking Irmgard all those times?" he asked, leaning in again. "Were you putting your hands on her neck?"

"She don't like nobody touching or going near her neck at all. If they did, she'd faint."

Later, Bryan asked: "How is Irmgard mixed up in this thing?" DeSalvo's shoulders drooped. "I don't know," he said. A few minutes later, Bryan ended the session.

As I drove Bryan back to Logan Airport to make a flight to Los Angeles, he seemed discouraged. "If we only had more time," he said. "This patient offers a unique opportunity to really learn something about homicide, to find out where in the personality the impulse arises—and why it's formed. I could work with DeSalvo for weeks and months; there's so damned much there. I don't suppose there's much chance of having him transferred to a California hospital, where I could see him on a regular basis?"

Maybe someday, I said. But there would be a long way to go before we could even think about a transfer. And we might never get that far. "There must be other Alberts walking the streets right now," I said, "and we have no way of recognizing them."

"Sometimes I suspect that I'm treating one of them," Bill said. "It takes so little to turn hostility into homicide. If only we knew more about the cause and the catalyst."

I nodded, and decided I'd do my best to see that someday a thorough study was done on Albert DeSalvo.

6. *AN INADMISSIBLE CONFESSION*

On May 6, 1965, we got over one obstacle. The Attorney General's office and I agreed on a guardian—attorney George McGrath, who had formerly served as one of the best commissioners of correction Massachusetts has ever had. I had worked with McGrath on prison matters, and had always found him to be both fair and imaginative.

In June, we began to climb over another obstacle. I was in the city of Salem defending George Nassar, whose chances looked slim. The only evidence against Nassar was his eyewitness identification by Mrs. Buote and her daughter. If he didn't testify, that would probably be enough to get him a conviction; if he did, the murder he had committed as a teenager would be thoroughly aired by the prosecution. And the jurors—even though instructed to the contrary—would in all probability decide that he had "done it again."

During the second week of trial I was approached by a tall, handsome man who introduced himself as Andy Tuney and asked if he could speak with me privately. We went into the library, and sat at the end of a long table that looked as if it had predated the witch trials. "I'd like to talk to DeSalvo," said Tuney. "I'm pretty well convinced that he's our man from some of the things I've seen and heard. But I have to talk to him to be sure."

"I'd be delighted to have the question settled," I said. "But how can I let you talk to him? If he gives the right answers, you'll be before a grand jury the next day, and Albert'll be staring at the electric chair."

"I know you can't let him make any confessions that could be used against him," Tuney said. "If you let me talk to him, I'll give you my word that I'll never testify against him without your consent. Check it out. I think you'll find that I keep my promises."

"Okay," I said, "I'll make a few inquiries. Let me talk to George McGrath, and see what we can do. But it would have to be just you—no stenographer, no recorder."

"That's fair," he said. "I'll check with you in a day or so."

I checked Tuney out with several lawyers, and I also talked to Sherry and Donovan. Nobody had anything to say about him that wasn't good. I especially liked one lawyer's summation.

"He's the damnedest guy I've ever seen," he said. "You can't win anything by cross-examining him because he sticks right to the truth. He'll tell the truth even if he ruins the state's case in the process. And he's driven a few prosecutors crazy by hunting up evidence after the trial that they convicted the wrong man. You can trust Andy. His word's as good as gold."

On June 26, the Nassar trial ended. George was convicted of first-degree murder and put in a death-row cell at Walpole. I took nearly a hundred exceptions, and announced that I would appeal the verdict.

Soon after the trial, George McGrath and I met with Tuney and John Donovan to work out the arrangements for DeSalvo's interrogation. We decided that Donovan and Tuney would question DeSalvo with McGrath present. DeSalvo would waive neither his right against self-incrimination nor his right to have counsel present. Whatever information the detectives obtained could only be used to help doctors involved in the case make their evaluations. The Boston Strangler would confess to police, but the confession would be inadmissible as legal evidence.

I'm afraid this arrangement has done a great deal to confuse the public—the general reaction being, "Well, if they know this guy is the Strangler, why can't they prosecute him?" And yet, what we did was not unprecedented. Under Massachusetts law, a doctor who takes information from a defendant in a criminal case is barred from using it against him. Otherwise, no defense lawyer in his right mind would ever permit his client to be psychiatrically examined. Also, the plan was the only possible solution under the circumstances. I wanted DeSalvo studied, not electrocuted; the authorities wanted to be able to end their investigation. In both cases, DeSalvo's identification as the Strangler had to be irrefutably established. And that was only possible if police examined him, if they matched his memory against the myriad details of thirteen murders.

By the time of the first interview, Bottomly had altered the arrangements "slightly." Before Tuney and Donovan began their interrogation, he would go in alone with McGrath. He had a few key questions he wanted to ask DeSalvo; he wouldn't take long.

On a day in July, five cars converged on Bridgewater. McGrath, Asgeirsson, and I drove up by ourselves. Tuney, Bottomly, and DiNatale arrived in Andy's unmarked state police cruiser, and Donovan and Sherry rode in a Boston police car. Tuney and DiNatale carried in racks of clothing and other evidence to use in testing DeSalvo. We gathered in Superintendent Gaughan's meeting room, and Bottomly and McGrath went into a private room with DeSalvo. Fifteen minutes would be sufficient, Bottomly had said. He stayed in the room for five hours.

No one was surprised when Bottomly decided that he would conduct all the interviews with DeSalvo. At the last minute, I agreed that he could use a tape recorder, provided I was given copies of the tapes. Transcripts of the interviews were turned over to the detectives, who checked the information both against known facts and against new material turned up by additional investigation.

Details piled upon details as DeSalvo recalled the career of the Strangler, murder by murder. He knew there was a notebook under the bed of victim number eight, Beverly Samans; he knew that Christmas bells were attached to Patricia Bissette's door. He drew accurate floor plans of the victims' apartments. He said he'd taken a raincoat from Anna Slesers's apartment to wear over his T-shirt because he had taken off his blood-stained shirt and jacket. Detectives found that Mrs. Slesers had bought two identical coats and had given one to a relative. They showed the duplicate to DeSalvo, along with fourteen other raincoats tailored in different styles. DeSalvo picked out the right one.

Then there was DeSalvo's addition of Mary Brown and Mary Mullen to his list of victims. Nothing had been known about the Mullen case; the eighty-five-year-old woman's death had been listed as due to natural causes when she was found in her Commonwealth Avenue apartment. But Tuney and DiNatale were able to check out the case, and DeSalvo accurately described the apartment's furnishings. He said she went limp in his arms as he was about to strangle her. She reminded him of his grandmother. "I tried to hold her," he said. "I didn't want her to fall on the floor."

He described an abortive attack on a Danish girl in her Boston apartment. He had talked his way into the place, and had his arm around her neck when he suddenly looked in a large wall mirror. Seeing himself about to kill, he was horrified. He relaxed the pressure and started crying. He was sorry, he said, he begged her not to call the police. If his mother found out, she would cut off his allowance, and he wouldn't be able to finish college. The young woman never reported the incident. With nothing to go on other than DeSalvo's memory, DiNatale found her. Not surprisingly, she remembered the incident vividly.

DeSalvo remembered an overstuffed chair in the living room of Miss Gruen, the woman who had fought her attacker off, as blue. By this time she had moved to another city, but Andy Tuney phoned her. No, she said, the chair was brown. A few weeks later he received a letter from her. She had found a color photograph of the room. DeSalvo was right, the chair was blue.

About all I could do while the interrogation was going on was wait. When I visited DeSalvo, I often found him depressed. Bottomly was kind to him, but the remembering took a lot out of him. And there was something else. "The guards around here are bugging the hell out of me," he said. "They keep telling me I'm going to wind up like some goddamn vegetable. Or they say I ought to get another lawyer—that you're just in it for the publicity, and you'll drop me. One guy keeps saying how Sheppard was ordered back to jail, and Nassar's going to get the chair. He says I'll get the chair thirteen times if I stick with you."

"Albert," I said, "this place is a garbage dump. And there are a lot of sadists posing as guards. The best thing you can do is write a letter of complaint to the superintendent every time one of these bastards starts annoying you. Do that for a while, and see what happens. And as for Dr. Sheppard and Nassar, both those cases will be reversed. Besides, don't worry about them. You've got enough headaches of your own."

"I've threatened to complain," DeSalvo said, "but they just laugh at me. They say I'm a nut, and nobody's going to take my word against theirs."

"Sure," I said. "That's how they've been getting away with abusing inmates for years. But you've shown some fairly important people that you don't make things up. Mr. Bottomly's one of them. If you don't get any satisfaction from Gaughan, send a copy of the complaint to the Attorney General's office. This hole has been spoiling for an investigation for a long time."

DeSalvo subsequently reported to the front office every instance of abuse he either suffered or witnessed. In a short time, the guards who had been bullying him found themselves writing answers to his complaints. He became a leader among the inmates, and some of the mistreatment at Bridgewater stopped. In future months, the Massachusetts Legislature held hearings on conditions at the institution. Although Bridgewater still stands as an ugly monument to the treatment of mental illness in this country, it's a better place than it was when DeSalvo was first confined there.

Bottomly interrogated DeSalvo for the last time on September 29,

1965. He had obtained more than fifty hours of tapes, which came out to more than two thousand pages of transcription. Tuney, DiNatale, and their aide, Sandra Irizzarry, continued to check and double-check everything DeSalvo had said. Meanwhile, Bottomly, Brooke, and I tried to set up ground rules for further proceedings if DeSalvo should be officially accepted as the Strangler.

7. LOOKING FOR THE MIDDLE GROUND

It's nice to think about lawyers on both sides of a criminal case working together to find a just solution. Quite often, both society and the defendant are better served by this process than they are by a jury trial. But this was no ordinary case; the central figure was a criminal whose actions the American public had taken as a blow to its psyche. The slightest suggestion of anything that could be misconstrued as a "deal" would cause a reaction of national proportions.

All of us were searching for a middle ground on which both the people and the accused could be justly served. We wanted to be fair, and we were prepared to be imaginative. But there were no ready answers, neither for me nor for Edward Brooke, who now was a solid contender for the U.S. Senate and quite properly concerned that no one be able to accuse him of using the Strangler case as a political bandstand.

If the state put DeSalvo on trial as the Strangler under circumstances that precluded the possibility of the death penalty, there would be all kinds of caterwauling about a fix. But DeSalvo's confession was inadmissible. Unless a capital result was out of the question, it seemed that the state would have no trial at all. As Brooke put it at one of our conferences, "I'm damned if I do and damned if I don't. The question is: What's the best way to be damned?"

We could bring the case before a grand jury, include DeSalvo's confessions, and hope for a finding of "no true bill"—after hearing evidence indicating guilt, the jury could nevertheless decline to indict. In this instance, the grand jury could file a report stating that it found the confessions to be true, but could not return an indictment because they were not usable in a jury trial. But there were pitfalls. Grand jury proceedings are secret, and the American public doesn't have much confidence in secret sessions. Besides, it was far from clear whether grand juries were empowered to rule on admissibility of evidence. Usually they indict if the *information* they hear is sufficient, at which point it's up to the trial judge to determine whether or not that information qualifies as evidence.

This led to another thought. The matter could be presented to a grand jury with the hope of an indictment. The trial judge would have to base his ruling on undisputed evidence that the confessions were inadmissible. The substance of the confessions would be made public during the admissibility hearing, and everyone would know about them except for the twelve jurors, who presumably would be forced to acquit for lack of proof. The trouble here was that no trial judge could be expected to be very happy about having to throw out the only damning evidence in the case, especially when the basis for his ruling had been set up in advance by the opposing sides. Under those circumstances, *everybody* would be yammering about a deal.

The third possibility was a trial in which medical opinion would show beyond a reasonable doubt that Albert was insane at the time of the crimes. If the jury found Albert not guilty by reason of insanity, the public probably would be satisfied. If they found him guilty despite clear instructions from the trial judge—which too often happens—the judge could set the verdict aside as unsupported by any evidence of sanity and order a new trial. There would be a fuss, but it would be minor compared to the uproar the grand jury solutions might trigger.

But there were problems here, too. Ostensibly the rule in Massachusetts is that the state must prove sanity beyond a reasonable doubt. If not, the defendant should be acquitted and, in a murder case, committed until he can prove his sanity has been restored.

It's a commendable rule, but it often turns out to be the exception. For one thing, juries frequently are reluctant to acquit criminals on insanity grounds, and this reluctance would be intensified in the case of a man who had killed thirteen women. For another, the Massachusetts Supreme Judicial Court had clobbered the rule in a 1962 case. The accused man, Charles Hartford, pleaded that he was insane when he killed his wife. The only psychiatric evidence at the trial supported his claim. But the jury found him guilty. His lawyers argued that the verdict should be set aside because the state offered *no* evidence that he was sane. But, the court upheld the verdict—ruling that the "presumption of sanity" was so strong that the state's failure to prove sanity was not fatal to its case.

Then there was Ames Robey. Relations between him and DeSalvo had deteriorated to the point where it seemed likely that if DeSalvo pleaded white, Robey would testify black—and vice versa. If the prosecutor failed to call Robey, he might be on the major networks within hours, yelling "fix." If he *were* called—well, it only takes one expert's testimony to sustain a guilty verdict.

There were personal considerations, too. If an insanity plea backfired, I had an excellent chance of being known as a lawyer who'd taken a perfectly protected client and steered him into the electric chair. Quite possibly, some of my colleagues might start yelling that my license should be revoked for risking a client's life to get publicity.

At one of our discussions, I put it this way to Brooke and Bottomly: "Look, when I met Albert, there were enough indictments pending against him to pretty much ensure that he'd never be walking the streets again. Now I've helped him disclose that he's committed multiple murder, and it's a certainty he'll never be released. Show me some way to avoid the risk of execution—I'll run the risk of conviction, but not execution—and you can have anything you want. I know damn well that neither of you really want to see him killed. Tell me, is that asking too much?"

Apparently Brooke didn't think it was. "Actually," he said, "you're not asking for a great deal, and in many cases, you'd be able to settle the matter on that basis. But I don't know of any case like this one. Right now, I'm not sure that I have either the power or the right to take the judgment as to Albert's life away from the people. We'll think about it some more."

We thought about it a lot more, without finding an answer. Then, without warning, on April 7, 1966, John Bottomly resigned. His reasons were never made clear, although rumors abounded. As far as I was concerned, it hurt the case. We'd had our differences, and some of them had been giant sized. But Bottomly had been a driving force in the efforts to resolve matters. He phoned me to convey his regret at being unable to speak for the state any more, and he wished me good luck. "We never found the answer," he said, "but we were on the right track." He was right.

Assistant Attorney General Bill Cowin, now in charge of the case, agreed that we should at least take one step that Bottomly and I had scheduled: the removal of DeSalvo's guardian. Although George McGrath had been outstanding in the role, the very presence of a guardian barred almost every legal step that might be taken. On April 12 there was a hearing at Bridgewater, and the judge ruled that DeSalvo no longer needed a guardian.

Around the same time, I had my final conference with Attorney General Brooke. By now, bygones were long since bygone, and I'd developed a great deal of respect for Brooke's ability as a lawyer. During the conference, we agreed that it would be a mistake to bring DeSalvo to trial as the Strangler in the middle of Brooke's campaign—unfair to DeSalvo, to Brooke, and to the electorate. Nor would it be right for Brooke to make any commitments that might be binding on a successor. The case of the Boston Strangler would have to be shelved for a while.

I could, however, bring the Green Man charges to trial. "By consolidating them and raising an insanity plea," I told Brooke, "I can at least test DeSalvo's evidence before a jury. And since the most he can get is life, there's no risk of execution. Besides, if it looks like we've reached an impasse, the district attorney's going to move those cases forward whether I like it or not."

"That makes sense," Brooke said. "In any event, whether I wind up in Washington, or at this desk, or in a private law office, I agree with your feeling that DeSalvo should be studied, that we should learn something about these impulse killings. If I can help, please call on me." We shook hands, and I left his office. The next time I saw him, he was a United States Senator.

8. *STRANGLER ON THE STAND*

June, 1966, was a fine month; I was on a dusty street in Dodge City, and the bad guys were falling left and right. My thirty-third birthday was June 10, but a cause for celebration appeared a few days before that. On June 6, the United States Supreme Court ordered a new trial for Dr. Sam Sheppard. And on June 7, the Supreme Judicial Court of Massachusetts handed down a similar ruling on behalf of George Nassar. Then, on June 30, Albert DeSalvo took the stand in Middlesex County Superior Court in a hearing to determine whether he was mentally competent to stand trial for armed robbery, assault, and lascivious and indecent acts.

The judge was Horace J. Cahill; the prosecutor was Donald L. Conn, a law school classmate who had become one of the stars of John Droney's staff. The witnesses would include Dr. Robert Mezer, whose expertise had become a thread running through my courtroom life.

And the room was dominated by the shadow of the Boston Strangler. We would never use the word "stranglings"; we would refer to DeSalvo's killings as "certain crimes." If DeSalvo were found competent, it was the Green Man who would go on trial, not the Strangler. But the crimes we could not discuss were a cloud over the ones at issue.

A white-haired bailiff opened the hearing: "Hear ye, hear ye, hear ye. All persons having anything to do before the Honorable, the Justices of the Superior Court within and for our County of Middlesex, draw near, give your attendance and you shall be heard. God save the Commonwealth of Massachusetts and this Honorable Court." God save Albert DeSalvo, too, I thought. All I can do is defend him.

Dr. Mezer, my first witness, said that although DeSalvo suffered from "chronic undifferentiated schizophrenia" and required commitment, he was capable of standing trial. He understood the charges against him, and was able to cooperate with counsel in the preparation of his defense.

Next I called Dr. Samuel Tartakoff, a psychiatrist who had been appointed to examine DeSalvo by Supreme Court Justice Arthur Whittemore. He was appearing for neither the defense nor the prosecution, but as an aide to the court. He, too, said DeSalvo was competent to stand trial. He said, however, that he had found no schizophrenia. Instead, he described DeSalvo as a "sociopath with dangerous tendencies." He defined a sociopath as "an individual who from early life has shown deviations from what are usually considered normal patterns of behavior, thinking, and emotional reactions." As far as I was concerned, all he had done was describe a schizophrenic who had contracted his disease at an early age. I had a feeling that by trial time, he would be testifying for the state.

Donald Conn then called Dr. Ames Robey, who said DeSalvo was incompetent to stand trial. "Over the last, oh, year and a half," said Robey, "I have seen him vacillate back and forth in terms of his chronic illness— at some times appearing almost like an acute anxiety hysteric, a neurotic, at times appearing much more obsessive and compulsive, again at other times appearing much more overtly paranoid and appearing very close to wild overt psychosis." When Conn pressed him to make his diagnosis more precise, Robey fell back on technical jargon: "The term we tend to apply particularly with this mixed alternating pattern," he said, "is 'schizophrenic reaction, chronic undifferentiated type.' And then descriptive phrases are added, as in this case—sociopathic features, obsessive features, hysterical features. At one time, depressive features, paranoid signs."

When my turn came with Robey, I was forearmed. It was common knowledge that his days at Bridgewater were numbered. According to DeSalvo, Robey had recently told him that he'd be entering private practice soon and would be available as—believe it or not—a defense expert if I wanted him. I expected a complete denial on cross-examination: but when I put the question to him, Robey surprised me.

"I said," he announced, "if Mr. Bailey, following my resignation, wants to employ me, then I would reexamine him (DeSalvo), and if I found an indication at that time that he was competent I would find him competent, just as I would testify today if I find him competent."

The next witness was a dark-browed, long-nosed man wearing a blue suit and tie, and a white shirt. He was a muscular man with an attentive manner and a charming smile. He had been brought to the courthouse in manacles from a mental institution. Now he was on the stand to prove that whatever else he was he wasn't a vegetable.

"State your name, please," I said.

"Albert H. DeSalvo."

"Where do you presently reside, Mr. DeSalvo?"

"Bridgewater MCI, Correctional Institution."

"How long have you been confined there?"

"Approximately a year and a half. . . ."

I moved fairly quickly to the subject of DeSalvo's competency to stand trial as the Green Man.

"All right. Albert, did you understand—do you understand the nature of these charges?"

"Yes."

"Do you understand what you might get for penalties?"

"Yes, sir, I do."

"And do you understand what your defense is?"

"Yes, sir, I do."

"What is your defense? Tell the court."

"My defense would be not guilty by reason of insanity."

"What do you mean by that, in your own words?"

"I wish to, in my own way, to release everything that is inside me, the truth," said Albert DeSalvo. "And whatever may be the consequences, I will accept because I have always from the very beginning wanted to tell the truth. . . ."

We discussed some of the problems he had run into with Ames Robey, and then I came back to his objectives and competence.

"Albert, when we first met, did you list certain things that you wished to have accomplished—legal matters?"

"Yes, I did."

"And are they clear in your mind today, the things that you then wanted?"

"Yes, sir."

"Have your objectives changed to any extent?"

"No. They are, as much as I can see, very increased."

A substantial portion of Albert's direct testimony touched on his experiences at Bridgewater. As he described it, the treatment he received wasn't always medical. I asked if he had ever been punished at the institution:

"I was sent to 'F' Ward for one month. That's where they throw you in the room naked and you stay there, depending on who you are and the situation. And this was first done to me because I was taken to Mr. Gaughan's office and I wasn't in there more than two seconds. I hardly got the seat warm, and he asked me a question—did I counsel this inmate? And when he used the word 'counsel,' I felt this was improper. The man had confided in me and I listened to him. But to counsel a person is to tell him what to do. . . . And it's been a proven fact that everything that I complained about was true. So Mr. Gaughan asked me again, 'I am asking you again, DeSalvo, did you or did you not counsel him?' I said, 'Let me explain. The man confided in me.' And the next thing you know, 'Take him to "F" Ward,' and they rushed me out of Gaughan's office, up to 'F' Ward. They stripped me naked, threw me in a chair, cut my hair right off—and I had already been there a year—shaved my head, threw me in the room naked, and that is it. They left me there. And then word come down, 'Oh Jesus, what did you do that for? Get him out right away.' "

When I asked Albert if he had made any complaints about conditions at Bridgewater, he said "yes," and told something of a horror story. "I'm in the so-called Medical Building, 'I' Building," he said. "Dr. Ross was there. A man had swallowed some paint. So Mr. Gaughan, thinking of the inmate, sent him off to Dr. Allen to take care of him and to have his stomach pumped out. But Dr. Allen was not present at the time and so Dr. Ross took over. And what he did was, he had the inmates— myself, as well as other officers—at first hold him down and he started pouring this stuff all down the man and pushed the tube down and the blood was squirting out. And all of a sudden the man is vomiting, can't breathe. And so this lasted about ten minutes. Finally the officers backed off. They wouldn't hold him because what he was doing was wrong. So finally Dr. Ross stood on a chair, pouring a gallon of water down the man's stomach, screaming, 'Where are the movie cameras now? Why can't they see me at my greatest height?'

"And the man was squirting blood, and the officers and the nurse ran out screaming. I vomited. These are the type of complaints that I have made."

"What happened right then?" I asked. "Did Dr. Robey come in?"

"No. The following day Dr. Robey came in and I asked to see him personally in the office and I explained to him what was going on. He said, 'I know it but can I complain about it?' I said, 'But these things are happening right in front of us. Nobody will go forward because of what will happen to them in the near future if they report it. But I'm going to report it.'

"And so right then and there, Dr. Ross comes in with IVs to feed a man who, they said, in 'F' Ward, who had just now had awakened and would not eat yet. I knew he would eat. So Dr. Robey said, 'Are you sure he will eat?' I said, 'Yes, I am.' He said, 'Show it to me.' I went down and got three bowls of cereal. The man ate it like he was starving to death. The nurse brought him a banana. He ate it.

"Dr. Robey said to Dr. Ross: 'Get out with your IVM stuff and don't ever get another IVM needle. I have so stated this here on the bulletin board, that you are not to touch needles or anything else to administer to patients because of'—because he's a sick doctor, Dr. Ross."

DeSalvo described other conditions at the institution, and then I asked him if he had understood the day's proceedings. He said he had. In answer to other questions, he said he was ready to stand trial; that he knew what his defense would be: that what he wanted was medical help.

"Would you rather be in Walpole or Bridgewater?" I asked him.

"I prefer not to be in any prison," he said. "I prefer to be in the hospital where I can at least get some type of treatment."

"Are you concerned about the possibility of conviction?"

"Yes sir, I am concerned."

"Do you realize there is a risk that you might be convicted?"

"Yes."

"Are you willing to assume that risk in order to have this matter thrashed out?"

"Yes, sir, I am."

On cross, Donald Conn referred to "certain disclosures" Albert had made to John Bottomly, and asked about the conditions that were imposed. When he pressed DeSalvo on this point, the judge warned him that he was on dangerous ground, and I broke in. "I will stipulate that the information was to be used for the benefit of the doctors in determining whether or not this man's history was fact or delusion."

"All right," Judge Cahill said. "Let it go at that."

Conn later asked DeSalvo what he meant when he talked about doing the "right" thing. What was "right" for him?

"I feel that what is right is to tell the truth. . . ."

When court reconvened, after the afternoon recess called at the end of Conn's cross-examination, I put DeSalvo back on the stand for redirect. First, I made it clear that he had been following my instructions in talking to authorities. "Have you for a year and a half followed my advice as to who to make disclosures to and who not to make them to?" I asked.

"I have listened to you on your advice, yes, sir."

"And notwithstanding your wish to tell Mr. Conn and this court this information, have you acted on my advice in not doing so in the last eighteen months?"

"Will you please say that question again?"

"Yes. Are you awaiting certain conditions to occur before you disclose this material?"

"That is true."

"You realize that if you disclose it, it will put you in jeopardy?"

"Yes."

"Do you have any desire to put your life in jeopardy?"

"I have none at this moment."

We discussed Bridgewater again, and DeSalvo mentioned a diary he had been keeping that was taken away by guards. He said that conditions had improved, and that he was being treated well. He was in the "I" Building, he said, where "you have a lot of sick patients who need a lot of care. I give the showers for the patients. I wash them up and I serve them and I do a little clerical work there and anything that—like, wash the floors, anything that has to be done, no matter what it may be."

For the final time, I brought up the disclosures. "Once again, Albert, you told Mr. Conn that you felt that, notwithstanding disagreement by counsel if that should occur, you nonetheless felt that you had certain things you wanted to get off your chest because it was the right thing to do?"

"Yes, sir, I did."

"Do you intend to continue following the advice of counsel as to whom you will make those disclosures to in the future?"

"I do," DeSalvo said.

A few days later, Judge Cahill ruled that Albert H. DeSalvo was competent to stand trial.

9. *A WITCH IS BURNED*

Donald Conn and I agreed that there was nothing to be gained by trying an already sensational case on the eve of a senatorial election, and my own court calendar was jammed. It wasn't until January 10, 1967, that Albert DeSalvo came to trial as the Green Man.

The basic strategy by which I hoped to convince a jury to find Albert not guilty by reason of insanity was simple: I would attempt to use the thirteen murders he had committed as the Boston Strangler to show the extent of his insanity. To do this, I would try to get both his confession and its corroboration by police into evidence.

There was no guarantee, of course, that I could get any part of the stranglings into evidence. And at the time of DeSalvo's trial, the law of Massachusetts, like that of most states, was governed by the 1893 McNaghten rule under which the accused must show that he was so mentally ill as not to know the nature and quality of his acts. This means he must show either that he had absolutely no awareness of what he was doing, or that he didn't know it was wrong.

A number of states that operate under the archaic McNaghten rule have extended the grounds for insanity through a modification known as the "Irresistible Impulse Doctrine": the defendant may have known what he was doing, and known that it was wrong, but nevertheless been physically unable to resist an overwhelming impulse to commit the crime. Some authorities consider the irresistible impulse doctrine to represent a great step forward, others condemn it as a silly and unworkable concept—how can you differentiate fairly between an impulse that was truly irresistible and one that simply was not resisted?

One criterion that has been applied to prove irresistible impulse is the "Policeman-at-the-Elbow Test." The idea here is that even if an officer were standing next to him at the time, the defendant would have been unable to resist committing the crime. Many prosecutors consider this a realistic test; many defense attorneys consider it just the opposite. In my opinion, the test is inescapably flawed by the fact that many people who suffer from severe mental illness are uncontrollable only when they're alone.

The search for a replacement for the McNaghten ruling has been as slow as beach-bound traffic on a hot summer day. One ruling offered real hope—the "Model Penal Code Rule." It provides that a defendant cannot be punished if his mental illness at the time of the crime was such that he lacked substantial capacity to conform his conduct to the requirements of the law. If DeSalvo were convicted, I felt we could use an appeal as a means of persuading the Massachusetts Supreme Court to replace the McNaghten Rule with the Model Penal Code Rule.

Such were the complications of an insanity defense as the trial opened. Before a jury was impaneled, Conn and I conferred with Judge Cornelius Moynihan on the crucial issue of whether or not I could use the stranglings to prove insanity. Because Conn was determined to keep them out, the judge would have to decide. Certainly the problem was unusual: I wanted the right to defend a man for robbery and assault by proving that he had committed thirteen murders.

"The psychiatrists," Moynihan said, "are of course allowed to give the basis of their opinions. Since it is common medical practice for a doctor to take into account the patient's history and background in arriving at a diagnosis, I see no reason to change the rule in this case. If Mr. DeSalvo has told these psychiatrists something of his activities in the years prior to these offenses which influences their judgment, they will be allowed to relate it. But only as part of that history, and for no other purpose."

"You get round one," Conn said, as we left the judge's quarters.

Following his opening statement, Don called four victims who had been attacked by the Green Man during the ten-month period between the last strangling and DeSalvo's arrest. All told similar stories.

DeSalvo would either knock at the door or jimmy it open. His usual line was that he was there to fix or inspect the plumbing. He would bind the woman, strip her, and start caressing her breasts. In two of the cases, this was followed by cunnilingus and in a third by fellatio—there were, as a matter of fact, no rape indictments before the jury. In each case, Albert threatened his victim into compliance with either a knife or a toy pistol. When he left, he took money or jewelry.

When the time came for cross-examination, I followed my own first rule: "Don't." There was, I felt, nothing to be gained by questioning these women. I was sure they were telling the truth, and I doubted that the jury would appreciate my pressing them. "No questions," I said.

After Conn had called police officers who had worked on the cases, the state rested.

In my opening statement, I said there was no question that Albert DeSalvo had committed the crimes described. The only issue was whether or not the Commonwealth of Massachusetts could prove that he was not insane at the time. I outlined the history my psychiatrist witnesses would offer as the basis for their diagnoses, and when I referred to the stranglings, Conn was up and objecting.

Moynihan settled the matter quickly. "The motion will be denied," he said. "I assume that Mr. Bailey is about to move along to something else."

My first witness was Dr. James Brussel, an assistant commissioner of the New York State Department of Mental Health. Dr. Brussel had achieved national fame in 1956 when he helped New York police trap George Metesky, the "Mad Bomber," by accurately describing the bomber's habits and appearance, and helping to draft an open letter that led to Metesky's arrest.

Dr. Brussel had been consulted by John Bottomly in the course of the Strangler probe. In April of 1964—three months after the last murder and almost a year before Albert DeSalvo revealed himself—Brussel had made an amazingly accurate diagnosis: the stranglings had all been committed by the same man, who was afflicted by a paranoid type of schizophrenia and who had cured himself to the point where he no longer was compelled to kill. It was unlikely that he would ever be caught by detective work alone; he was too clever to have left any substantial clues.

But he was tormented by an overwhelming desire to confess, and sooner or later he would come forward.

I'd had Dr. Brussel examine DeSalvo three months before the trial, and again on the day before it opened. Also, one of his aides had given DeSalvo a battery of psychological tests. Dr. Brussel testified that his previous diagnosis was confirmed. DeSalvo was schizophrenic. In terms of criminal acts, he could not distinguish right from wrong and he was suffering from an irresistible impulse.

Did DeSalvo, I asked him, lack "substantial capacity to conform his conduct to the requirements of the law"?

Judge Moynihan excluded the question. A bench conference followed, during which the judge said he was not allowing the question because the Model Penal Code Rule had not yet been expressly approved by the Massachusetts Supreme Court.

Conn pressed Dr. Brussel for clinical opinions on almost every act DeSalvo had committed other than the stranglings. Conn scored often as he and the psychiatrist cut and parried, especially when he drew curt answers from the doctor that some jurors obviously felt had "wise guy" overtones.

During the cross-examination, Conn suddenly asked to approach the bench. He told the judge that he had just gotten word that two men in a bar on Cambridge Street in Boston were brandishing a pistol and threatening to kill Mr. Bailey so he couldn't get DeSalvo off.

Judge Moynihan directed the court officers to clear the corridors outside the room, where would-be spectators were crowded up against a rope barrier. A police cordon was thrown around the building. Wicki was in the courtroom, but police went to my home and took my son and his baby-sitter to the home of Wicki's mother. The trial continued without incident. The gun wavers apparently were just big talkers.

The next morning, I had Dr. Robert Mezer give a complete picture of DeSalvo's background—his home life, his early sexual activity, his voyeurism, his introduction to crime, his acts of cruelty. As a boy, he said, Albert had imprisoned dogs and cats in orange crates and shot arrows through the boxes until the animals were dead or dying.

He then described DeSalvo's army career and his marriage to Irmgard; Judy's birth and her leg ailment. He said that DeSalvo's wife had never been willing to satisfy her husband sexually until late 1964.

After mentioning various jobs DeSalvo had held, and saying that his bosses found him a good worker, Mezer described DeSalvo's career as the Measuring Man. When DeSalvo was released from jail in 1962, said Mezer, Irmgard rejected him at first and told him that he would have to prove that he had reformed. Soon afterward, the stranglings began. When the homicidal impulses ebbed, DeSalvo still needed sexual gratification outside his marriage, despite the fact that things were much better at home. The result was the Green Man.

Mezer said that DeSalvo suffered from chronic, undifferentiated schizophrenia. At times, he said, DeSalvo would feel "little fires" inside his abdomen and would gradually be overcome by a desire—which he could not control—to obtain some sort of sexual relief. The Green Man's crimes were the result of an irresistible impulse.

On cross, Conn invoked the Policeman-at-the-Elbow Test. Would DeSalvo have been able to resist his so-called impulse if a policeman were right there with him?

"Yes," said Mezer, "I believe that he would." Mezer had told me there were some points he would have to concede. He did not believe the Policeman-at-the-Elbow Test was valid, but he would have to answer yes.

Conn scored again when he asked about the nonsexual aspects of the Green Man's crimes—the locks jimmied, the ruses used to gain entrance, the theft of valuables. Were these the result of an overwhelming impulse? No, said Mezer, they were not. Only the sexual assaults were.

It was good, intelligent cross-examination, which is what I had expected. I was not overly concerned about the charges of breaking and entering, and armed robbery; they were not connected to the stranglings. It was the sexual acts that were important—the caresses, the fellatio, the cunnilingus. If only the jury would find that these actions resulted from the "little fires" that burned inside DeSalvo, there was every chance that a jury might reach the same conclusion when it came to homicide.

On redirect, I asked Mezer to name the central force behind each incident. The sexual attack, he said. The breaks and robberies were excuses that enabled DeSalvo to tell himself he wasn't a sex deviate.

Then, to protect the record, I asked Dr. Mezer a question I had forgotten on direct examination. Did DeSalvo qualify under the Model Penal Code Rule? At the time he commited the acts, did he lack the capacity to conform his conduct to the requirements of the law?

As Conn rose to object, the judge surprised both of us. "No," he said, "I think we will take a step forward. I will allow it."

Conn asked to be heard, but the judge stopped him. "I am aware of the grounds of your objection, and I have considered them. I will allow the question."

Mezer had no trouble answering. Under this test, DeSalvo was clearly insane while committing all criminal acts involved in the case.

A recess was called for the weekend. In the corridor, Conn told me I was way ahead. "I think the judge is right," he said, "but I didn't expect him to anticipate what you and I both know the Supreme Court is likely to do. He's a hell of a judge, though, isn't he?"

"He's too good," I said. "I had a good appeal until this happened.

Now, I don't know. I suspect that when this trial's over, I may have nothing to complain about. Good trials usually don't make good appeals."

"Sure," said Conn. "You won't have anything to complain about except an acquittal."

I also talked to Ames Robey, who had been brought in to testify for the state. At Bridgewater, Robey had been a champion of the Model Penal Code Rule and he was happy about Mezer's testimony. "Tremendous break," he said. "I tried to tell these judges for years that it was the only fair and workable test."

"You may recall, doctor," I said, "that in June of 1965, we discussed the subject, and you said that under the Model Penal Code Test, Albert was certainly not responsible."

"You're quite right," said Ames. "There's no question about that. I would have to say you've won your case."

On Monday, Conn called his rebuttal witnesses. The first one, Stanley Setterlund, had been in Bridgewater with DeSalvo. He said DeSalvo had admitted to him that he was the Strangler. DeSalvo also told him that he cased the apartments before entering; that if the woman made a lot of noise he strangled her to "shut her big mouth"; that he was always careful not to leave any marks or prints.

DeSalvo, Setterlund said, had talked a lot about "getting a good lawyer" who could arrange for him to go to a hospital, where he could get a head operation and be set free. He quoted DeSalvo as saying he expected to make a lot of money out of being the Strangler—that magazines and movie companies were fighting for his story.

I couldn't do much with Setterlund on cross-examination. His appearance came as a complete surprise, and I suspected that much of his testimony was at least partly true. Ironically, I had once defended him on a charge of escaping from the House of Correction.

After Setterlund, Conn called a series of jail officers and former employers of DeSalvo, all of whom testified that DeSalvo was an apparently stable man who didn't cause trouble. Then Ames Robey was called.

Although Robey had not examined DeSalvo since the competency hearing, he had changed his diagnosis somewhat. For the most part he stuck to professional jargon as he discussed his various diagnoses. His latest opinion was that DeSalvo had a sociopathic personality disorder, antisocial type, with sexual deviation and schizoid features. At all relevant times, DeSalvo knew the difference from right and wrong, and did not suffer from irresistible impulses.

Okay, Dr. Robey, I thought as I got up to cross-examine, here's your chance to score one for the Model Penal Code Test. Did DeSalvo, I asked him, have substantial capacity to conform his conduct to the requirements of the law?

"Yes," said Ames Robey, "he did."

Robey was something, all right. I asked him about the conversation we'd had on Friday, and he admitted it in substance. But he said he'd thought about it over the weekend and decided that DeSalvo had "conned" him very badly. In view of that, he didn't think DeSalvo was insane under *any* test.

Robey was followed by Dr. Samuel Allen, who had been his assistant at Bridgewater. Allen said DeSalvo was suffering from schizophrenia and was legally insane. But, he said, DeSalvo knew right from wrong and was not a victim of irresistible impulse.

As I'd expected, Dr. Tartakoff also testified for the state. He described DeSalvo as a psychopath with schizoid features who, he said, nonetheless knew right from wrong.

That was it. I tried to introduce testimony from John Bottomly and Phil DiNatale, but Judge Moynihan refused to allow it on the grounds that we had gone far enough into murder cases that were not before the court.

The jury went out early in the afternoon. We waited for the verdict in the Esquire Bar. The majority opinion was that DeSalvo would be found not guilty by reason of insanity on all charges. I thought we would lose on everything but the sexual assaults. That, I thought, would be enough. My goal was to see the Strangler wind up in a hospital, where doctors could try to find out what made him kill.

The jury took four hours to find Albert Henry DeSalvo guilty on all counts.

10. EPILOGUE

Albert DeSalvo, sentenced to life imprisonment, was remanded to Bridgewater and eventually sent to Walpole. His prisonmates there include George Nassar, who was convicted at his retrial.

DeSalvo's sentencing was not his last public appearance. Shortly after midnight on Friday, February 24, 1967, he and two other prisoners left blankets and pillows folded in the shape of bodies on their cots and escaped from Bridgewater.

Albert had been very despondent in the wake of his conviction; it meant he couldn't get the medical help he wanted. He said he could "walk out" of Bridgewater any time he felt like it. "Don't try it," I told him. "There'd be the biggest manhunt you ever saw, and some trigger-happy cop or citizen just might kill you."

This time, my advice was ignored. DeSalvo left a note for Superintendent Gaughan on his bunk: he was breaking out to dramatize his own predicament and focus attention on conditions at Bridgewater. He had found a way to unlock his cell and those of the other two men, one a convicted burglar and the other a wife killer. They clambered down an elevator shaft under construction, and used planks to climb a twenty-foot wall to freedom.

They stole a car and abandoned it when it stalled. DeSalvo called his brother, Joe, who drove him to Chelsea, where another brother gave him some clothes. The two other men left. After drinking their way through the day, they turned themselves in Friday night.

Meanwhile, the manhunt I had warned DeSalvo about was in progress. The Boston Strangler was loose; the city was terrified. Television and radio stations, and the newspapers, had a field day. There were reports that DeSalvo had been seen in Ohio, that he was escaping to Canada, that he was on his way to Mexico. Border patrols, the FBI, even the Royal Canadian Mounted Police joined the search.

All the time, Albert DeSalvo was riding buses around his home town and listening to news of the search on a transistor radio. At one point, a policeman asked him if he was DeSalvo, and he said no, that his name was Johnson, and he lived in a nearby building. "Check with my wife, if you want," he said. "She's home." The cop was satisfied.

When DeSalvo escaped, I was in South Carolina defending an Air Force captain accused of molesting four small girls in the swimming pool at Charleston Air Force Base. My first notification of the escape came in the form of an early-morning phone call from a newspaperman. Later in the day, I learned that the *Boston Record-American* had offered a $5,000 reward to anyone who directed the newspaper to DeSalvo, dead or alive, before the police found him. I told Charles Burnim, an attorney working with me at the time, and Andy Tuney, who by now was running the investigation service, that I was afraid the offer was an invitation for open season on DeSalvo. I instructed them to post a reward that referred to the newspaper's reward and offered $10,000 to anyone who had both the power and the legal right to kill DeSalvo and could prove that he had refrained from doing so in an effort to bring him in alive.

DeSalvo spent the night in the cellar of a house he had broken into. At 2:40 P.M. Saturday, he walked into a clothing store in Lynn and asked for a telephone. "This is an emergency," he said. "I got to call

185

F. Lee." The people who owned the store subsequently claimed our reward, to which they had no right. The case is pending trial.

And Albert DeSalvo is in a state prison. It is a penitentiary, not a mental hospital. The psychiatric help he wanted is denied him. And society is deprived of a study that might help deter other mass killers who live among us, waiting for the trigger to go off inside them.

Did the system work? Not on your life.

V

Love, Hate
and
Carl Coppolino

PROLOGUE

Like all men, Carl Coppolino made mistakes. His most costly mistake was that suburban cliché, an affair with a neighbor. Her name was Marge Farber, and she was eighteen years older than Carl. When the affair ended, she turned her passion to a different kind of drama. She caused him to be brought to trial twice for murder. At Carl's first trial, I offered this perspective to the jury:

"This woman drips with venom on the inside, and I hope before we are through you will see it drip on the outside. She wants this man so badly that she would sit on his lap in the electric chair while somebody pulled the switch, just to make sure he dies. This is not a murder case at all. This is monumental and shameful proof that hell hath no fury like a woman scorned."

1. *BACKGROUND TO INDICTMENT*

The first newspaper story ran on July 9, 1966, in the *Sarasota* (Florida) *Herald-Tribune:* "2-State Probe Launched in Death of Sarasota Doctor."

The doctor was Carmela Coppolino, a thirty-two-year-old mother of two small daughters, who had died August 28, 1965, apparently of a heart attack. Now, more than ten months later, authorities were investigating the possibility that she had been murdered—killed with a mysterious drug called succinylcholine chloride. The drug's effect was similar to that of curare, the nerve-paralyzing poison with which South American Indians coat the tips of their arrows. Used by doctors to paralyze certain areas of the body during surgery, succinylcholine chloride possesses a property that makes it an ideal murder weapon: after entering the bloodstream, it breaks down into separate components normally present in the body, becoming virtually undetectable.

The story was tailored to the public fancy. A young wife, a deadly drug . . . a darkly sinister husband. The husband, Dr. Carl Coppolino, was a thirty-four-year-old anesthesiologist who suffered from a heart condition and had moved his family from Middletown, New Jersey, to Sarasota in 1965. As an anesthesiologist, he was familiar with succinylcholine chloride. Also, Carmela was heavily insured. And just forty-two days after her death, Coppolino had remarried, taking as his second wife a good-looking divorcée he'd met in a bridge studio a few months after moving to Florida.

This was only half the plot. The other state referred to in the head-line was New Jersey, where authorities were looking into the death of William E. Farber, a fifty-four-year-old insurance executive and retired Army colonel who had died in Middletown on July 30, 1963. Again, almost three years later, police were considering the possibility that he had been smothered. The suspect was Farber's former neighbor, Dr. Carl Coppolino.

In each case, Coppolino had been accused by the same person— Marjorie Cullen Farber, a slim, black-haired woman who could still wear a bikini at fifty-two. She was William Farber's widow and Carl Coppolino's ex-mistress, and she claimed that Carl, an expert hypnotist, had mes-merized her both into intimacy and into helping him kill her husband.

On July 21, 1966, Coppolino, a dark-haired, heavy-browed man with an imperious expression and sharply angled face, was indicted by a Monmouth County Grand Jury in New Jersey for the murder of William Farber. Four days later, a Sarasota County Grand Jury in Florida indicted him for the murder of Carmela Coppolino. The elements of death, mys-tery, sex, and suspense inspired predictably sensational newspaper coverage. And national magazines like *Newsweek, Life,* and *Time* unveiled much of what was supposed to be evidence—information that could only have been released by public officials whose clear legal and ethical duty was to keep their mouths shut.

For example, in December of 1965 an autopsy had been performed on Carmela's body by Dr. Milton Helpern, New York City's chief medical examiner. Helpern noticed an apparent needle puncture in the buttock, and took a section for microscopic examination. He also filled eleven cans with tissue and gave them to Dr. C. Joseph Umberger, head of his office's toxicology laboratory. Umberger was told to look first for general un-known poisons, but if his findings were negative he was to test for succinylcholine chloride. There was no known test for the drug, and by the following July, Umberger's findings were not conclusive and tests were continuing. Nevertheless, *Life* magazine reported that the Sarasota indictment had resulted from positive findings of succinylcholine chloride in Carmela's body.

Other news stories drew attention to Monmouth County Medical Examiner Malcolm Gilman, who was said to have injected several rabbits with succinylcholine chloride and buried them in his backyard. Eventually he dug them up and tested for traces of the drug. His findings were said to have triggered the decision to disinter Colonel Farber. What was not reported was that the tests were scientifically and legally meaningless— as it turned out, they were so meaningless that they would not even be offered as evidence in either the New Jersey or Florida trials.

In Arlington National Cemetery, a few paces from the Tomb of the Unknown Soldier, Farber's body was exhumed on July 14, 1966. An autopsy was performed by Helpern two days later. Helpern found that the cricoid cartilage—a hard, narrow ring that circles the lower portion of the larynx—was fractured in two places. Farber, he said, had died of manual strangulation. The fractured cartilage got good coverage. What was not disclosed was the strong likelihood that the fracture was post-mortem and had nothing to do with Farber's death.

If the situation hadn't been so serious it would have been ludicrous. No trial had been held, but many people were already convinced that Carl Coppolino had committed two murders. And yet the essential question was not who did it. The question was: had any murder been committed? On the evidence, neither case should have gotten as far as a grand jury indictment. Both went to trial.

Carl Coppolino grew up in Brooklyn, where his father was a barber who worked hard in other men's shops. Carl, intelligent and ambitious, worked summers to earn his tuition at Fordham University. He met his expenses with the five-dollar-a-week allowance his parents scraped together and his profits from a ten-cent-limit poker game played daily in the school cafeteria. In 1952, he started dating Carmela Musetto, a premed student at Trinity College in Washington, D.C., and the daughter of a successful physician.

After graduating in 1954, Carl enrolled at the Downstate Medical Center of the State University of New York in Brooklyn. Carmela enrolled at the Women's College of Medicine in Philadelphia, but transferred to the Downstate Medical Center in 1956. She had a good reason—she and Carl had gotten married that summer. By the time they graduated as doctors in 1958, they were the parents of an eleven-month-old daughter who was in the care of Carmela's mother.

By 1960, the Coppolinos had their daughter with them and owned a home in Nutley, New Jersey, where Carmela was employed as a consultant for a pharmaceutical firm. Carl was chief resident in anesthesiology at Methodist Hospital in New York. In 1962 he became a staff anesthesiologist at Riverview Hospital in Red Bank, New Jersey, and the Coppolinos moved to a split-level in a new development off the Garden State Parkway in Middletown. That October, Carmela, who was pregnant again, entertained neighborhood housewives at a tea in her home. The guests included a trim, friendly, forty-eight-year-old woman who lived in a house down the street. Her name was Marjorie Farber.

The following January, Carmela gave birth to a second daughter. Carl had suffered two heart attacks and learned that he had a coronary insufficiency, a condition that forced him to resign from Riverview and to apply, successfully, for the benefits of a disability policy he held.

Near the end of January, Marge Farber told her friend Carmela that she wanted to give up smoking but hadn't been able to break the habit. "Perhaps Carl could help you," said Carmela. Carl explained that his system would consist of hypnotic suggestion, and on February 4, 1963, he went to the Farber home and gave Marge her first treatment. He conducted a follow-up session the next day, and the treatment worked— Marge stopped smoking for two years.

But if one vice was cured, another developed. As Marge would tell it, the two were in her bed in a matter of days after the hypnotic session. As Carl would tell it, they didn't make it to bed until they went on a ten-day trip to Miami Beach in mid-March. In explaining the trip to Carmela, who had gone back to her job after a maternity leave, Carl said that the New Jersey winter was bad for his health, and that he needed a warm climate. But because of his heart condition, he was afraid to travel alone. Good neighbor Marge could go along as a sort of nurse.

Carmela was either the world's most unsuspecting or most understanding wife. Or perhaps she was just complacent. She not only approved the idea, she had Bill and Marge come to dinner so they could all discuss it. Farber argued with Marge about it that night, but eventually he gave in.

As things developed, that trip was the first of several for the lovers. They relaxed in Atlantic City together the weekend after Bill Farber's death in the summer of 1963. And in 1964, they traveled to Sarasota and to San Juan.

Carl and Marge later contradicted each other about the frequency of their coupling. "In reference to Carl's heart condition," Marge would tell Sarasota authorities, "I had often wondered how he could be as strong as he appeared to be, because we had intercourse at least once a day, and while we were on these trips it was at least three times a day. I don't know how he did it." Carl said she was exaggerating. But both agreed that the affair ended sometime around the end of 1964.

When Bill Farber had died on July 30, 1963, Carmela signed the death certificate, and listed a coronary thrombosis as the cause. Farber left Marge well provided for, and that fall she decided to sell the large house in Middletown and move somewhere else. Her decision triggered the trip to Sarasota, where she purchased a bayfront homesite on Longboat Key. Carl, who wasn't thinking about moving at the time, bought an adjoining lot as an investment.

But in October of 1964, he suffered his fourth heart attack. When he recovered, he took Carmela to Florida and showed her the homesite on Longboat Key. And in April of 1965, the Coppolinos moved to Sarasota.

The move south was not without setbacks. Carmela failed to pass a test for obtaining a license to practice in Florida, and Carl lost about $15,000 in two real estate ventures. He also found that keeping himself occupied was a problem. In July, he enrolled at a bridge studio on St. Armand's Key; at his third lesson he was matched with a fellow student who would become his usual partner, a thirty-eight-year-old divorcee named Mary Gibson. A poised and lively Alabama girl, Mary had two teenage daughters, a moderate income, and a new home in Sarasota. She also had plenty of suitors—she had, in fact, turned down several proposals of marriage, including one from her ex-husband.

It was not exactly the worst of times for Carl. A good home, a pleasant bridge partner, and the Florida sunshine. And then on Sunday, August 22, the widow Farber, who had sold her house in Middletown, arrived in Sarasota with her two daughters to build a new home on the lot adjoining Carl's. Carl was at the bridge studio when she drove up to the Coppolino home, where she and her children spent the night.

It wasn't until the following Friday that Marge was able to satisfy some of her curiosity about Carl's bridge partner. Near the studio she spotted Carl and Mary talking in Mary's car after an afternoon lesson. Carl introduced the two women, and Marge left after a brief conversation. When Carl got home he learned that Marge had telephoned Carmela to tell her about seeing him and Mary in a parked car. Carmela, who knew about the bridge lesson, was not upset.

That evening Carl played bridge again. Mary had brought one of her daughters with her to the studio, and after the lesson Carl treated them to root beers at a nearby restaurant. When he got home some time between 11:00 P.M. and midnight, Carmela was still awake. She told him she'd been sick earlier in the evening, that she'd had chest pains and nausea. Now she was feeling better, she said, and suggested that they have a nightcap. After finishing their drinks, the Coppolinos went to sleep— Carmela in the master bedroom, Carl in a guest room. Around 5:00 A.M., Carl woke up and walked restlessly through the house. He looked into the bedroom where Carmela was sleeping, and as he would explain later, "I knew at once something was wrong, she didn't look natural." He hurried into the room and reached for her wrist. Carmela was dead.

Dr. Juliette Karow, who was called to the house by Carl, listed a coronary occlusion as the cause of death. After talking to her, Sarasota County Medical Examiner Dr. Millard White ruled that there was no reason for him to perform an autopsy, and Carmela's body was embalmed that afternoon in a Sarasota funeral parlor. Marge Farber came to pay her respects.

The morning of Carmela's death, Carl asked Mary Gibson if she would look after his children. She picked them up that day and continued to care for them while Carl lived alone in his months-old house. After a few weeks, Carl proposed. Mary thought about it for a couple of days and then accepted. But she said that for the sake of both his children and hers, they should hold the ceremony as soon as possible. They were married October 7.

Before October had ended, Marge Farber visited Dr. Karow and said she believed Carl had murdered Carmela by injecting a drug into her body. She said she knew about the drug because, two years before, Carl had mesmerized her into trying to pump it into her husband, whom he had finished off by suffocation the following day. It was quite a story, and the next person Marge told it to was a priest. In November, she went a step further—she took her suspicions to county law enforcement authorities. On December 6, she made a formal statement.

Nine days later, Carmela's body was exhumed. Carl Coppolino was six months away from a murder charge.

2. *ENTER THE DEFENSE ATTORNEY*

On July 24, 1966, Bill Bryan, the hypnosis expert, called me on behalf of Carl Coppolino, who had lectured at one of his hypnosis seminars. He said Coppolino had been arrested the day before on a New Jersey murder warrant. "I haven't known Carl for long," he said, "but I know him well enough to be convinced he's no killer. I promised his wife you'd help him."

He gave me Mary's phone number in Sarasota. When I reached her she was calm, almost casual, as we discussed the case. She told me that her husband was suspected of killing Farber, and that he was also under investigation in the death of his first wife in Florida. "It seems they've been investigating Carl for six months," she said, "and nobody's bothered to ask him a question. You'd think that if they suspected him of murder, they'd at least have the decency to ask him if he did it."

Almost two weeks later, I landed my plane at Sarasota-Bradenton Airport. Mary Coppolino was waiting for me, and I liked her the minute she said hello.

"How do you do," she said. "I'm the rich fifty-two-year-old divorcee who married the murderer." She was making fun of a *Life* magazine article that apparently had confused her age with Marge Farber's. "For thirty-nine," Mary said, "I look pretty ordinary. But for fifty-two, I look pretty good. So I guess I'll be fifty-two if they want me to."

Andy Tuney and I talked to Mary during the day, and that evening we met Carl Coppolino in the chief deputy's office of the Sarasota County Jail. Carl looked haggard but managed a smile when we shook hands. I had pretty much anticipated his first question. "When do I get the hell out of here?"

"You misunderstand," I answered. "I'm just a guy who goes through the motions so that when they give you the juice, an appellate court can pontificate on how you've had due process of law. There is, of course, no way to win these cases. I've read all about them in the papers."

"Great," he said. "How much does it cost to get burnt with Lee Bailey's blessing?"

"Ah, yes," I said. "The fee. The fee will be very substantial, I'm afraid. There's some work involved, and the executions will look bad on my record. But I'll give you your money's worth."

Carl's reaction was a belly laugh, and I felt that we were establishing rapport. As we talked, I asked questions at random, without trying to get the whole story. That's Andy's job; mine at a first meeting is to size up the accused and decide how difficult he'll be to defend. Carl sized up well.

"This New Jersey thing is straight bullshit," he said. "I treated Bill Farber before he died, and he had a coronary. He refused to go to a hospital, and Marge wouldn't send him. I got disgusted and pulled out of the case, and I made her sign a written release. I don't see how the hell they can get around that. Marge may have let him die, I don't know. I know she hated him—"

"Wait a minute," I said. "What did you say about a release?"

"You know. A release. She agreed that her husband had probably suffered a heart attack, and that he wouldn't go to the hospital. She released me from all responsibility in the case."

"If the Farbers were friends and neighbors," I said, "why did you think it necessary to get a release?"

"Because I thought Bill was in tough shape, and that Marge was just the type to hit me with a malpractice suit if he died. Besides, I wanted it to be clear that I only gave emergency treatment. Because of my disability insurance, I wasn't supposed to be practicing."

"And you think that's going to give you a complete defense?"

"Sure," said Carl. "It shows that Bill Farber had a heart attack, and that I recommended—"

"It could also show," I pointed out, "that you and Marge conspired to knock off the old man and cover you neatly in the process. Also, as a doctor you would have to explain why no specialist was called. You're no cardiologist."

"Now, wait a minute," Carl said. "I know a helluva lot about hearts because of my own condition, and the point is that I did try to get him to a hospital."

"Carl," I said, "there's something you'd better understand right now. You'll never be convicted or acquitted on the truth. You'll only be concerned with what the *evidence* is, understand? The evidence. False testimony is evidence just as surely as honest testimony, and if a jury fails to guess which is which, you can be convicted on lies. If someone lied to accuse you of murder, she can just as easily lie about that release. It could even be used to hurt you."

I could tell by Carl's face that he got the point—and that the idea of a jury's believing false testimony had never crossed his mind before.

"We tell absolutely no one about the release," I said. "There's a bare possibility that Marge has forgotten about it. If she has, we may be able to cut her to pieces with it. But don't count on anything."

The next day, Andy returned to the jail to talk to Carl while I nosed around town, picking up scuttlebutt. The people I talked to included Gene Miller, one of the country's top crime reporters, who was with the *Miami Herald*. He told me that according to his sources the New Jersey case was the rough one.

"The Farber woman will claim that she held her husband's arm while Coppolino injected this succinylcholine chloride stuff," he said. "When that didn't kill him, they suffocated him with a pillow."

"Christ, that's wonderful," I said. "And why did they kill him?"

"I couldn't find that out for sure. One possibility is that they were shacking up."

"Carl admits that," I said, "but that's no motive for murder."

"It could all tie in," he said. "First they kill Farber, then they wait for a while and kill Coppolino's wife. Then they can get married and shack up happily ever after."

"Except that Carl married someone else," I said. "There's one extra woman—Mary Coppolino. If Carl and Marge set something like that up, he wouldn't have dared throw her over. Either she'd be Mrs. Coppolino now, or she'd be dead herself."

Later that day, two things happened to strengthen my growing belief that Carl Coppolino was innocent. The first was Mary's response when I hit her with what Marge Farber was supposed to be claiming. "It doesn't sound good to me," I said. "What do you think?"

She looked right at me. "I'll tell you what I think," she said. "I think the man I've lived with for the better part of a year is no killer. We've known for months that he was being investigated, and he's never given me the slightest sign that he was hiding anything. But I have no way of *knowing* that he's not guilty. If you ever find out he is, I want to be the first to know. I mean, do you realize that I've adopted his little girls? My God, what in the world could I tell them?"

"Look, Mary," I said, "I can only act as Carl's lawyer. If I learn that he's guilty, I can't tell you. And if he is guilty, and I win him an acquittal, I still can't tell you, and you are going to be in a hell of a fix. But that will be your problem. If you should offer to pay all or part of my fee, I couldn't accept. As a lawyer, I can only serve one master."

"I see," Mary said, taking stock. "I suppose I should thank you for laying the cards face up. At least I know what to expect—or what not to expect. For now, I think he's innocent, and I'm sticking with him. If I think otherwise, I'll let you both know."

"Before any verdicts are in, you'll know far better than any court whether Carl killed anyone," I told her. "You have your intelligence, your experience, your intuition, and something more—unlimited access to Carl. Sooner or later, you'll know."

The second indication of innocence came when I visited Carl. "Marjorie Farber may testify that she held the colonel's arm while you injected him with succinylcholine chloride," I said. "When that didn't work, you smothered him with a pillow." I paused. "How do you like those apples?"

If the jurors who eventually tried Carl for the death of William Farber had been there, they might not have bothered with the evidence offered at the trial. Just looking at Carl's face, I was satisfied that Marge Farber's story was absolutely false. "How in the world can they let her testify to that?" he asked finally. "It never happened, it just never happened. Can't you stop her?"

"Not if the state of New Jersey wants to use her as a witness," I said. "But if she's lying, there'll be weaknesses in her story, and it'll be up to Andy to find them and me to use them."

"You know," he said, "I might as well commit suicide. I mean it. Mary's going to go through hell, my family's going to go through hell, my defense will probably take every dime I own. And I'm not sure my heart can take the strain of two trials. I should just let you go back to Boston, and jump out a window or something. I'm serious."

"Stop being a crybaby," I said. "You didn't kill anyone. You worry about your heart, and let me worry about the evidence. Marjorie Farber can be had in more ways than you've had her. But if you're serious about giving up, make up your mind now. After all, I'm a reasonably successful lawyer. I don't propose to have it known that any client of mine had so much confidence in me that he knocked himself off rather than go to trial."

Carl turned sheepish. "Okay, okay," he said. "I'll stick around. But you'd better be some lawyer, or I'm gone. Jesus, how did I get into this mess?"

I grinned. "Unlike some other things you've gotten into," I said, "this was quite by accident."

3. *GETTING READY*

Carl Coppolino's first trial would not open until December. Meanwhile there was a preliminary hearing in Sarasota, and months of pretrial investigation. Before I was through representing Carl, I would put in about a thousand hours of study on the medical facts of the case, and Andy Tuney and Teri Plaut—who had joined the investigative bureau in September, 1963, while attending law school at night—would drive up and down New Jersey and Florida collecting a couple of casebooks on the Coppolinos and the Farbers.

As we put the evidence together, I was also kept busy with legal moves and countermoves. At the start I ran into trouble with the Florida prosecutor, Frank Schaub, whom I called on before leaving Sarasota after my first visit. At issue was Carl's constitutional right to a speedy trial. Serious questions of federal law were involved—could the governor of Florida deprive Carl of his right to face the New Jersey indictment by blocking extradition? My position was that Carl should have his choice of which trial to undergo first by insisting on a speedy trial in one jurisdiction and waiving it in another. I mentioned this to Schaub, and then asked him how he felt about bail.

"I might not oppose bail," he said, "if I thought Coppolino would stay here until trial—not go running up to New Jersey the minute he makes bond."

"Let's get something straight right away," I said. "If I want Carl in New Jersey, I'll try to move him by court order. If I tell you that in exchange for unopposed bail he's going to stay here, he'll stay here."

"I'll count on that," he said. "We'll think it over, and when the judge gets back we'll set a date for a bail hearing. If we can agree on bail, we won't need a hearing."

I smiled at him. "If we don't have a hearing, I just might have to go to trial without knowing anything about your case. I'll think about that as well." We shook hands and I left.

The next day, Andy Tuney and I flew back to Boston. At my office there was a message waiting from Mary Coppolino, who wanted me to phone her right away. No sooner had I left Sarasota than Frank Schaub had subpoenaed her to appear in his office for questioning—a move he had never mentioned during our conversation.

I immediately got in touch with James M. Russ, an Orlando, Florida, attorney who had worked with me in the past. Russ had spent four years as a prosecutor, and he'd been belted with almost every technicality devisable by defense lawyers. He made Frank Schaub's life tougher. Every paper Schaub filed was found defective; it was six months before he was able to serve a valid subpoena on Mary Coppolino.

Russ filed the necessary papers, and a hearing was scheduled for September 12 before Circuit Judge Lynn Silvertooth in Sarasota. Schaub eventually filed notice saying he would not oppose bail, but by now we had requested a preliminary hearing. At such a hearing, under Florida law, the prosecutor must demonstrate that he has sufficient cause to hold the accused on the indictment. I doubted that Judge Silvertooth would dismiss the case, but I wanted to force Frank Schaub to show what had to be a lousy hand.

On September 1, at Carl's arraignment, I demanded a bill of particulars from the state as to how it would attempt to prove that Carl had committed a murder. The response was a statement saying Carmela had died from succinylcholine chloride, through the criminal agency of Carl Coppolino. I was well into my studies on the drug, and I felt Schaub couldn't make his thesis stick. The hearing would not only show me how he planned to try, it would give me a chance to evaluate Milton Helpern, who would be a key prosecution witness at both of Carl's trials.

I didn't think that even the famous crime doctor could positively link Carmela's death to a drug that broke down in the bloodstream. He couldn't —but that didn't stop him from trying. In his direct testimony at the hearing, Helpern said that his office began its postmortem investigation into

Carmela's death on December 17, 1965, when he performed the autopsy. But he said the finding as to cause of death was "finally determined in June of 1966." He cited the various studies involved in the postmortem, including a toxicological examination conducted by "trained chemists." He said he had concluded that the cause of death was "an injection of succinylcholine."

In response to Schaub's questions, Helpern said that the only abnormality turned up by the autopsy was a puncture wound in the left buttock. He said the puncture was consistent with the sort of wound made by a hypodermic needle, and that it did not appear to be self-inflicted.

"Are you a chemist?" I asked Helpern in cross-examination.

"No."

"Then I take it that the conclusion that you gave this court is in fact a conclusion of your chemist, Dr. Umberger?"

"May I explain?" he said. "The chemist reported what he found, and his report, being positive as it was, is not necessarily conclusive of the cause of death. The responsibility for concluding about the cause of death is that of the pathologist who does the postmortem examination. I might explain that toxicological examinations are only part of a postmortem examination."

"Then apart from the report that you got from your chemist, what did you find as evidence of the remnants of succinylcholine?"

"I found a normal body, a puncture wound, and a track in the buttock. Nothing else."

"Then from your own findings you can't say what went in the puncture wound?"

"That is correct, as far as naked-eye examination of the tissues is concerned," Helpern conceded. "As for microscopic examination of the tissues, I could not conclude what had been injected or introduced into this body. That was determined by the chemist, and on the basis of his determination I made my conclusion."

I established that the chemist was C. Joseph Umberger, and asked if I could see his report. I noticed that each of the two reports Helpern gave me stated that it was "possible" that the choline and succinic acid found in Carmela's tissue were derived from succinylcholine. I called this to Dr. Helpern's attention.

"Well, don't take one phrase that he said," said Helpern. "Take the whole report."

"I have taken the whole report. The strongest word I see is 'possible.'"

He read the amended report. "That might sound like a mild statement to you," he said, "but to me it is a very definite statement because the report does not indicate any other possible source and very clearly excludes any other possible source of these compounds."

"Wait a minute," I said. "You say it excludes other possible sources of compounds which you agree are always found in the body?"

"But by this method of analysis they never show up," he said, adding: "In other words, under normal conditions these substances are not detected in the chemical analysis."

It was a sizable opening. "Why not?" I asked.

"I am sorry, I cannot tell you," admitted the normally informative Dr. Helpern.

In response to subsequent questions, Helpern also could not tell me what constituted a lethal dose of succinylcholine, and, more important, he could not tell me how much succinic acid had been found in Carmela's organs.

The hearing lasted two days. When it ended, Carl collapsed at the counsel table while attorneys for both sides were in the judge's chambers He spent the night in a hospital, but was back in court the next evening when bail was set at $15,000. The following month, Florida Governor Hayden Burns ordered his extradition.

It was New Jersey's turn.

4. FIRST, FREEHOLD

A few days before the preliminary hearing, I had called Carl Coppolino long distance from my office. After we finished our business, I told him another client was with me who wanted to say hello. Then I handed the phone to Sam Sheppard. "I know how it feels, buddy," he said.

Less than three weeks after Sam's acquittal, I came to Freehold, New Jersey, to defend Carl Coppolino on a first-degree murder charge in the death of William Farber. The trial began December 5, 1966, in the Monmouth County Courthouse before Superior Court Judge Elvin R. Simmill, a former Speaker of the New Jersey State Assembly. The prosecutor was Vincent P. Keuper: sixty-four years old; a tall, gaunt, unemotional man who preferred to work alone in the courtroom. My aides were Joseph Mattice, a veteran Monmouth County attorney, and Joe Afflito, a young Boston Law School graduate who had just started practicing in Wayne, New Jersey. During jury selection, my screening team also included Bill

Bryan, who, in addition to specializing in hypnoanalysis, is an expert in interpreting unarticulated response, or what it has become voguish to call body language. Carl also was involved—he suggested that I pick one woman simply because of the way she was looking at me, and I accepted her without asking a single question.

The jury selection was not without its light moments. One man said his only knowledge of the case came from reading the *New York Daily News*. When I asked his opinion of that publication's reliability, he said, "I think it is not generally accurate." I said that a man with that much discernment should make a good juror, and Keuper made no objection.

Then there was George Phillips, a square-faced mining engineer who said that evidence of extramarital activity would not prejudice him against Dr. Coppolino. "We're all human beings, and I step off the line myself," he said.

I was as surprised as I was pleased. When I leaned forward and looked at him, he followed up. "I bet you step out of line yourself," he said. "You're the type."

Laughter filled the courtroom. "No further questions," I said. "I'll take the Fifth." I also took the juror. Later, I told someone in regard to Phillips: "There's my foreman." Sure enough, when the jury held its lottery, Phillips's name was drawn as foreman.

We made our opening statements on Friday morning. Keuper asked for a verdict of murder-first, with no recommendation for mercy. He said Carl had broken not only the commandment "Thou shalt not covet thy neighbor's wife," but also "Thou shalt not covet thy neighbor's life. . . ." My statement lasted just seven minutes. "William Farber was not murdered," I said, "and therefore Carl Coppolino could not have done it. The hoax was created by a fifty-two-year-old woman who was cast aside and who initiated a plot to destroy Coppolino. . . ."

When I finished, I gestured toward Marge. I walked back to the defense table, and Vincent Keuper called his first witness.

"I call Mrs. Marjorie Farber," he said.

5. THE WOMAN SCORNED

Marjorie Cullen Farber was dressed for church or a charity lunch—royal blue knitted suit, white blouse, navy blue leather pumps and purse, even short white gloves.

Keuper led her through her first meetings with the Coppolinos in the fall of 1962, the hypnotic session at her home, and the follow-up session on the next day, a Tuesday. On Wednesday, she said, "I did my shopping, and I had this overwhelming feeling that I just had to get back to Wallace Road and I couldn't understand what it was, and the whole thing was based on the fact that I wanted to get back to see this Carl. And when I went past his house, he was sitting out there in the driveway in a folding chair, and I got out of the car, and my whole feeling was of this tremendous overwhelming—I couldn't understand it, but I just had to be with this man. . . . He got me a chair and I sat down next to him, and I had to touch him.

The touching was confined to hand-holding, but the next day in her home, said Marge, "I told him that I had a very strong feeling that I wanted to be close to him, and he just sat there and kept saying, 'Yes, yes' to me. And the next thing I knew we were in each other's arms embracing, kissing each other."

Because of her concern for Carl's heart condition, she said, they didn't go to bed. They saved that mutual discovery for the following day, Friday, February 8, and according to Marge, "I saw him constantly from that time on." Their intimacies had taken place in her home, while her daughters were at school and her husband was at work.

Now Keuper got to Marge and Carl's Miami Beach jaunt. During the trip, Marge said, Carl worked out "a love plan. He had written down things that I was supposed to do when I got home. . . . That my husband and I should not sleep in the same bedroom. That we should live as brother and sister and that I should try to either get an annulment or a divorce." About a month after she got home, Marge said, she was able to implement the separate bedroom plan.

That June, Carl told her about a drug "that was not traceable, that caused instantaneous death," and suggested she use it to get rid of her dog, who had been fighting with other dogs in the neighborhood. But when he obtained the drug from a friend, Dr. Edmund Webb, he started talking about Bill Farber.

"I didn't know what he was talking about at first," Marge testified, "and then he said, 'That man has got to go,' and I was very upset and shocked by this suggestion of Carl's. I told him he must have been crazy or out of his mind to even think of such a thing. . . . Carl set a date. He said, 'The first of July, he's got to go.' "

She said that Carl had given her the drug—whose name she couldn't pronounce—in a vial with a screw top. It was in an envelope that also contained a disposable syringe or hypodermic needle. On Saturday, July 27, she mixed the drug in water according to his instructions. But after filling the syringe, she dumped its contents. "I didn't want—I just—I—this was very objectionable. I just couldn't do this thing. . . ."

Marge testified that she saw Carl the next day, but could not remember whether they discussed her faltering with the drug the night before. The following night, Monday, July 29, she tried again. She said she mixed the solution and filled the syringe. After pacing back and forth, she went into her husband's bedroom.

"He was lying on his side," she said. "His legs were exposed and I bent over him with this syringe in my hand and I—I started to push the plunger down and I couldn't—I just couldn't. . . . And then my husband jumped up and he said he had a charley horse and I helped him into the bathroom and he sat on the toilet and said he felt—well, he was ill. He had a form of diarrhea. He was gasping. He fell off the toilet and he fell on the floor. I tried to help him and I couldn't lift him. . . . So I called up Carl to 'come up, please help Bill.' "

When Carl arrived with his medical bag, Bill was back in bed. Carl injected a sedative he said would make Bill sleep. Then, testified Marge, Carl asked her to get a plastic bag. "Well, I got the plastic bag. It happened to be one of the dry cleaner type things and I gave it to him and he put it over Bill's head and started to suffocate Bill and Bill was nauseated and I told him to stop it, leave him alone, and he did. I wanted to change the pillow case because it was soiled and he said all right, I could do that but not to wash the pillow case. Then we left Bill. He was resting and I guess we went into the . . . the TV room." When Carl left, she said, it was five or six in the morning.

At that point, Judge Simmill called a morning recess. "I think we all need a respite," he said.

When we returned, Keuper picked up Marge's story on Tuesday, July 30. She said Carl came to her home around noon or 1:00 P.M. and announced that he was going to give the colonel another sedative. While it was taking effect, she said, Farber and Carl got into a discussion. "And

Bill was quite groggy and he said something to the effect that he wanted Carl to leave him alone, get out of here, and Carl picked up the pillow case that he told me not to wash during the night and showed it to Bill, and he said, 'You ungrateful bastard, I saved your life last night,' and then he threw the pillow case at me and I went out of the room." She heard angry voices, she said, and then Carl joined her in the TV room.

"He said, 'That bastard's got to go. . . . He has threatened me and my family. Nobody is going to talk about me like that, and he has got to go.' "

"Did you say anything in response?" Keuper asked.

"I begged him, leave us alone, leave Bill alone. And while I was telling him this, he was filling the syringe with more of whatever he was taking out of a bottle. And he went into my husband's room and I just stood there in the TV room, like I was frozen to the spot." She said that when she entered the bedroom, Carl had finished the injection. "He said, 'He is a hard one to kill. He is taking a long time to die,' and then he pulled this pillow out from underneath my husband's head, and he put it over him—just put it over him, and he leaned full weight right down on him like this, and I just stood there and looked at him."

Marge started sobbing, and an attendant gave her smelling salts. When she continued, she dramatized the smothering by going to a small table below the judge's bench and making believe she was holding a pillow. She put the heel of her right hand against the table top, put her left hand on her right hand, stiffened her arms and leaned down. ". . . and he just leaned down like this. . . ."

She quoted Carl as saying he wanted to turn Bill over so he'd look like he died in his sleep. "Before he turned him over," she added, "he opened his eye and said, 'He is dead.' "

Next, she said, she wrote a note for her children at Carl's bidding that said, "Daddy is sleeping. Don't disturb him." She pinned it on the door, and she and Carl walked down the hill to the Coppolino home, where they sat in the back yard. She said she asked Carl what they should do, and "He said that there was nothing to worry about, everything was all right; and he told me at that time when Carm got home from work, that I should call her and have her come up and take a look at Bill . . . but not to call until after they had dinner, which would be around 6:30."

Sometime between 6:30 and 6:45, she said, she called Carmela, who came to the house and examined the body. Funeral arrangements were made, and William Farber was buried at Arlington National Cemetery. After establishing that Carl did not attend the services, but that Carmela did, Keuper walked back to the prosecution table and turned to me. "You may cross-examine," he said.

I stood behind Carl and put my hands on his shoulders. "Mrs.

Farber," I began, "will you look at the defendant, please? Is it fair to say that you hate the defendant?"

"No."

"Do you like him?"

"I don't have any feelings one way or the other about him."

We were off. Quickly, I established that Marge was appearing voluntarily and that she had paid her own way to Freehold. I asked if she was in love with Carl at the time of her husband's death, and she said she thought she was. I made her state her age and Carl's age, and asked if she had been in love with her husband. She said she had. "Did you do anything to interfere with his demise?" I asked. She said she couldn't.

"You couldn't, why?"

"Because of the hypnosis. I had no free will."

"Are you representing to this jury," I asked, "that while your husband was murdered you were unable to interfere because you were under hypnosis?"

"Yes, sir."

"Tell us at what time on July 30th Carl put you under hypnosis."

"It wasn't necessary to be putting me in a so-called trance because his influence was such that it wasn't necessary."

"Were you under hypnosis at all times with Carl Coppolino?"

"As far as I'm concerned I was."

"You don't say that Carl ever placed you in a trance, told you to relax and went through the usual preliminary steps and then said, 'Marjorie, I want you to kill Bill?' He didn't do that, did he?"

"If he did," she said, "I don't remember it."

A minute later, I asked: "When did you first feel a compulsion to kill your husband?"

"After the series of suggestions that Carl was giving me about 'That man has to go.' "

"Is that all you say Carl ever said about killing your husband?"

"Yes."

I kept pushing for a specific date on which she realized that she intended to kill the colonel. She said she was in "a constant, what they call a waking trance." Finally, she said, "well, it would have to be the morning of July 30th." But she couldn't remember when Carl had last put her in a trance and given her hypnotic suggestions. Nor could she explain why the trance had failed on July 27 and worked on July 30, when she claimed to have gone at Farber with the needle. She said she could not remember the name of the drug, but recognized "succinylcholine chloride" when I named it for her.

I asked if she had cared about whether Farber died a painful death, and she had trouble answering. "All right," I said. "Well, despite this compulsive trance in which you found yourself, did you have any thoughts about what a nasty thing it was to kill Bill Farber? . . . Do you have difficulty answering that question?"

"Yes, because . . ."

"Is it because, Mrs. Farber, you never thought about killing your husband?"

"That's true. I didn't want my husband dead."

"You never thought about it at all?"

"No."

"Until Carl Coppolino brushed you aside and then for the first time you thought about the death of your husband as a killing? Isn't that true?"

Marge lost her temper. "No," she yelled. "It is not true!"

I came back to the "waking trance," and Marge said that Carl had lost control of her, "when he and his wife and family moved to Florida."

I asked her what had happened to the poison left in the vial. "It disappeared," she said, "I don't know where it went."

"Carl didn't tell you what to do with it, did he?"

"No."

"Just walked out of there," I said, "and left the poison, whatever it was, sitting in the house? Is that right?"

"I don't recall what happened to it."

I kept pressing, and brought her back to her original position—that the drug had disappeared. Then I reviewed her "compulsion" with regard to the hypodermic needle.

"You had some affection for your husband," I said. "You didn't want him to die, you said."

"That's right."

"But at some point you were overcome, and you took this needle and injected it into his leg for the purpose of killing him, an attempt to murder?"

"That's right."

"And how long before you did this act did you have a change of heart so that you could do it?"

"As I told you earlier," said Marge, "it was during the evening of Monday, on the 29th, that I knew that this thing that I had to do had to be done."

"And the thing you had to do was kill your husband?"

"I was supposed to inject the drug into my husband. I don't know if I had the thought of kill in my mind."

We went around the mulberry bush on this for a while. "Did the needle get under his skin by compulsion and against your will?" I asked finally.

"Yes, sir," she said.

"Did you push the plunger under compulsion?"

"I started to push the plunger."

"Did you get some of the fluid into him?"

"Apparently."

"But it didn't kill him?"

"That's right, it didn't."

"When Carl came over did you say, 'Look, Carl. What about this poison? I gave him a little bit and it didn't kill him?' Did you have a conversation about why it wouldn't work?"

"No," said Marge, and she made a mistake. She smiled.

"Why did you smile?" I asked immediately. "Is there something funny about this case?"

"I think it is very serious. I am sorry I smiled."

"You won't smile again, I hope." I went on with the questioning. When I came to the plastic bag incident, she repeated that she had asked Carl to stop. I asked how she could do this if she were under Carl's control. "I would like to think that the real me was coming through," she said.

"That the real you was coming through! Was the 'real you' the homicidal you, or the nonhomicidal you, Mrs. Farber?"

Keuper objected, but was overruled. "I am not a homicide," said Marge.

"You never participated in any killing, did you?"

"Never."

I moved closer to the stand and leaned at her. "Never! This whole story is a cock and bull story, isn't it?" This time, the judge sustained Keuper's objection. I finally asked if there was any confusion in her mind as to whether she was a participant in the murder.

"It isn't a real situation as far as I am concerned," she said.

Soon, we got to motive. She said she never asked Carl why Farber "has got to go." I kept at her, and she said Carl might have been jealous.

"Of Bill?"

"Yes."

"Of course," I said. "Carl could have you pretty much any time he wanted, couldn't he?"

"Yes."

Now I went to the day Farber died. Marge said her daughter Victoria, then fifteen, had discovered the body but, "she wasn't aware of what the situation was." She told Marge that "Daddy looks funny," and Marge diverted her attention. This was at 5:00 P.M. Then Marge waited until 6:30, when she was supposed to call Carmela.

"How long did you have to sit round with this cadaver before you made the phone call?"

"I went upstairs with my daughter, Victoria, and cooked her dinner."

"With a dead body lying in the bedroom, you cooked dinner?"

Marge didn't help herself. "I cooked her a hamburger," she said.

Later, she said that it was only after Carl's spell had worn off that she realized she'd been involved in a killing.

"Prior to that time had you any real awareness of your participation in this murder?"

"I knew what had happened," she said, "but I could not relate to it as it relates to me sitting right here."

"Well, is it fair to say that you viewed the whole affair like a TV program?"

"Yes," she said, "it was like something that I had observed. I was like another person observing this whole scene."

I asked if it was hard for her to accept the fact that it was real. She said no, "but I cannot . . . all I can say, I was in a trancelike state when I was with this man, and the relationship was broken off—the hypnosis, and this terrible conflict within me that was me and this other person that was dominated by Carl."

"That other person within yourself that Carl used to dominate, what happened to it? Is it still around?"

"It is gone," she said, and testified a few minutes later that she had been acting of her own free will since October, 1964.

She conceded that she didn't want to fall back under Carl's spell, and I asked her why, then, had she moved to Florida in 1965. Well, she said she had bought property there and wanted to live on it. When I asked her why she hadn't been afraid that Carl would put her back under a trance, she said, "I didn't think about it."

Marge also testified that she no longer loved Carl when she came to Sarasota, but looked upon him as a friend. She only became angry with him, she said, when he failed to view Carmela's body in the funeral parlor.

"You were angry about that, so you went to see her?"

"I went to see her because I loved the girl," Marge answered.

"I see," I said. "Had you loved her back when you were running around with her husband?"

She returned to her crutch. "That again has to do with this relationship that was forced on me by Carl and the hypnosis. I had a normal, friendly relationship with Carmela." When I pressed harder, she said she loved Carmela "like a sister."

A short while later, I took a chance with a "why" question. "Now, Mrs. Farber," I said, "will you explain to the jury why you have come, not knowing what the consequences are that may await you, to testify against Carl Coppolino, why you were willing to take this risk to testify against this man on trial for his life, voluntarily and without promise of leniency, tell them please, tell the jury."

"Because," she said, "based on my suspicions of Carmela's death, the knowledge of my own husband's death, I felt that this man might kill his present wife, and I wanted to stop him."

"So, you are here today to protect the present Mary Coppolino?" I asked. "Is that right?"

"Maybe myself," she said. "I don't know."

"Carl never made any move against you even after he found out you were making these accusations, did he? Did he?"

"No."

After a recess, I established that Marge, after Farber's death, had made Carl the godfather of her children.

"At the time you asked Carl to become the godfather of your children, and he accepted and did become the godfather, did you still remember the killing of your husband by Carl Coppolino?" I asked.

"I have never forgotten how my husband died," she said.

"And notwithstanding the fact that you say he killed your husband, you made him the godfather of your children?"

"I was still under his influence."

"Was this because of the trance, Mrs. Farber?"

"Yes, sir."

"Well, since you escaped this trance later that year, did you take any steps to change your status with respect to the church, after the influence was gone?"

"I have continued to be a Roman Catholic," she said. She added that she returned to the church of her own free will (she'd left it when she married Farber), but that making Carl godfather resulted from his hypnotic powers. Minutes later, she was even more confused.

"I am asking you," I said, "whether or not that decision to ask Carl was induced by his trancelike mystic hypnotic power?"

"I don't believe so."

"Didn't you tell us a little while ago that the only reason you made the man you say killed your husband the godfather of your children was because you were compelled to do so because of the trance? Didn't you just tell the jury that?"

"If I said it, I certainly didn't mean it the way that you have interpreted it."

"You say now that the decision was made of your own free will?"

"At this point I don't know. All I know is that they [Carl and Carmela] were godparents of my children."

"And you are unable to tell us now whether you deliberately made them godparents of your own free will or whether Carl caused it by making you request it through his mystic power. Is that right? Is that the way you want to leave it?"

"That's right."

"You don't really know what the reason was?"

"They were the only Catholics I knew," said Marge.

Now I had to close some loopholes.

"When he left the house a little after noon on the 30th day of July, 1963, didn't Carl say to you and your husband, 'I'm backing out of this if you won't go to a hospital and you reject my advice'?"

"No, he didn't say anything like that at all."

"Do you say," I asked, "that Carl did not in the afternoon of the 30th at any time tell you, 'Don't call me. I won't have anything more to do with this case because he should be in a hospital and you won't go there'?"

"Carl did not say anything like that."

"Was anything like that ever mentioned by either of you?"

"Not at all. No. Not by Carl."

I gave her a last chance, and she repeated her denial.

"You swear that?"

"Yes," she said, and I had her. The gamble had paid off; Marge had forgotten about the release. I walked over to the defense table and picked up a sheet of lined yellow paper that Teri had gotten out of the casebook. I showed it to Marge. "Is that your signature, Mrs. Farber?"

"Yes," she said, and then looked around as if bewildered. "But I have never seen that piece of paper before."

"How did your signature get on it?"

"I haven't any idea."

"Do you say it's a forgery?"

"I don't know how it got on there. I don't even remember signing any paper."

"Did you sign—"

"It's Carl's handwriting on it."

"Did you sign a paper on the 30th day of July 1963 with the following: 'I hereby release Carl A. Coppolino, M.D., from all responsibility for the case of my husband, William Farber. Dr. Coppolino wishes to be released because Mr. Farber refuses to be hospitalized even though he may have had a coronary. Dr. Coppolino only gave emergency care. Signed, Marjorie C. Farber.' Do you remember that now?"

"No, sir," she said. "I do not remember signing that—that is my signature, yes, but I do not recall."

"Look at it," I said. "Study it, and tell the jury how it got on that piece of paper under those words. I would like you to tell me how it got there."

"I don't know . . . ," she said. "I have no recall of ever signing this paper, and I am telling the truth."

"You are telling the truth?"

"I am telling the truth, Mr. Bailey. I have never seen this piece of paper before in my life."

It was almost four o'clock, and the judge recessed court until Monday. That evening in the American Hotel, across the street from the jail where Carl Coppolino was staying, a reporter asked Marge Farber if it had been rough on the stand.

"As rough as it can get."

6. *DR. HELPERN, I RESUME*

On Monday, Marge spent another hour on the stand. One of the questions I asked her was whether Carl had suggested any means of murdering Farber other than a drug injection.

"No," she answered, "but he did say, he suggested that I first wrap a towel around a baseball bat and knock my husband unconscious before I used the drug."

"Did you have a baseball bat?"

'Oh yes. Several of them."

"Did you follow that instruction?"

"No, I did not."

"I take it then, you were not under his control to the extent of using the baseball bat. Is that right?"

"I couldn't do it."

Later, I gave her a pillow and had her demonstrate the alleged smothering on a table. I also diagrammed her version on a chalkboard to show how difficult the act would have been. I ended the cross-examination by asking about a phone conversation she'd had with a reporter after Carl was indicted. In the course of that conversation, hadn't she said, "Wouldn't it be funny if somebody dreamed this whole thing up?"

"Yes," she said, "Because I was—"

"That is all," I said, turning to Keuper. "Your witness."

On redirect, Keuper asked Marge about circumstances surrounding Carmela's death and called six more witnesses. Only the sixth was a major factor in the prosecution's case. He took the stand after lunch; a white-haired man with a professorial manner who had been the subject of an article in the *New York Times Sunday Magazine* the week before. In the article, a law enforcement official had been quoted as saying that this man could "smell a homicide." It was my second encounter with Dr. Milton Helpern.

The New York medical examiner described his autopsy findings like a lecturer, noting, for example, that the openings of the coronary arteries "are called ostia, or ostium in the singular." He said that he found minimal arteriosclerosis in some places, but nothing approaching a critical nature. And he said there was no evidence that Farber had suffered a coronary thrombosis. When he came to the cricoid fracture, he oozed authority, explaining that he had handled "thousands and thousands of these larynxes. . . ."

Helpern dramatized his testimony with visual aids. Displaying a photograph, he left no doubt as to who was in charge of his office. "That," he said, "is a photograph that was taken of the larynx by me with one of my associates working the camera." When it developed that the photograph only showed one side of the fracture, he had an assistant bring him a glass jar which contained Farber's yellow-white larynx. The doctor took the larynx out of the jar, dried it with a towel, and showed it to the jury.

When Helpern finished his lecture, Keuper asked for his opinion as to the cause of death. I immediately objected.

"In the first place," I said, "we have nothing so far but an injury to the cricoid cartilage and some discussion of the arteries. Now the doctor has given no indication that he knows whether that injury was antemortem or postmortem. He has not indicated whether he was given a history and no indication whatsoever that he knows how this body was dug up or whether a spade was stuck through the neck, and I think this is critical to the foundation before he can reasonably give an opinion as to whether this had anything to do with the cause of death."

Keuper quickly rephrased the question. "Doctor, assume that this defendant, and I am pointing out the defendant here, Carl Coppolino, did on the 30th day of July, 1963, lean his full weight down on the head, face, and chest of the body of William E. Farber with a pillow, assuming these facts, do you have an opinion within a reasonable medical certainty as to whether or not that act on the part of this defendant could have caused the condition you observed when you autopsied the body?"

I objected again: " 'Could have' isn't good enough in this business, your honor," I said.

Judge Simmill asked Keuper to rephrase the question again, and this time he asked whether an act of Carl's *did* cause the condition Helpern observed in the autopsy.

"In my opinion," said the doctor, "death resulted from the compression of the neck as indicated by this double fracture of the cricoid cartilage."

"And your opinion," Keuper said, "is that this act upon the part of the defendant could have caused that condition which resulted in his death?"

"Yes."

Then he was mine.

After establishing the frequency with which the doctor performed autopsies (some twenty thousand in his thirty-five years as a medical examiner), I moved quickly to the exhumation of Farber's body. Under questioning, Helpern said that when the body was brought to him in a tarpaulin, the scalp was missing.

"All right," I said. "Did you talk personally with any of the people that exhumed that body to find out how it was accomplished?"

"Not directly, no."

"Somebody gave you information that the coffin was caved in?"

"I was told by the man who brought the body to our place and identified the body that the sides of the coffin and the outer box were supposed to have collapsed."

Next I got him to concede that the cricoid cartilage can be fractured after death. "Now, after the time you discovered this cartilage, and prior to the time you formed an opinion, did you make any effort to get any of the details of the exhumation? Just yes or no."

He said yes; that he was told that the grave was wet at the time and that "when they took the outer board of the—the outer box in which the coffin was contained, that these boards were collapsed; but I was also told that the top of the coffin was intact. And not only that, but the inner lining of the coffin was intact, and that there was no soil on the body when it was first observed."

"When you got the body, it was covered with soil, wasn't it?"

"It was mixed with soil, yes."

I soon switched to questions about whether any postmortem signs of strangulation such as bruised skin were visible on Farber's throat. Helpern said he'd been told there were no such marks, but that he wasn't surprised because in many cases no such bruising occurs. I asked if he had checked for bruises, and he said he hadn't made a specific check, but that nothing was said to him about them.

"Did you make inquiry?" I asked.

"I did not make specific inquiry."

"You say it was unimportant?"

He was annoyed. "No, it is important, but I just assumed if they had been there I would have been informed about it, so I assumed they weren't there."

"Your assumption," I told him, "was correct." I then asked Dr. Helpern if he had brought with him the slides of cross-sections of the coronary arteries from which he had determined that the colonel's arteriosclerosis was not critical. He had them, but the showing had to be postponed when it turned out that there was no suitable projector available. I used what was left of the afternoon to solidify the foundation for what would be a vital part of my cross-examination. The most important exchange concerned the sort of pressure that can be applied through a pillow.

"Isn't it fair to say," I asked, "that there is no way through that pillow to concentrate pressure sufficient to break the cartilage?"

Helpern said it would be easier without the pillow, but that it could be done, and that there had been cases where the cricoid had been fractured in smothering attempts. In this case, he said, the injury spoke for itself.

"You say this injury by itself is proof of homicide?" I asked. "All by itself?"

"Yes."

"No question about it?"

"Yes, in this case."

I tried not to show my satisfaction. A fracture of the cricoid that occurs during life invariably leaves substantial traces of hemorrhage in the tissue of the larynx. I was certain I could show that the injury itself was not proof of homicide.

On Tuesday, Helpern exhibited his slides. The show would have bombed on or off Broadway, and it didn't play too well in Freehold. The slides seemed interminable, as did Helpern's monologue: ". . . this is the atheromatous plaque, and normally the intima, or the lining, is this thick. . . . It's extrinsically placed. That is, it's not concentric but excentric and . . ."

When the projector was turned off an hour or so later, two jurors appeared to be dozing. I asked if that was the end, and Helpern said yes, unless I wanted to see slides of other tissues. "I have 107 slides in all of the tissues that I sectioned," he said, "but I think you wanted to see the coronaries."

"We won't terrify the jury with a hundred and seven of anything," I said. "If you will resume the stand, I will resume the role of counsel and we will continue."

After a ten-minute recess, I began a key series of questions: "Now, if you were to exert pressure on my cricoid cartilage right now, and push in hard enough to break it, what would you expect to happen to the tissue inside?"

The doctor showed his rapier wit. "I thought you were going to ask what I would expect to happen to me."

I showed mine. "Well," I said, "I can promise you I wouldn't defend you."

"I'm sorry, Mr. Bailey."

I pushed the question. What would happen to the tissue inside the larynx? "It would hemorrhage, wouldn't it?"

His answer boiled down to yes.

"Now, a dead person doesn't bleed, does he?" I asked.

He said that you could bruise the tissues after death and produce hemorrhage, "but generally speaking, if the heart stops, it isn't the kind of bleeding that we think about in a live person."

"Now, in attempting to determine for yourself whether or not the injury to this larynx with which we are concerned occurred before or after the death of Colonel Farber, did you examine the tissue for hemorrhage?"

"I examined the tissue very carefully," Helpern said, "but the state of the tissue precluded any observation of hemorrhage. In other words, whatever hemorrhage there was, was no longer discernible in the tissue as I saw it. . . . The fact that I couldn't find it after three years of death would not permit me to conclude it wasn't there, and I found no evidence of it after three years of death."

The day before, he'd said the fracture itself was proof of homicide. Now he was saying that traces of hemorrhage would once have existed if the injury occurred during life. Since no such traces were visible, he was assuming that they had once been there. "So what you are saying," I asked, "is that if there ever was hemorrhage present in the lining you couldn't see it after three years?"

"That's right."

"And you don't have any evidence that there was hemorrhage that has disappeared?"

"I don't have any evidence of hemorrhage as such."

As the cross continued, I kept the doctor backpedaling on the hemorrhage issue, finally getting him to admit that he could not form any opinion about the presence or absence of the hemorrhage.

My last question came shortly afterward. "Is it fair to say, doctor, that apart from this larynx, just assuming you found no differences, that you would be unable to give us a cause of death at this time apart from that?"

"If I didn't have the larynx in this case," said Helpern, "I would have to say I did not know what this man died of."

At which point the doctor left the stand. "If your honor please, said Vincent Keuper, "the state rests."

7. NEITHER MURDER NOR HYPNOTISM

I dried off William Farber's larynx and handed it to the first witness for the defense, who examined and returned it. The witness was not unfamiliar with such objects; his name was Dr. Joseph W. Spelman, and he was the chief medical examiner for the city of Philadelphia.

"From your examination of that larynx alone," I asked, "do you have an opinion as to whether or not that fracture occurred prior to or subsequent to the death of the person whose larynx that was?"

"In my opinion," said Doctor Spelman, "that fracture is undoubtedly postmortem." He elaborated by saying that hemorrhage invariably accompanies fractures of the larynx, and that he had seen evidence of hemorrhages in exhumed bodies many years after burial. "I believe that if any hemorrhage which had occurred during life had been present," he said, "it would still be visible in this specimen."

In giving his qualifications, Dr. Spelman had mentioned that he'd taught courses in coronary disease at the University of Vermont. I asked him about the severity of the arteriosclerosis indicated by Helpern's slides. "The degree of arteriosclerosis that I saw," he said, "is a competent cause of death in and by itself."

Next on the stand was Carl's friend Dr. Webb, who described the container for the succinylcholine he'd given Carl in 1963. He said it was designed for use with an infusion bottle, the type from which medication drips into the patient's vein. It was not meant for injection with a hypodermic, though it could be adapted for such use.

The third witness was Dr. Richard Ford, senior medical examiner for Suffolk County, Massachusetts, which includes Boston, and a man of extensive experience in forensic medicine. His opinion was that "there was sufficient arteriosclerosis in Colonel Farber's coronary arteries to account for his death." Discussing the fractured cricoid, Dr. Ford said that Farber's larynx wasn't damaged in life. "There is no hemorrhage," he said. "There is adequate tissue there, and I have found through the years that in no case of pressure on the larynx, or the windpipe below it, in no case where there is pressure applied can you say that death occurred unless you find some hemorrhage to indicate the force of that pressure. . . . In view of the state of preservation of that specimen of the larynx, any hemorrhage occurring in life should be visible now in that specimen."

I also asked if he thought pressing down on a pillow with the heels of the hands could cause a double fracture of the cricoid cartilage. "It is unlikely," he said.

I had two other experts ready to discuss hypnosis, but first I called Carl's mother, Mrs. Anna Coppolino. Small and soft-voiced, she testified that at Longboat Key, after Carmela's death, Marge Farber told her several times that she wanted to marry Carl. She said that on one such occasion, "I told her she was crazy, that she was old enough to be his mother."

My hypnosis experts were Dr. Leo Wollman, an obstetrician-gynecologist who used hypnotherapy in his practice, and Dr. James A. Brussel.

Dr. Wollman said he'd found it impossible to make a subject perform an act "which they felt they are morally unable to do," and that there was no such thing as a continuing trance lasting for weeks or months. He said that in his opinion Marge wasn't hypnotized. Dr. Brussel said that no amount of hypnosis could cause a person to commit a criminal act "if he or she did not want to commit it without hypnosis, and the unconscious was also against it."

My next-to-last witness was Leo Clark Foster, a funeral director who had supervised the exhumation of Farber's body at Arlington, and had transported it to the Bellevue Hospital morgue in New York City for autopsy.

In describing the exhumation, he said there was water in the outer box that held the casket, and that the lid of the casket had to be removed in pieces. The workmen didn't want to touch the body, and Foster had to remove the satin lining covering the face and upper torso. Then the workers found that it was impossible to lift the body out of the casket because of the pressure of the moist earth against the box. The men dug a second grave alongside Farber's, the side of the casket was broken up and removed, and a disaster pouch was spread in the second grave. The diggers used L-shaped hooks to pull the body into the disaster pouch— attaching one to Farber's right shoulder, and one between his hip and knee. The idea was to slide the body into the pouch, but when the body was pulled, said Foster, it "turned over from his left to his right and landed on his face. . . ."

On cross, Keuper showed a signed statement in which Foster had made no mention of the body "landing" on its face. Foster said he meant that "he turned over from his back, face down." He also said he never saw any part of the casket fall on the upper body.

On redirect, I established that the casket lid was intact when Foster arrived, but had to be broken up for removal. He couldn't recall if he'd seen the actual breaking, but agreed that shovels were used for the job.

"Shovels jammed right down into the top of the casket?"

He hedged a bit, and then said: "Shovels were used, but I know they weren't jammed."

"Did you watch them being used?"

"No, sir."

"You didn't? Then how do you know they weren't jammed?"

"I don't know," he said.

I felt that Foster's testimony had been especially effective when coupled with Helpern's statement about Farber's scalp being missing. Foster was excused, and I called my last witness—Dr. Carl Coppolino.

8. *HIS OWN WITNESS*

Early on the morning of July 30, 1963, said Carl, he was awakened by a phone call from Marge Farber. "She told me that her husband, Bill, was ill, and could I rush right over." When he arrived, Carl found the colonel seated on the toilet with the lid down. Farber told him that he felt very weak, and could hardly move or breathe. Carl said he and Marge got her husband back into bed, and he took Farber's pulse and found it quite irregular. Farber was still gasping and holding his chest.

Carl went home for his medical bag and rushed back to the Farbers. He took the colonel's blood pressure, which was low, and listened to his heart with a stethoscope. The sounds were muffled. "From what he had told me and from my clinical observations," Carl testified, "I made a tentative diagnosis that the man obviously had suffered some sort of coronary episode."

I took him through his treatment of Farber step by step: Demarol, to relieve pain and apprehension; Pronestyl, injected to decrease the irritability of the heart; Nembutal, to induce relaxation and drowsiness. After about an hour, Farber's pulse became regular and he was able to talk. The colonel kept asking if he were going to die. Carl told him no, but said he was very ill and that an ambulance should be called to take him to the hospital.

Carl said Marge immediately said no, and that instead of answering him the colonel "went into a long harangue with Mrs. Farber that was not complimentary to her." Carl cut the argument short and told Farber he had to go to the hospital, but the colonel refused. A few minutes later, Farber vomited and began choking. Carl cleaned out the vomit and administered Sparine, a drug that acts as a tranquilizer and prevents nausea. Again he asked Farber to go to a hospital; this time, both the colonel and Marge said no. Carl took Marge into the den, where she told him that she had to respect Farber's wishes. Carl told her that since Farber was a sick man, the responsibility was hers to assume. "And then I asked her would she please let me call an ambulance and send him to the hospital. She refused."

At this point, said Carl, it was 6:00 A.M., and he left the house. When he returned between 10:00 and 10:30, he found the Farbers arguing. He got them to stop and reexamined the colonel. Farber's blood pressure was still a little low and his pulse was irregular. He told Carl he felt "lousy," but still refused to go to a hospital.

Carl stayed at the Farber house for about two hours this time. "I told Bill," he testified, "and I told Marge . . . that I could no longer render any aid whatever to Colonel Farber, because both of them refused to get what I considered proper medical attention for this patient, and that, under the conditions, I was going to withdraw from the case, and that I wanted Mrs. Farber to sign a release removing me from any responsibility for this case whatsoever. And I told Bill Farber the same thing."

He said Marge returned to his house with him, staying there while he wrote up notes on the treatment he'd given Farber. He also wrote the release and had Marge sign it.

"Did she put up any fight about signing?" I asked.

"No," he said.

Carl testified that Marge left sometime between 2:00 and 3:00 P.M. At about 6:30, she called Carmela. Carl said he had not left his home again until after Carmela found the colonel dead and phoned him from the Farber house. He said that when he looked at the body he estimated that Farber had been dead for anywhere from three to five hours.

I knew Keuper would bring up the death certificate, so I brought it up first. First, I had Carl testify that Carmela had signed the report, and that he had been present when it was filled out.

"Now," I said, "I notice that it says here above the signature: 'I attended the deceased from 3:30 A.M. to 6:00 A.M. Last saw him alive at 1:30 P.M., above date. Death occurred at approximately 4:00 P.M. on

the date above from the best of my knowledge from the cause as stated.'
Did Carmela attend from 3:30 to 6:00?"

"No."

"Did Carmela attend at 1:30?"

"No."

"Where did she get the information to put in there?"

"From Mrs. Farber and from myself."

"Prior to the time that she put her signature on this death certificate,
had you given her whatever history and diagnosis you had in the case?"

"I told her when I got home at 6:00 A.M."

He denied that there had ever been a "love plan" or that he had
said anything about Farber having to die. He said he had discussed
succinylcholine with Marge only as a means of putting away her dog, and
he never gave her either the drug or a syringe.

When Keuper got to the death certificate, he hammered at the fact
that Carmela had signed it although she had not taken care of Farber the
day he died. "Now doctor," he asked, "why didn't you sign the death
certificate?"

"I had withdrawn from the case."

"And that is your only answer?"

"That is right."

Keuper established that the afternoon before Carmela's death, Marge
had seen Carl and Mary Gibson in a car near the bridge studio and had
phoned Carmela about it. Carl admitted that he called Marge to complain
about her action. He said he told her he didn't like her spying on him.

"What else did you say, doctor?"

"I told her that Carmela knew Mary and that it was no surprise for
her to find out that I was with Mary."

"Did Carmela also know that you were intimate with Mrs. Farber?"

"Not to my knowledge."

"Did she know you had been out on many occasions with Mrs.
Farber?"

"Oh yes."

"Never objected to that?"

"Never."

"Never objected to your being out with Mary?"

"Never."

I objected to any further questioning along that line, and the judge
sustained me. Minutes later, Keuper was finished.

It was shortly after 12:00 noon on Wednesday, December 14, and all
the evidence was in.

9. *ONE DOWN*

My summation took less than an hour. "This is not a murder case at all," I said. "It is something that was dreamed up—something that never happened.

"Marjorie Farber," I said, "speaks of mystic powers and strange compulsions, of a black cloud, of exotic electricity, not that simple chemistry that draws woman to man. . . . She would have the world believe that out of her slumber comes the robot, the automaton guided and directed by that master of the black art, her controller! Her convenience of slipping in and out of hypnosis is exceeded only by the convenience of her forgetful memory.

"This woman who goes for all or nothing," I told the jury, "her story is not persuasive, it is an agony of contradiction." At another point I asked; "What kind of a woman would unfold this grisly story to the daily tabloids and put her children through the ordeal? Yes, a woman with two teenage daughters spilled this mess. . . . And maybe she spilled the beans when on the stand she told us of 'the other me.' We have no evidence that Marge snuffed him out. I wonder if she just let him die."

In discussing the evidence, I mentioned the release Marge had signed, and then got to the injury to the larynx. "What is important is that it occurred after death. No one could bend over the head of a bed and fracture the cricoid with the heel of his hands, even forgetting the pillow." As for Milton Helpern, I said that "this grand opinion, when challenged, crumbles down and is meaningless."

Keuper took half an hour. He said he held no brief for Marge, but that she was not on trial. He called her acts "disgusting, deplorable, and disgraceful," and said he felt that she and Carl had conspired to kill the colonel. He said hypnosis was involved in the case in that Marge was Carl's "willing subject" and hated her husband and wanted to kill him. "She reached the brink and prepared the solution, and rebelled. . . . She could go just so far. She couldn't do it."

He said Carl got Marge to sign the release because he didn't trust her—"he did not know at what time she would blow the whistle." He defended Helpern's testimony, and closed by calling for the death penalty.

The jurors were out for just four hours and thirty-four minutes. "It's

222

impossible for them to be back that soon with a guilty," Joe Mattice said to me as they entered the courtroom, and he was right. Asked for the verdict, George Phillips stood and said: "We the jury find the defendant Carl Coppolino not guilty."

When court adjourned, Anna Coppolino ran to her son. Carl was crying. "Mamma," he said, "I didn't do it." Then he hugged Mary. "I never did anything," he told her.

Later, I was greeted by autograph seekers in the hotel bar. I looked at one of them, and did a double take. It was an aunt of Wicki's from New York. "You're kidding," I said.

"No," she said. "It's for a friend, and I don't want to forget it."

Later, I learned that I had signed a slip of paper saying, "I promise to buy my wife, Wicki, a mink coat for Christmas, 1966."

The case had ended in time for a happy holiday. But Florida was yet to come.

10. EPILOGUE

For a short while, Carl and Mary Coppolino enjoyed the present, and allowed themselves the luxury of contemplating a future. The Freehold verdict had given Carl confidence—he felt fairly certain he would be acquitted in Florida.

I shared Carl's optimism, but I had some reservations. I figure that normally, the odds against winning a murder case are about nine to one. When the defendant is on trial in a second murder case, the odds are about eighty-one to one. Although Carl had been found not guilty in Freehold, his innocence had been blemished forever by the simple fact of indictment. And the thinking of a Florida jury might be influenced by the feeling that "well, he beat the rap in New Jersey, but he won't get away with it here." Also, the case was complicated by the intensely technical nature of the evidence—this was the first time anyone had been tried on a charge of committing murder with succinylcholine chloride. For the average juror, the evidence was sure to be as clear as a course in advanced biochemistry.

When the second trial opened, I asked for a change of venue, hoping for a much larger city than Sarasota. The bigger the city, I thought, the less chance of local gossip and slanted newspaper coverage prejudicing jurors. In February, Frank Schaub announced that he would agree to a change of venue, but suggested another county seat in his Twelfth Judicial Circuit, such as Fort Myers or Naples. At a hearing later in the month before Judge Lynn Silvertooth, who would preside at the trial, I asked that the venue be changed to Dade County, which would mean going to the mat in Miami, the state's largest city and one in which newspaper coverage of the Coppolino case had been least prejudicial. If the trial couldn't be held in Miami, I said, I'd prefer Sarasota to any of the other county seats in the Twelfth Circuit. But when the judge asked if I was withdrawing my request for a change of venue, I had to say no.

The trial was set for April—in Naples.

During the selection of the jury, Schaub used one of his peremptory challenges on a retired organic chemist who would have been able to understand the technical evidence and explain it to other jurors. I strongly objected to the challenge. I was angry, and I got angrier when Schaub accused me of "making a play for the press." I was fighting for a man's life, and we were being deprived of a capable juror precisely because of his ability to understand the evidence. Judge Silvertooth said that a peremptory challenge was an arbitrary right; I said I knew it was considered as such, but that I was challenging it nevertheless. "I think it is prejudicial to my client," I said, "for the state to use a peremptory challenge to deprive the jury of the one man who might be able to interpret the state's evidence against the defendant." The judge overruled me, and the chemist was removed from the panel.

As the trial got underway, and the jury got soaked with a mess of medical testimony, it became painfully evident what the chemist's presence might have meant to the case. Helpern and Umberger had tried to recoup from the preliminary hearing by experimenting with succinic acid; my experts had concentrated on choline. And although Helpern and Umberger had focused their efforts on finding an excess amount of succinic acid in Carmela's brain, their testimony left two points unresolved. One was whether a "blood-brain" barrier exists in the brain that's capable of keeping succinylcholine out of the blood in that organ. The other was whether the succinic acid found in the brain by Umberger represented material that was normally present or came from an outside source.

The jury's task is illustrated by a section of Umberger's direct testimony. He was describing how he developed a test for the detection of succinic acid in a sample of Carmela's brain: "All we had to do was convert the acid over to the anhydride, take the single crystal, and add to the solid another crystal of hydroxamic imide to it, and heat to about

120 degrees, and then come back with a drop of the ferric chloride reagent. . . ."

He went on in this vein until Assistant Prosecutor William Strode finally asked if Umberger's tests enabled him to say "with reasonable medical certainty" whether his findings indicated "a toxic overdose of succinylcholine."

"Well," said the toxicologist, "I would say that the chemical findings are consistent with—now I use the term 'consistent with' meaning that it is reasonable that death could have occurred from succinylcholine."

"Could have?" I interjected.

"Could have," Umberger repeated. "I don't establish the cause of death. I'm speaking from the chemical point of view. Could have."

We went around on this, and Judge Silvertooth searched for clarity: "Do you make a positive finding of this drug in a toxic dose?"

Umberger went into another complicated explanation. Finally, he said that "I think the term should be 'reasonable scientific certainty,' and not 'medical certainty.'"

In cross-examination, I established that Umberger had relied solely on finding succinic acid, which he was *assuming* had been injected into Carmela's body.

"I'm not involved in that," he said, referring to an injection. "I don't care, really."

"Well, we do, we do," I said.

"I know you do."

I pushed. "And the jury does."

"Yes," Umberger said, switching positions, "and I do too."

"All right. You changed your mind on that?"

At the least he was convivial. "Yes," he said, smiling, "I backtracked on that quick."

We discussed his meaning of the word "possible." "So when you say a succinylcholine injection is possible," I asked, "what you are really saying is that: 'If there is proof she was shot with a drug my findings are consistent with those facts'?"

"Well, yes. I would say that 'consistent with' is probably the most reasonable language between the lawyer and the chemist. If it were a discussion between two chemical people I don't think the word 'possible' would raise any question. They'd understand what I mean by possible."

"Well," I said, "use our language, if you will, since again I remind you that we have no chemists on the jury, unfortunately."

"Well," he said, "say 'consistent.'"

The core of his testimony was that he had found four and a half milligrams of succinic acid in one kilogram of Carmela's brain, and that his experiments enabled him to conclude that this represented twelve milli-grams originally existing in the sample, or about eighteen milligrams in her entire brain. He was unwilling to concede that the succinic acid he found could have been present in the brain without an injection, but he didn't rule out the possibility. He agreed that the human brain normally contains about forty milligrams of succinic acid, but said this was "bound" succinic acid. I asked him what it was bound to, and his answer was: "Well, I don't think anybody knows." I then tried to find out if embalming fluid might free bound succinic acid. Umberger said he had never run enough tests on embalmed brains to say for sure that the fluid would have no effect on bound succinic acid, although it was his opinion that it wouldn't.

On redirect, the assistant prosecutor asked Umberger if it was his finding, "to a reasonable scientific certainty, that the body tissues of Carmela Coppolino indicated a toxic overdose of succinylcholine?"

"Yes," said Umberger. "After considering all the circumstances, all the facts available to me, I can't arrive at any other conclusion."

Strode asked what Umberger, as a chemist, meant by the word "pos-sible." "Well," answered Umberger, "in chemical language, 'possible' means there is no other explanation until or unless someone comes up with something to disprove it."

This surrealistic approach to semantics also characterized the ap-pearance of Dr. Milton Helpern. In his direct testimony, Helpern said that based on his autopsy and on Umberger's findings, it was his opinion that Carmela had died as the result of an injection of succinylcholine into her left buttock. During cross-examination, I got around to the various versions of Umberger's report that had come up at the preliminary hearing, citing the chemist's statement that it was "possible" that the succinic acid and choline found in Carmela's body were derived from succinylcholine.

"He put down this as a possibility," Helpern testified. "That was not a speculative possibility, that was an exclusive possibility, and that was chemist talk. And then he indicated that the only explanation for this combination was succinylcholine."

When I asked Dr. Helpern what part findings of choline had played in his conclusions, he said that choline was very often found in dead bodies, but that "we are using the choline fraction in combination with the succinic acid to arrive at the conclusion."

He didn't know how much choline Umberger had found, and I asked him whether the amount of choline was of any significance in helping him toward his opinion.

"No," he said, and added that "if it were absent, I would say it was significant, but the fact that he found choline makes it significant, but not by itself. In other words, it's the combination."

After Helpern left the stand, I made a motion asking that his and Umberger's testimony be stricken. Neither the medical examiner nor his toxicologist had offered any proof that succinic acid from an injection of succinylcholine could pass the blood-brain barrier. Neither could give normal brain levels for either choline or succinic acid. And if Helpern's opinion were based on Umberger's opinion, his testimony should be inadmissible—in a court of law, opinions are supposed to be based on facts, not on other opinions. The prosecution argued that if the judge supported the motion, he would be rebuffing modern chemical techniques.

Judge Silvertooth took the motion under advisement and rejected it the following day. Meanwhile, the state produced another expert witness—Dr. Bert La Du, Jr., chairman of the pharmacology department at New York University Medical Center. Dr. La Du had analyzed a tissue sample from Carmela's buttock. Along the needle track area, he'd found "material that had the same properties as succinylcholine in amounts that would correspond to about thirty gamma per gram of tissue." Dr. La Du's testimony struck me as inconclusive, though damaging. A gamma is one-millionth of a gram, and the doctor had not said he had found succinylcholine, only that it "had the same properties." Also, he'd said he was unable to obtain enough material to make a definitive test.

Our roster of experts was headed by Dr. Francis Ference Foldes, chief of anesthesiology at New York's Montefiore Hospital, and Dr. John Crispin Smith, a research biochemist at the same place. Using radioactive succinylcholine in experiments with rats, both men had done pioneer work in finding out what happens to the drug when it enters the body.

Smith described an experiment involving an intramuscular injection of a large dose of succinylcholine: seventy-six per cent of the drug would show up at the injection area after death, and only three-tenths of one per cent would reach the brain. These studies, he said, showed that the blood-brain barrier was a reality. He also testified about experiments demonstrating that embalming fluid has a significant effect in freeing bound choline in the brain. The free choline found in Carmela's brain could not, he testified, have come from a succinylcholine injection.

Dr. Foldes said that only minute amounts of succinic acid and choline could get past the blood-brain barrier, and that the choline found in Carmela's tissue was not sufficient to indicate a succinylcholine injection. Asked what importance he attached to the four and a half milligrams of succinic acid found in Carmela's brain by Umberger, he had a simple answer: "Nothing."

I also called Dr. Richard Ford, the expert who had helped damage

Helpern's testimony in Freehold. He discounted the validity of Dr. La Du's tests as an indication of the cause of death.

Later in the trial, as a result of information I'd gotten from some concerned members of Umberger's staff, I recalled Umberger. He conceded that he had probably not come up with his finding of four and a half milligrams of succinic acid in Carmela's brain until 1967. As I told the jury in my summation, the evidence against Carl hadn't even existed when he was indicted in July 1966. "Searching for truth is one thing," I said, "but searching for evidence to support an indictment already voted is another."

I then asked Umberger if he expected to publish a report on the tests that enabled him to come up with his finding. "No," he said. "I don't think it would be accepted for publication. It is not complete enough." My feeling was that if his evidence wasn't good enough for a scientific report, it surely wasn't good enough for a murder conviction.

The nonmedical witnesses included Marjorie Cullen Farber and Mary Gibson Coppolino, both of whom were called by the prosecution. This time, Marge's role was limited—early in the proceedings I had won a fight to exclude matters involved in the Freehold trial. Marge, deprived of her hypnosis routine, testified that she and Carl had been lovers and described their trips to Florida, Atlantic City, and Puerto Rico. She also testified that she had seen Carl and Mary together in Mary's car the day before Carmela's death and had sized Mary up as "just so-so."

Marge told another story that only Carl—if he took the stand—could contradict. She said that after Carmela's death, she and Carl had a conversation in which he told her he had left home for three days early in August to think about his marriage. He'd also told her, Marge said, that when he returned he told Carmela he didn't love her any more.

On cross-examination, I tried to show Marge's vindictiveness. I got her to admit that she had tried to block Carl from obtaining a license to practice in Florida, and that she had conspired with a state investigator in an unsuccessful attempt to trip Carl up with a bugged phone call.

Mary was called as a hostile witness for the prosecution. In answer to Schaub's questions, she described meeting Carl at the bridge studio in July. She didn't remember how many times she had seen him the following month, or how many times he had been at her home. At the time of their marriage, she said, her income was between $600 and $800 a month. I had just one question. "From the time you met Carl in July until August 28, did he ever make inquiry into your financial status?"

"No," Mary said.

Dr. Musetto, Carmela's father, also testified for the prosecution: Carl had told him there had been an autopsy, and that it had revealed that

Carmela had suffered a bad heart condition. On cross, he conceded that he remained friendly with Carl after learning there had been no autopsy. He even wrote Carl a letter containing the names of two women who might make good second wives for his son-in-law.

The defense witnesses included Dr. Webb, who demonstrated his belief in Carl, and Carl's mother, who told of her conversations with Marge Farber. Schaub had called several witnesses in an attempt to suggest pre-marital hanky-panky between Mary and Carl. I called Mary's daughters, who testified that Carl never stayed at their house overnight before his marriage to Mary.

One of the best witnesses I had produced at Freehold did not appear at Naples. He was Carl Coppolino, and it was his own decision not to testify. It was a terrible mistake.

In Freehold, there had been a self-purported witness to the alleged crime—Marge Farber. And Carl had testified to counter her wild story of what happened the weekend her husband died. But in Naples the case was purely circumstantial, and Carl convinced himself that it was a mistake for a defendant to take the stand in a circumstantial case. Ironically, the Sheppard trial influenced his decision—he'd been impressed by the fact that Sam hadn't testified, and he wanted to know why. I didn't tell him that Sam was in no shape to go on any witness stand, but I did tell him everything I could think of that might change his mind.

In most instances, the defendant should stay off the stand in a circumstantial case. But there are exceptions to every rule, and as I tried to tell Carl, this was one of them. If he took the stand Carl could explain away the one incriminating factor, the needle track in Carmela's buttock: Carmela took vitamin B–12 shots and administered them to herself in the buttocks. But unless Carl testified, there was no way to get that fact before the jury.

I told Carl there was a long difference between his case and Sam Sheppard's. And I also told him that he should give some consideration to the fact that he was a fine witness, and Sam a poor one. But the night before he would have gone on the stand, Carl came to his final decision. He would not testify.

Nevertheless, when the jury went out at 5:15 P.M. on April 27, I thought we would win. The state's case was built upon a cobweb of inference and conjecture, and its key witness had admitted that his findings weren't even solid enough for publication. "This was a brand new case to all law and all medicine," I said in my summation. "There is no certainty in it. There is no competent evidence on the cause of death."

At 10:20 P.M., the jurors took an overnight recess. At 9:00 the next morning, they resumed deliberations. Half an hour later, they had a verdict. "We the jury," read the court clerk, "find the defendant guilty of murder in the second degree as charged. So say we all."

The second-degree conviction was a strange verdict. In all states, premeditation is necessary for a first-degree verdict. But in Florida, second-degree murder specifically must involve a *lack* of premeditation. It's difficult to see how a poisoning could be committed without premeditation.

Judge Silvertooth imposed the maximum sentence. "You shall be delivered to the custodian of the state prison at Raiford, Florida, for the remainder of your natural life," he said as Carl stood before him.

After the verdict, Marjorie Cullen Farber composed a statement for the press. "Although I have sympathy for the parents and children of Carl Coppolino," she said, "please keep in mind that my husband is dead and my children have no father because of this man's action." It was as if Freehold had never happened.

We appealed in the state courts, and were turned down. Since then, Carl has not tried to apply for the remaining remedies. At least, if he's doing anything, he's doing it without my knowledge.

So far as I know, both Marge Farber and Mary Coppolino still live in the Sarasota area. In the end, Marge Farber got her revenge, but I wonder if it satisfied her. There are all kinds of hells.

VI

When the Defender Stands Accused

On April 24, 1968, I wrote a letter to Richard Hughes, the governor of New Jersey. It read in part:

I am writing to call to your attention a matter which I consider to be of most serious consequence to the man I represent and to the State of New Jersey. I am about to commence a trial wherein the prosecutor presenting the case is fully aware that the only witness he has intends to lie and give a fully fictional account of a murder allegedly committed by my client.

Harold Matzner of Denville, New Jersey, was indicted in June, 1967, for the murder of Judy Kavanaugh and in October, 1967, for the murder of Gabriel DeFranco. I have represented him since the first indictment. I have never, in any state or federal court, seen abuses of justice, legal ethics, and constitutional rights such as this case has involved. The "witnesses" to each murder are convicts and both have been pressured or bribed by the prosecution to give their stories and thus knowingly jeopardize the lives of five completely innocent people, all of whom have been cleared by polygraph tests administered by nationally recognized experts.

One trial involves three defendants and one involves four: two, including my client, are defendants in both cases.

It was my original intent that the trial itself be the medium of exposing this disgraceful situation. However, some weeks ago, there suddenly appeared a special prosecutor in the person of James Dowd. The DeFranco trial was scheduled for April 22. A week prior to its commencement, Mr. Dowd attempted to obtain a continuance to "further investigate" the case with which he had become recently acquainted. I objected, and his motion was denied. I conferred with him privately in the presence of his assistant, Richard McGlynn. Upon his representation that (1) he was in charge of the case, and (2) he had a sincere desire to determine whether or not his chief witness was a perjurer, I reversed my original stand and assented to a continuance.

Mr. Dowd was as good as his word. He did determine that Edward Lenney, the alleged eye-witness, had in fact offered a completely perjured story, and that he had been assisted in its concoction by officials of the State of New Jersey. Mr. Dowd wished that the indictment immediately be dismissed and the defendants be cleared of all suspicion. The defendants agreed. Before this could be done, however, representatives of the office of the prosecutor, John Thevos, made contact with Edward Lenney as a result of which he reverted to his false story. The State of New Jersey now proposes to go forward with this trial in order that those officials guilty of felonious conduct may be to some degree protected. My client, therefore, is offered the opportunity to fall into the classic American syndrome of the damnation of an acquittal. I do not propose that this be allowed.

Should this trial proceed as is presently planned, the stench arising from it will hold the State of New Jersey up to ridicule such as has beset no organ of government since the abolition of Star Chamber. Although there would be a certain pleasure in bringing to book these officials in the spotlight of a murder trial, I believe it to be in the best interests of my client to urgently request that an immediate investigation be made to determine whether or not Mr. Dowd is being forced by orders from superiors to offer in an American courtroom a man he knows to be a liar. The money and effort of which the taxpayers will be defrauded in such a trial could much better be spent in conducting the investigation that would lead to the disbarment and incarceration of those responsible for this travesty.

The press has been throttled in this case to the extent that the public is almost wholly unaware of what is being perpetrated. As of the day our trial jury is sequestered, I intend that the entire matter be aired. I hope that some action on your part will precede such an unfortunate event. Thank you very kindly for your attention to this matter.

In its essentials, the letter speaks for itself. But it did not obtain the desired result. Instead, ostensibly because it was leaked to the press, it triggered my being censured in Massachusetts and suspended from practice in New Jersey. The underlying hows and whys illustrate the fact that, as a maverick, the defense lawyer is a constant target.

Unlike the state prosecutor, the defender has always been at a marked disadvantage when it comes to protecting his professional status. Except in very unusual circumstances, almost no machinery exists for controlling a prosecutor who transgresses ethical, moral, or legal bounds in the exercise of his office. People are indicted for predominantly political reasons most weeks of the year, but the prosecutors who contribute to this sort of miscarriage of justice are seldom brought to task. The defense lawyer who takes honest shots at official diddling doesn't have a grand jury to shield him, and he has no authority to take action against an individual. He is only sanctioned to defend those persons against whom action is taken. Consequently, he often winds up as the dart board.

For example, Clarence Darrow was tried twice in California and at one point his attorney, Earl Rogers, was indicted. Most advocates who have made news as criminal lawyers have either been prosecuted or scrutinized and threatened by bar associations.

I'm no exception. Early in my career, I ran into muttered warnings that I was running the risk of grand jury investigations by continuing to prosecute certain cases with "inappropriate vigor." Then, in the fall of 1966 and the winter and spring of 1967, my target potential increased with a spate of national magazine stories. From comments my brothers in the Boston legal community were making to interviewers, I deduced that my notoriety had engendered a certain hostility. But there was no brush with the Boston Bar Association or any other agency until June, 1967.

It occurred in the wake of Carl Coppolino's conviction in Florida. In order to appear in another state, an attorney has to obtain a certificate of good standing from his home state's highest court. I needed such a certificate to petition the district court of appeals in Lakeland, Florida, to allow Coppolino to go free on bail while we appealed his conviction. To my surprise, my secretary was informed by the clerk's office of the Supreme Judicial Court of Massachusetts that although no official complaint had been brought against me, a "matter of concern" was lodged with the Boston Bar Association and would have to be cleared up before any certificate could be issued.

I immediately asked the aid of my colleague Joe Balliro, who contacted the bar association. An informal meeting was set up with that group's grievance committee. The "matters of concern" were:

1. A report that I intended to play myself in a movie about the Sheppard case.

2. A contract I had signed with David Susskind's Talent Associates for an ABC-TV series that fall.

3. My appearance on CBS radio in Boston to discuss the Chicofsky affair with a local interviewer named Paul Benzaquin. (Chicofsky was the man who had come to me during the Mail Robbery probe with a report that the postals were behind a plot to kidnap Tom Richards and have him tortured into disclosing the whereabouts of the loot.)

4. My appearances on the Joey Bishop and Johnny Carson TV shows after Carl Coppolino's conviction, during which I attacked the verdict. I had discussed on the air the implausibility of poisoning as the means of second-degree (unpremeditated) murder, and had quoted the prosecution's expert witness Dr. Umberger to the effect that he had never meant his testimony to be used as the basis for conviction.

5. The fact that I had contracted to write what would become this book, and had engaged a literary agent.

With Joe's approval, I discussed each matter in detail before the grievance committee. I had indeed been asked to play myself in a documentary about the Sheppard case. I had replied that I would have to see the script and that I could only make such a decision after conferring with bar association officials. (I never did play in the film.) As for the TV series, it was to be totally unrelated to the practice of law, but would involve interviews with celebrities somewhat in the manner of Ed Murrow's *Person to Person* program. (This format was followed throughout the seventeen weeks the show lasted.)

I accept, as any lawyer must, the principle that statements in print or on the air which might influence the outcome of a trial are unethical—that is why, for example, my defense of Captain Ernest Medina is not discussed in this book. But in the case of the radio broadcast concerning Richard Chicofsky, there was no upcoming trial that I could prejudice. Further, I believed Chicofsky was telling the truth, and I was worried about Tom Richards. Exposure of the plot might help stop the use of such government tactics to elicit information. In publicizing the affair, I believed I was exercising the right of free speech in an extraordinary situation.

Nor could I see grounds for objection to my appearances on the Bishop and Carson shows. I felt that Coppolino had been unfairly convicted, and I knew how much his family was suffering as a result of national publicity about the verdict. (I doubted that the media had understood the evidence against Carl any better than the jury had.) More important, I was hoping through publicity to attract people in the scientific community who could furnish me with new expert evidence. Since Coppolino had already undergone two jury trials, and Judge Silvertooth had passed on his motion for a new trial, I felt there was very little danger of an appellate court's being influenced by anything said on a national television show—especially in view of conjecture and speculation by the press over the course of the better part of a year.

Finally, I was planning a book and had indeed contracted with a literary agent: any author who tries to represent himself in the publishing field is in the same league as that lawyer who represents himself in court —he has a fool for a client.

Apparently, my explanations satisfied the grievance committee at the time. When the conference ended, the bar association terminated the proceedings and the certificate of good standing was issued. I heard no more about the matter for two years.

Meantime, the Matzner case was developing. In 1966, the New Jersey papers were running stories about the murder of a young housewife named Judith Kavanaugh. The case was getting sensational treatment for at least two reasons: there were allegations of wife-swapping, and the victim's husband, Paul Kavanaugh, worked for Matzner Publications of Wayne, New Jersey. Harold Matzner, a young publisher, had spurred a series of articles that tried to link the office of Passaic County Prosecutor John Thevos with underworld elements.

On June 29, 1967, Harold Matzner was indicted for the Judy Kavanaugh murder. The next day, his father retained me as defense counsel. What followed was a case characterized by more dirty tactics than any in which I have ever been involved.

The brunt of the case against Harold Matzner rested on the story of a convicted prostitute named Jacqueline Natoli. She said that a small-time hood, Gabriel (Johnny the Walk) DeFranco, had said Matzner claimed to have killed Judy Kavanaugh. Unfortunately, DeFranco was unable to speak for himself; he died on October 6, 1966, from a slit throat, the victim of a gangland-style killing. Although hearsay evidence such as Miss Natoli's would be ruled inadmissible in any court, Matzner was held without bail to stand trial.

There was more. The prosecutor's office, dominated by an investigator named Joseph Muccio, kept harassing people associated with the defense. Some were hauled before the grand jury without warning after midnight and as much as told that unsatisfactory testimony could land them behind bars. When Matzner came up with an alibi for the night of the murder, the alibi witness was quickly indicted for false swearing. At one point my investigator, Stephen Delaney (who, like Andy Tuney, had come to me from the Boston Strangler Bureau), ran into trouble. It started with back trouble, which got worse when he went to a chiropractor—without knowing that the chiropractor's partner was a member of the grand jury. Suddenly Steve was indicted for attempting to interfere with the grand jury. And throughout the case, threats of indictment were made against defense counsel—including myself and New Jersey attorney Leonard Garth, now a U.S. district judge.

On October 11, 1967, Matzner was also indicted for the killing of Gabriel DeFranco. Matzner, a man named Vincent Kearney, and John DeGroot, a detective sergeant in the Clifton, New Jersey, police department, were fingered by a thirty-year-old felon named Edward Lenney. He told a muddled story that belonged in an old Jack LaRue crime movie. He had been with the others when the murder occurred, and DeFranco had been rubbed out because he "did some beefing" involving the Kavanaugh case.

Then on January 10, 1968, Harold Matzner's wife, Dorothe, was indicted as a codefendant in the Kavanaugh murder. The state's stone-thrower was none other than Jacqueline Natoli, who had made a change in her story—she now claimed to have been an eyewitness to the killing. She said she had seen Harold and Dorothe Matzner shoot Judy Kavanaugh with a pistol some distance from where the body was found.

The harassment continued, and I assigned Steve Delaney to a full-time station in New Jersey just to keep up with the case. On occasion I sent him two or three other investigators from the Boston office. If the Matzner case was one of the most frustrating in which I have ever been involved, by the spring of 1968 it was also one of the best prepared.

As part of the trial preparation, I saw to it that all the defendants submitted to polygraph tests. At a pretrial hearing to determine whether polygraph findings would be admitted into evidence, I produced a chain of experts who laid a solid foundation for scientific reliability. They included several members of the New Jersey State Police, none of whom knew of any instance in which a man had been prosecuted after being cleared by polygraph tests. The state was unable to produce any evidence damning the polygraph, but Judge Gordon Brown ruled that until the Supreme Court decided otherwise, the tests would be inadmissible.

The hearing, held in March, signaled another important development—the appearance of a new attorney for the prosecution. James T. Dowd, a former Justice Department lawyer who had worked on the Jimmy Hoffa case, had been appointed by the state as a special prosecutor for the Kavanaugh and DeFranco trials.

It was finally decided that the DeFranco murder case would be heard first, and trial was set for April 22. Although I felt that both cases were pushovers for the defense, the DeFranco case seemed the more ludicrous. The prosecution was depending on Edward Lenney, whose credibility was about as solid as a soft-boiled egg. Lenney had been serving a five- to seven-year term in Rahway, New Jersey, when he told a cellmate that a man named Ventura had ordered the DeFranco murder and that he had committed it. Then he was brought to Passaic County, where he changed his story and implicated Matzner, Kearney, and DeGroot. His conduct under custody as a state witness had included one attempt at escape, which was surprising—the prosecution had provided Lenney with private quarters, steaks from one of the best restaurants in town, music, and feminine company. All of which promised to give us a heyday before a jury.

On April 10, in an appearance before Judge Brown, Dowd and his young assistant Richard McGlynn urged a postponement of the trial. I had wanted to proceed as planned, and Judge Brown indicated he would rule in our favor. But during a recess, a conversation with Dowd changed my mind. I told him that I would be able to place Lenney in a city some three hundred miles from the scene of DeFranco's murder on the night in question. If he got a continuance, I asked, would he be willing to make his own investigation into Lenney's story? He said he would. He also said that if the case turned out to be a fraud he wouldn't hesitate to say so, but that he wanted to satisfy himself as to the facts. Equally important, he told me that he had been appointed to the prosecution on the recommendation of U.S. Attorney General Ramsey Clark, and that his authority in the case was complete. After conferring for half an hour or so, we went back before Judge Brown and obtained an indefinite postponement. I told the judge I was now persuaded that "further investigation will probably militate in favor of my client and that the prosecutor is sincere in his efforts."

Dowd was hopeful. "Well, all I can say, your honor, is that the postponement of this case as heretofore discussed in every regard can only serve the interest of justice."

Justice. That's what the system is supposed to be all about. And that's what both Jim Dowd and I were after. I agreed to give him the results of my investigation and all of my files in the case. On his part, he would make every effort to get the truth out of Lenney. And if the truth absolved Harold Matzner, Dowd would stand up in open court and move for dismissal on the grounds that Matzner was innocent. He also agreed not to oppose bail for Harold, now in jail for close to a year, and the day after the hearing Harold was released on relatively modest bond.

A week later, I got a call from Joe Afflitto, who was serving as cocounsel for the Matzner defense. Lenney, he said, had admitted to Dowd that he'd lied about seeing the DeFranco murder, and Dowd had called the defense attorneys and gone with them to the home of County Court Judge Theodore Rosenberg late that night to arrange for a hearing the following morning. At the hearing, Lenney's recantation would be recorded in open court as the basis for a motion to dismiss the indictment. For reasons never made entirely clear, the hearing was postponed, but Dowd took a retraction from Lenney under oath the next day.

When he first sang, Lenney had made a forty-two-page statement implicating Kearney, DeGroot, and Matzner, and had followed that up with a four-pager to straighten out seeming inconsistencies. As I've indicated, he showed a real flair for melodrama. He said that Matzner sat in a car while he and the others stepped onto the porch of his old friend "Johnny the Walk" DeFranco's apartment. Lenney even threw in dialogue; he quoted Matzner as saying: " 'Now hurry and make sure it's done right.' " He said they knocked on the door, and DeFranco opened it, saying, " 'What the fuck you want this hour of the night?" Then, he said, Kearney spun DeFranco around, and DeGroot "come up with an upward swing . . . and the Walk like made a funny sound and that was it, you know." Lenney further embellished his tale by saying that a gob of DeFranco's blood "hit me right in my face and like a speck was on my jacket." It was some story. But now he was telling Dowd that none of it ever happened—that he wasn't even in New Jersey that night. The sworn retraction that Dowd took from Lenney says a lot about the case that the prosecutor's office of Passaic County had compiled against Harold Matzner.

Q. (by MR. DOWD) Would you state your name for the record, please.
A. Edward Lenney.
Q. And how old are you, Mr. Lenney?
A. Thirty.
Q. I am going to direct your attention to what has been marked as

S–1, which is a statement consisting of forty-two pages dated September 1, 1967, and ask you is that your signature?

A. Yes.

Q. And I direct you to what has been marked as S–2, statement dated October 10, 1967, and ask you if that is your signature on that statement consisting of four pages?

A. Yes.

Q. I direct your attention to a copy of affidavit dated October 13, 1967, styled in the matter of State of New Jersey v. Vincent Kearney, Jr., Harold Matzner, and John C. DeGroot, Indictment No. 64–67, and ask you if that's your signature?

A. Yes.

Q. Now, referring to the S–1 exhibit, Mr. Lenney, there are allegations in there that on October 6, 1966, at about 1:15 A.M. you were on a porch in Paterson, New Jersey, near Apartment 4, 297 5th Avenue. Were you there on October 6, 1966?

A. No, sir.

Q. And where were you on that date?

A. In Baltimore.

Q. Baltimore, Maryland?

A. Yes.

Q. And what were you doing at that time?

A. I was working as a bartender.

Q. And where were you working?

A. Spierle Cocktail Lounge.

Q. Do you know Vincent Kearney, Jr.?

A. Yes.

Q. To your knowledge was he on the porch at 297 5th Avenue, Paterson, New Jersey, on October 6, 1966?

A. No.

Q. Do you know Harold Matzner?

A. No.

Q. To your knowledge was he on the porch at 297 5th Avenue, Paterson, New Jersey, on October 6, 1966?

A. No.

Q. Do you know John C. DeGroot?

A. No.

Q. To your knowledge was he on the porch at 297 5th Avenue, Apartment 4, Paterson, New Jersey, on October 6, 1966, at 1:15 A.M.?

A. No.

Q. Do you know whether or not they are at all in any way involved in the murder of one Gabriel DeFranco on October 6, 1966?

A. No, sir.

Q. I direct your attention to State Exhibit S–2, which is correction of S–1 that you signed subsequent to your statement marked as S–1, and ask you are the facts in that statement correct?

A. No.

Q. Why was it that your brother testified that he picked you up in New York on October 5, 1966?

A. I asked him to lie. . . .

Q. Are the statements concerning the murders in the Kavanaugh case and the DeFranco case in Exhibit S–1, are they correct or incorrect?

A. Incorrect.

Q. You make this statement, Mr. Lenney, freely and voluntarily?

A. Yes, sir.

Q. And what you are saying now under oath before this certified shorthand reporter, is this the true story?

A. Yes, sir.

MR. DOWD: No further questions.

It was plain that Dowd wanted to move quickly. I figured he anticipated pressure from local authorities, who could be tagged with suborning Lenney's perjury. But I also figured he had the power to make his own moves, and to make them stick. I was wrong. If Dowd had ever had complete authority in the case, it was soon gone. There was no motion to dismiss the indictment, no court move in that direction. But there were reports that the prosecutor's office was threatening to indict Dowd and the defense attorneys for coercion with regard to Lenney. And then Judge Joseph Crane, the assignment judge for Passaic County, returned from a trip abroad and reset the DeFranco trial for May 20, 1968.

I was outraged. I had released all of my information to the prosecutor, thereby forfeiting any chance of catching Lenney by surprise with our evidence. I learned that the trial had been reset at Thevos's request, and that Thevos had gotten Lenney to say his recantation was false—although he apparently had made no such statement under oath. On April 24th I went to Paterson, and, in company with co-counsel and Jim Dowd, sought to see Judge Crane. The judge refused to give us an audience. I asked Dowd what had happened to his authority, and he shrugged. He was honestly puzzled; I don't think even he knew what had happened. The most I could find out was that John Thevos had made a trip to Trenton, the state capital. But I couldn't find out just whom he'd seen.

In any event, I was hurting. It wasn't just a matter of my responsibility to the Matzners; I also felt I'd let down the other defense lawyers involved in the case. I'd taken the responsibility for trusting Dowd's authority at our first conference; now I felt I owed it to all concerned to try and implement the agreement he and I had made. I asked my fellow counsel if there was any way we could enforce the bargain through a judicial proceeding; they thought not. (They later proved the point by bringing a motion that Judge Brown denied and the New Jersey Supreme Court refused to review.) I returned to Boston after Judge Crane declined to meet with us, and composed my letter to Governor Hughes.

Obviously, I was angry. I told my secretary to send copies to U.S. Attorney General Clark, New Jersey Attorney General Arthur Sills, the president of the state's bar association, and the state's U.S. Senators and Congressmen. After dictating the letter and without waiting for it to be transcribed, I left for Atlanta and Baton Rouge, Louisiana. On my way out the door, I asked my secretary to make up a list of New Jersey's state senators and assemblymen in case a mailing to them should seem necessary in the future. Unfortunately, she misunderstood; she not only compiled the list, she also sent copies of the letter to every name on it.

Within forty-eight hours of its mailing, the letter was in the newspapers. The evening of the day the letter was published, I took a phone call from a New Jersey reporter. I get a lot of news that way, and it usually comes in question form. His was a winner: would I comment on the fact that the New Jersey Supreme Court had ordered my removal from the Matzner case unless I could show cause as to why I should be allowed to remain?

At this point, I was beginning to feel like a pacifist at a war rally—the proceedings bordered on the incomprehensible. I had this crazy idea that a man has a right to avoid the destructive experience of a first-degree murder trial if he can prove that the state knows he's innocent and is going ahead with the trial to save the hide of its own officials.

Pursuant to the court's order, I went to Paterson, where a private hearing was held in Judge Brown's chambers. The Matzners and Joe Afflitto were with me. I had notified Judge Brown that as part of my effort to show cause why I shouldn't be removed, I wanted to demonstrate the truth of everything in the letter. This included the fact that the defendants had been framed, and that the prosecution knew it. But the judge, whom I respected, ruled that the only question before him was the propriety of my conduct. "We are not meeting to talk about Mr. Thevos or Mr. Dowd or Edward Lenney," he said. "We are meeting to talk about you."

He also said that the Constitution had no place in our discussion. "You have no constitutional right to appear in this case," he said. "You are in New Jersey as a matter of grace or privilege. You can insist upon nothing, you can demand nothing. You can only plead for continuation of a discretionary grant of authority. You and I arranged for your appearance as an attorney directly between ourselves and in private. You satisfied me that you were in good standing in Massachusetts. Now the question is, are you in good standing here? That's for me to decide. No one else in the world has any part to play in the issue."

The hearing lasted about an hour. Most of it was taken up by Judge Brown's cross-examination of me, which centered on my letter to the governor. "I will ask you the sixty-four-dollar question," the judge said a third of the way through. "Did you deliver or cause to be delivered a copy of the letter to any news media?"

"Absolutely not, your honor."

When the judge said the letter had been published in full in two Paterson daily papers, I suggested that an inquiry be made to find out how they got it. Joe Afflitto said at this point that he had questioned the two reporters involved, and that he "was met with a smile."

Judge Brown said that the issue was whether the letter represented any evidence of unethical conduct on my part, and I asked him whether, as a judicial officer, he would say that "the allegations of that letter, whether true or not, have no bearing on my right to write it?"

"Yes," said Judge Brown. "I think we have reached an ultimate issue in that respect." A few minutes later, he ruled that by writing the letter I had moved "out of the courtroom into an extralegal field of action" where, as an advocate, I had no right to go. "In that respect you have, I think, displayed a shocking contempt for the basic rule which is respected by New Jersey lawyers," he said, "namely, that cases in which they are advocates will be tried and disposed of inside the judicial branch of government and not elsewhere." He also found that I had violated orders of his not to discuss the Kavanaugh or DeFranco cases with press or public, or to mention polygraph tests in regard to them. He ordered that I be removed as counsel in both cases.

And that, I'm afraid, is when I lost my temper. I felt that I had neither done anything unethical nor violated Judge Brown's orders. I said heatedly that he had deprived my clients of counsel, and that I regarded his order as a nullity.

I also filed suit immediately in U.S. District Court in Newark to restrain Judge Brown from removing me. The suit was heard by U.S. District Judge Robert Shaw. "I think that the cardinal error in Judge Brown's proceedings," I said in my opening argument, "was to rule that under no circumstances could such conduct ever be justified, and then to rule that it was totally irrelevant whether or not in fact the state was guilty of the charges lodged against it—that is, subornation of perjury and fraud, and whether the state intended to order one of its lawyers to put a man on the stand to say my clients committed murder before his eyes, knowing that man was a liar."

By the end of the day, I thought we had won on points. Both Dowd and McGlynn had testified to pretty much everything that had happened.

Also, both said in effect that if they were prosecuting the Matzners, ethical considerations probably would stop them from putting Edward Lenney on the stand. The opposition argued that I should have sought some sort of judicial remedy before writing letters to public officials. Under questioning, they insisted that there were such remedies, but they did not describe them.

In the course of the hearing, Judge Shaw made the point that it is not the prosecutor's function to convict: "It is the prosecutor's function to protect the innocent as well as to prosecute the guilty." He also indicated that any attorney in his court who found the prosecution suborning perjury would find a quick judicial remedy if he brought the matter to Judge Shaw's attention. Listening to him, I felt sorry that we hadn't been in federal court in the first place.

Judge Shaw also expressed what appeared to be some doubts as to the wisdom of removing a defense attorney on the brink of trial in such a complicated case. But he made no ruling on that issue. Like most federal judges, he was reluctant to interfere in a state criminal proceeding until all state courts had an opportunity to act. "Upon careful consideration of this matter," he ruled, "it is concluded that the federal court . . . should not resolve the question presented, but should stay its hand until petitioners present the opportunity to a state court for appellate review. Moreover, nothing herein stated is to be construed as indicating any opinion this court may have as to the merit of petitioner's application. A proper respect for the state judicial system dictates such restraint."

A hearing was set for the following week before the New Jersey Supreme Court. I appeared for the Matzners, and tried to interest the state's high court in what I thought was a fairly strong argument. The use of perjured testimony in a capital case is nothing short of attempted murder on the part of lawyers, and should be designated as such. My argument was that letter-writing by defense counsel paled before attempted murder by the prosecution.

I made little impression. The chief justice, Joseph Weintraub, suggested that my claim that I hadn't intended my letter to go to the press was incredible. Considering that my secretary's mistake about the state legislators had resulted in a mailing of some 150 letters, I could understand his feelings. And although I had never intended to involve the media, I have to admit that I considered the case a classic example of the sort of situation in which the press *should* be involved. In any event, the Supreme Court of New Jersey affirmed my removal as defense counsel, and ordered the removal of Dowd and McGlynn as prosecutors—an action taken on the correct if tenuous grounds that both men might be called as witnesses in the Kavanaugh and DeFranco trials.

More than two years later, I was to appear before Chief Justice

Weintraub on the question of whether I should be prevented from practicing in New Jersey. "You know these cases had to be tried by a jury," he said. "There was no other way." That was the crux of my disagreement with New Jersey's judicial authorities: a trial is not—and should not be —always the only way. Whenever it's possible to ascertain without a trial that truth absolutely favors the defendant, he should be spared the hell and uncertainty that a trial holds, and the stigma that follows him even if he is acquitted.

We tried to go back before Judge Shaw, but he refused further hearings and filed a brief opinion ratifying the New Jersey Supreme Court's action. I subsequently appealed to the Third Circuit Court of Appeals and the U.S. Supreme Court. Neither appeal was successful, and by the time the latter was heard, the first Matzner trial was already under way without me.

Meantime, back at the Boston bar, interest in me had revived with the flap in Jersey. My first official notice was a letter from Haskell Cohn, then chairman of the Boston Bar Association's Grievance Committee, saying that the group wanted to see me again. At this conference, held in April, 1969, we discussed the DeFranco letter. I went into the details of its mailing, and for a while, I heard nothing further. But in September, the Boston Bar Association filed a complaint against me with the Supreme Judicial Court of Massachusetts. There were three basic charges of misconduct. Two were repeats—the Chicofsky broadcast in 1964, and my comments on the Johnny Carson show in 1967 about the Coppolino case. The third was the DeFranco letter. If the matter had been something other than a legal proceeding against a lawyer, I suspect I could have argued successfully that the first two charges had already been disposed of. But in Massachusetts, there are almost no rules for the discipline of attorneys, and, in fact, the state has never formally adopted the Canons of Ethics published by the American Bar Association.

In any case, Supreme Judicial Court Judge Paul Kirk, who was assigned to the case, said in effect that even though the rules may not have been defined in print, we all know what the right thing is for lawyers to do. I felt that at best it's difficult to establish a level of professional conduct with such vague guidelines; at worst, it's impossible. But we couldn't convince Judge Kirk.

When New Jersey got back in the picture, I began to feel like a man whose picture is on a post-office wall. As far as some of my fellow attorneys were concerned, I was wanted in two states. I received a copy of a complaint filed by a prosecutor in Bergen County, New Jersey, at the direction of the state's Supreme Court. In addition to the allegations that had caused my removal from the Matzners' defense, it contained additional counts alleging insolence to Judge Brown.

Normally, the rules of the Supreme Court of New Jersey provide that no attorney can be disciplined unless a group of lawyers appointed by the bar association hear evidence and recommend such action. But in my case, the court had sidestepped what amounted to a jury trial and had named Judge Morris Pashman of Bergen County to act as a one-man grievance committee. I felt that if I were being held to the standards of ethics expected of New Jersey lawyers, I should be given the same rights. I also felt that there was something unfair about designating a judge of an inferior court to hear charges that had already been determined by the state's Supreme Court—trial judges are not usually invited by their state's highest court to overrule it. Judge Pashman didn't agree.

Although the Massachusetts proceedings were held in open court, the New Jersey hearings were held in absolute secrecy. Presumably, the intention was to benefit the attorney-defendant, but it didn't work that way. At one point, evidence was entered in the New Jersey record that we wanted to bring to the attention of Judge Kirk in Massachusetts. We sought permission from Judge Pashman, who referred the request to the New Jersey Supreme Court, which turned it down. Consequently, Judge Kirk never heard that particular evidence. And the secrecy rule prevents me here from going into any of the details of the hearing before Judge Pashman—except to say that he's one of the most evenhanded jurists I've ever encountered, and that he bent over as far as possible to be fair. So did Judge Brown, who testified at the proceeding.

The Massachusetts action was the first to be concluded. Hearings were held at the Suffolk County Courthouse in Boston on February 10–12, 1970. I was represented by Monroe Inker and Joe Balliro. The prosecution included Hiller Zobel and Chief Prosecutor Calvin P. Bartlett. I'd have to say that Mr. Bartlett prosecuted me with a certain zeal—even to the point of trying to find out about the contents of my book and to convey the impression that my literary agent was a publicity agent. It began when I said that in answer to a prosecution request, I had asked my agent to furnish me with a copy of the contract for my defunct television show:

Q. What is the agent's name?
A. His name is Sterling Lord.
Q. He was your agent in 1967?
A. Since 1966 he has been, yes.
Q. Was he your publicity agent at that time?
A. He is not a publicity agent, sir, he is a literary agent.
Q. A what?
A. A literary agent. . . .
Q. How long did he continue as your agent, literary, publicity, or otherwise?

MR BALLIRO. I object, your honor.

THE COURT. I will exclude that as to the form.

Q. What duties did this gentleman perform—?

MR. BALLIRO. I object.

Q. —for you in '67?

THE COURT. Admitted.

MR BALLIRO. My exception.

THE COURT. Noted.

A. A literary agent acts in contractual negotiations.

Q. Describe to the court what that means?

A. A literary agent, sir, is a person who on behalf of authors or prospective authors negotiates with and eventually contracts a publisher, if he is successful.

Q. In what field did this literary agent work for you?

A. In the field of literature.

All of this indicates how far afield a hearing of this nature can go. Not that the specific charges against me weren't discussed—they were well covered in both direct and cross-examination. In many instances, I feel that my answers reflected the gut realities of a defense lawyer's professional life. Two segments from the hearing transcript make the point. The first concerns my radio discussion of the Chicofsky affair—the disclosure of a plot against Tom Richards. This is under cross-examination by Bartlett:

Q. Did you say, did you broadcast over the Paul Benzaquin Show in 1964, WEEI, as follows:

There is only one power that I know of that is greater than that of a politician or a governmental appointee, and that's the people. And so we take this case to the people.

Did you say that?

A. Certainly.

Q. Why did you elect to take the torture and threats on the life of your client to the people rather than to the court of law?

A. How does one take a cause to the courts of law with a complaint when one cannot find an audience?

Q. You felt very keenly that your client's rights, Mr. Richards, Tom Richards's rights, constitutional rights, were being very seriously prejudiced by this torture and these threats, did you not?

A. No, sir. I felt that his life was in imminent danger through the government.

Q. And through the deprivation of his rights, to life and liberty, didn't you?

A. He certainly was in danger of losing those.

Q. You now say that the courts, at that date, would give you no recourse, that you had to take your case to the people; is that your testimony?

A. I felt that in order to prohibit the United States Post Office from kidnapping and murder, it would be a good device to expose them.

Q. In connection with the deprivation of Tom Richards's constitutional right to live, did you prepare or file one single paper in any court?

A. No.

Q. Why?

A. Because the only witness that could be used [to tell of the plot] against Mr. Richards was a convicted criminal; because in prior instances, prosecution against the federal officials had been blocked at each turn, sometimes by the federal government overtly because there were matters already pending in court; because I hardly thought it appropriate to get an injunction to prohibit the United States Government to order them not to murder a citizen.

The second segment of the transcript contains an attempt to explain my actions in New Jersey, under direct examination by Monroe Inker:

Q. Mr. Bailey, will you again tell us why you sent the letter, and tell us slowly so that we can copy down your words?

A. Yes. Because it was apparent to me that someone in the state of New Jersey had ordered to trial a capital case, knowing that the only linkage between the crime and the defendants was perjured testimony from a criminal, and intended to proceed toward conviction, if it could, notwithstanding knowledge of these facts.

I wrote the Governor of the state of New Jersey because, as I understood, he appointed the county prosecutor and is the chief executive . . . and the head of the executive branch.

I wrote the Attorney General because it was on his name that Mr. Dowd had obtained the authority that he represented to me and made his promise which he could not keep.

The President of the Bar Association because I assume the subject of perjured testimony is of interest to him.

To the United States Attorney because I felt that a federal offense was involved, and to the Senators and Congressmen because I was hopeful that if some officials in New Jersey were disposed to cover up this matter, others would be disposed to take some kind of appropriate action.

I did this because I was informed, and it has since been ruled by New Jersey, that the Judge in New Jersey does not have the privilege to entertain a motion which interrupts a criminal proceeding, even if it's taken as true that the evidence of the state will be perjured.

Q. Mr. Bailey, did you think that by doing what you did that you would be violating Judge Brown's order?

MR. BARTLETT. I object.

THE COURT. Admitted.

A. No, sir.

Q. Why not?

A. Because I felt that I had a right to take the action I did because of the admitted perjury and that it should be called to the attention of the officials; and as I said, under New Jersey law, I was powerless to act. I did not anticipate that the letter would be released by anyone.

Q. Now again, Mr. Bailey, tell his honor what your feelings were about your client's being put to trial after the representation that had been made to you at the time you wrote the letter.

A. First of all, I felt that they had a right not to go to trial under all the circumstances, that they had a right to avoid financial expense and other distresses that accompany every homicide prosecution regardless of the result; that if the perjured testimony as a result of the trial going forward were believed by a jury and a sentence of life or death should result, there would be no remedy in the hands of any counsel that would assure its reversal—despite the obvious injustice inherent in such a result if one took as true, which I did, the recantation of the chief witness, that he knew that he was committing perjury and that the defendants were wholly innocent.

After the hearings, we submitted briefs challenging the entire proceeding. Finally, Judge Kirk handed down his decision. The verdict: Censure.

My first reaction was to appeal. I was particularly disturbed by some of the language in the ruling, which suggested that disbarment might not be wrong, but that since I had only been practicing for a limited time perhaps censure would be sufficient punishment. Then I began to get a lot of phone calls—many of them anonymous—from people who felt that Judge Kirk had given me relatively light punishment, and who suggested that the situation might get worse if I pushed any higher. I refuse to believe that the full bench of the Massachusetts Supreme Court could have made a judgment before getting the record. But there was discomfort among members of my staff who had suffered as a result of the censure, and I decided that the best thing to do was drop the matter where it was.

That left New Jersey. After the closed hearing was completed, Judge Pashman found me not guilty on all charges other than those arising from the mailing of the letter. He agreed that the Canons of Ethics provide that contact with the press is improper *except* in extreme circumstances

But he did not think the circumstances in the DeFranco case were extreme.

We next appeared in New Jersey Supreme Court. Monroe Inker said this was probably as far as we could go; he didn't think the U.S. Supreme Court would hear the case. He also felt that the New Jersey high court wasn't looking for blood—especially since the Supreme Judicial Court of Massachusetts had already punished me for the same things. Monroe told the New Jersey court that he was waiving none of his prior arguments, such as my right to trial by a jury of lawyers. "I suggest that Mr. Bailey speak," he said.

I reiterated that it had not been my purpose to go to the news media, but that I felt the circumstances were indeed extreme. Chief Justice Weintraub said that one of the things that had upset the court during my previous appearance was an attitude of arrogance. I tried to explain that what they had taken for arrogance was actually profound indignation about the way in which I felt the crucial issue had been switched around: my action in writing an absolutely true letter was under investigation, while the fact that state officials may have been trying to put somebody in the electric chair with perjured testimony was being overlooked.

The court handed down a one-year suspension prohibiting me from practicing in New Jersey courts. After that, I could be readmitted to practice—providing a trial judge found that I had been a good fellow during the intervening year.

EPILOGUE

Censure in Massachusetts, suspension in New Jersey. It may appear that I'm bitter about New Jersey justice. Not at all. I couldn't have asked for better justice than I got in the first Coppolino trial, which was held in New Jersey. As for my own case: in retrospect, I concede that it would have been wiser and of more benefit to my clients if I had done even more poking around before sending a letter. It would also have been wiser to have delivered by hand such a letter to the governor and other high officials. And the New Jersey Supreme Court's suggestion that in writing a letter of this sort one should say it is not for publication makes excellent sense.

I do think that Passaic County could stand a housecleaning, and that people like John Thevos should be the object of grand jury investigations. I went both to Washington and to the U.S. Attorney's office in Newark to outline the facts in the DeFranco case and ask for an inquiry. I was told that the matter had been under scrutiny, but that the U.S. Attorney involved had since been promoted to the bench. Also, the office was busy looking into organized racketeering.

There is one other thing that makes an epilogue all by itself. The Matzners were tried twice. They were acquitted in both cases, after long and protracted trials.

They should never have been indicted. The fact that they were illustrates a serious flaw in our system. It's not the only one.

VII

The State
of
the Law

Let's start with a hypothetical case. Two men, inmates in the same prison, write my office for help. Both have been convicted as participants in the same loan company holdup. The first man says he's innocent. He was tucked in with his girl friend at the time of the robbery, but the jury didn't believe her. The second man doesn't deny taking part in the crime, but complains that he was never told that as an indigent he had a right to free counsel. Jailhouse lawyers have told him this is sufficient violation of rights afforded him by the Miranda decision to win him a new trial.

We write the first man: there is nothing we can do for you; innocence is not important once you're in the can. But we tell the second man he has a sixty-forty chance of winning a new trial. He writes back to say that's fine, and that a relative will be in with a retainer. "By the way," he adds, referring to the robbery, "the other guy who wrote you wasn't there. I know, because I was."

That revelation won't change anything.

In the course of this book, I've touched on specific problems—the harm done by police lineups, the untrustworthiness of eyewitness testimony, the inanity of not permitting defense counsel to examine prosecution evidence until the middle of a trial. But the system's overriding fault is the one I mentioned at the outset of the book—the fact that as the wheels of justice grind on, innocence becomes progressively less relevant.

Let's take two more hypothetical defendants. Both are convicted. In one case, the jury made a mistake—the man didn't commit the crime—but the trial was impeccably conducted by the judge. In the other case, the jury was right—the man was guilty—but the judge made a mistake. As a lawyer, I can do nothing for the first man. I can probably obtain a new trial for the second man.

Defense lawyers usually know very soon whether a man is innocent or guilty, and they certainly find out long before the jury gets even a peek at him. There is something very wrong with a system that forces me to inform an innocent man that his innocence may not mean much in a court of law.

"First of all," I feel obligated to tell him, "you'll have to pay me a sum that probably will stagger you if I'm to do the kind of a job that needs to be done—to give you every possible chance to spin the roulette wheel so that the ball will fall on the red instead of the black. Second, you'd better know that if you get acquitted because the evidence against you is thin, and you happen to be innocent, a majority of the public will always say that you were guilty but that I got you off. Third, I want you to face the possibility that you may have to go to prison and do time for a crime you never committed. And worse, I want you to understand that once a jury finds you guilty, if the proceedings have been correct I will not be authorized in any court in the United States of America to suggest that you're innocent—because such a suggestion would be irrelevant to the court, whether it be an appellate or a reviewing court."

The frustration of being an arm of the criminal law is doubled by the small space in which trial lawyers have to work. If anything infuriates me, it is the corrosive lack of imagination shown by those elder statesmen of the legal profession who react to change the way the Prudential Insurance Company would react to the destruction of the Rock of Gibraltar. And it's so goddamn stupid because we all know the system isn't working.

What all the hypocrisy comes down to is the promise of a fair trial. If you give a man a fair trial, justice has been served. Even though he didn't do what you say he did, you may convict and execute him. That's what we call due process. The late Justice Felix Frankfurter described it accurately: "Due process is not a yardstick. It is a process. It is a delicate process of adjustment inescapably involving the exercise of judgment by those whom the Constitution entrusted with the unfolding of the process." It serves that purpose well, but it doesn't necessarily do much for factual accuracy. If after the execution of the defendant you should discover an error of fact—well, you could dig down six feet or so and hand him the certificate that says he's won a new trial.

The system is screwed up from indictment on. To start with, there is nothing less grand than a grand jury. The typical grand jury is a flock of sheep led by the prosecutor across the meadow to the finding he wants. Then, if he finds it politically expedient, he can always say: "Hell, don't blame me; the grand jury got the indictment." Meanwhile the target of all the potshotting learns that although the state didn't come around to ask if he was having tea with the Pope on the day in question (this is considered a fair alibi in legal circles), he's just been accused of knocking off his business partner. Now he has to hire counsel. If he's rich, the chances are that he will get good counsel. If he's not rich, he may or may not.

He goes to trial, which puts the load on the lawyer. Pity that poor bastard. Under the canons of ethics, counsel is required to be prepared. Before he goes into court, he should interview the witnesses and find out whether they're telling the truth. If they're not, he should learn why. He should review all documents and exhibits. He should examine the scene of the crime, and, in short, obtain as much information as possible. But often these are the very things he's prevented from doing. In the first Sheppard trial, for example, defense attorneys were denied free access to his house. After the trial, they were able to send an expert criminologist there. He obtained new evidence, but it was too late to do Sam any good.

Or take the second Coppolino trial. At Naples, I wasn't able to get a look at the autopsy report on Carmela until the trial was in progress—more than a year after the autopsy had been performed. Federal courts are no better. The rule in the federal system is that after a witness finishes his direct examination, the defense lawyer is handed a ream of paper embodying all the witness's prior statements and possibly his grand jury testimony. If the lawyer asks the judge for a two-day recess so he can assimilate and check the information, the judge may hold him in contempt. If he asks for thirty minutes, the judge may scowl. And yet if the lawyer doesn't ask, he's violating the canons of ethics. Whatever that is, it's not justice. It's a game, and I don't know why it's played. Unless the operating theory is that defense lawyers should be entrusted with what's supposed to be the truth only when they don't have time to get a good look at it.

Nor are those hallowed words "trial by jury" synonymous with justice. First, there's the problem of who serves on a jury. Most people put jury duty in a class with measles and root canal work. Quite often, intelligent, successful people who would make good jurors are the ones who get out of serving. And there are the problems that crop up during jury selection. At Coppolino's second trial, the prosecution was able to keep a chemist off the jury even though he was the one candidate capable of thoroughly understanding the evidence. This was about as just as Madame de Pompadour was chaste. But it was our system that enabled the prosecution to get away with it.

What this all comes down to, of course, is that more often than most of us would like to admit, juries convict the innocent.

Last year I ran into a jury that took all prizes for stupidity. My clients were a pair of narcotics agents accused by a dope peddler-informer of having taken a bribe. There are few forms of human life lower than the creatures who earn their living selling heroin. And yet the government often marries these subhumans by making them informants in the hope of catching bigger dope peddlers. Anyway, they are a particularly vicious group, and one of them decided to get at two agents by accusing them of accepting a bribe. On the night the payoff was allegedly made in New York, one agent was in Kansas City. After the bribe had been offered, the other agent turned in a written report saying he'd been offered a bribe and suggesting that the bureau set up a trap. The government, instead of looking into these facts, got an indictment, and we went to trial in Brooklyn. We wound up with a jury whose combined intelligence would have trouble hitting 700 on the Wechsler-Bellevue test. When they were in the mood, they listened to the evidence—I figured that some of it had to have seeped through. When they went out, there seemed little doubt about the verdict. The prosecutor walked over to me and said that he hadn't lost a case in a long while, but that he'd surely lost this one. The judge said. "They're going to be back in an hour with an acquittal."

They weren't. They sent the judge a note saying they would halt deliberations at 6:00 P.M. and resume the next morning at 10:00. The note was signed, "By order of the jury."

"Judge," I said, "I think we've got trouble."

I was right. An hour later, they sent another note. "Please have the stenographer prepared in the morning to read all of the testimony so we can review it." The trial had gone on for two weeks. Judge and counsel for both sides felt that little would be accomplished by the jury's rehashing the testimony they had heard the first time around, so we squelched that idea. The next day they deliberated into the afternoon and came up with a verdict. "Your honor," said the forelady, "on all counts, we find all defendants guilty with a recommendation of clemency for each."

"I didn't authorize you to recommend clemency, this isn't a capital case!" said the judge. He turned to me. "Do you want to poll the jury, Mr. Bailey?"

"Most assuredly." I had started to poll them when juror number two, Mrs. M., asked the judge if she could say something. He told her to go ahead.

"Your honor," said Mrs. M., "they didn't exactly force me, but push me they did."

The judge sent the jury back to the deliberation room and told Mrs. M. to stay in the box.

"Mrs. M.," I asked, "what was your original vote in this case?"

"Not guilty," she said, adding that the prosecution witnesses had confused her. She'd felt that at least part of the time, they weren't telling the truth.

"How was it you changed your vote?"

"Well," she said, "they all promised me that if we recommended clemency, the judge could only give a ten-dollar fine."

The offenses carried maximum sentences of twenty-five years in jail. "If you'd known that the judge could send them up the river," I said, "what would you have voted then?"

"I would have stuck to not guilty."

"Do you have a reasonable doubt about their guilt?"

"Yeah," said Mrs. M., "that's why I was voting not guilty."

"Do you still have it?"

"Yeah."

"Is it fair to say," I asked, "that the verdict we've just entertained in this courtroom amounts to not guilty with a recommendation of clemency because of reasonable doubt?"

Mrs. M.'s face lit up with the delight born of true communication. "You said it!"

We questioned a few more jurors, who corroborated Mrs. M.'s statements. The judge sent the jury home; he wouldn't record the verdict. We'd wasted our time; we would have to retry the case.

Nobody of even minimal intelligence could have doubted that at least one defendant was 1,250 miles away from the scene of the alleged crime when it allegedly happened. But for reasons known only to the jury, justice went down the drain. The system simply can't be counted on. In my opinion, despite all the criticism leveled at the military, the odds are that a military court will produce a more accurate verdict in a disputed issue of fact than a civilian jury. The members of a military court are likely to be better disciplined and better educated than civilian jurors, and they don't require the fiction of unanimity for their verdict. In the military, a two-thirds vote is necessary for conviction. Consequently there are no hung juries, worthless exercises that victimize civilian justice all the time.

Okay. In all of this, I've been concentrating on the defendant who's innocent and pleads not guilty. It's important to remember that a plea of not guilty means, "Prove it." By no stretch of the system does it mean "I'm innocent," because no judgment of a jury can ever show innocence. Now let's take a look at how the system treats a man who pleads guilty. A guilty plea can be translated as "I did it, sock it to me." The object is to work out a deal—the defendant pleads guilty to, say, one count instead of three or four, or five or ten. Because overloaded court calendars have crowded the jails with men awaiting trial, this practice has become more and more the rule. A Detroit judge who was quoted by *Newsweek* put it right on the line. "They don't try cases anymore," he said, "they negotiate convictions."

So the system becomes a trading mart. And once the defendant goes to jail, the system becomes a travesty. In effect, what the law says is that we're going to put this felon into a place where there are plenty of others just like him to stimulate his criminality, and others who aren't quite like him and can teach him criminal acts he hasn't yet conceived. We throw murderers, pimps, dope pushers, and bank robbers all together in crowded cell blocks so they can combine their respective specialties in what amount to colleges of crime. And we put innocent men in among them.

About eighty-five percent of the country's criminal acts are committed by repeaters. As ex-Attorney General Ramsey Clark explains it: "We manufacture crime." And we damn well do. We allow little credit even for rehabilitation, which at best is only a beginning. Actually, we should be going far beyond rehabilitation—all *that* consists of is bringing convicts back to where they were before they went to jail. Our purpose should be to turn them into decent citizens.

We allow almost no options, especially in the case of the guilty man convicted after a trial. The emphasis is on appeals. There is no possibility of his reconstruction as a citizen unless he can first look at himself in the mirror and say, "You did it, you son of a bitch, and you should try to change yourself." But he's held back from doing this because the minute he tells somebody in authority he did it, he's jeopardizing the possible success of the postconviction appeals he's entitled to pursue.

All of which gives you an idea of what's wrong. Now for some thoughts on setting things right—or, at least, moving in that direction. First of all, we've got to start putting the emphasis on justice rather than game playing. In many cases, justice might be better served if a man had the option of waiving safeguards he doesn't need so that he could go in and plead innocent. By way of illustration, he might not need the Fourth Amendment—it might annoy him to have his house searched, but perhaps he'd rather have that done to negate suspicion than have police allege through a "reliable informant" that he has something in his house that was never there.

This plea of innocence would not be the same as a plea of not guilty, and would not involve the onus of publicity. A man would be informed that he was under suspicion, and he would be given a chance to absolve himself. He would be given full access to all government witnesses so that he could demonstrate without the fiction of a jury trial why the government shouldn't proceed against him, why it shouldn't blacken his name with a formal accusation. The presumption of innocence has never existed in the public mind; this way the defendant who could demonstrate his innocence at the start would be spared an indictment. If a trial should be necessary, let this man go to trial on the plea of innocence—and forget those safeguards he doesn't need as he did in the pretrial procedure. Often a trial would *not* be necessary, and the key element there would be judicious use of the polygraph.

That has to happen. If justice is the objective, it's about time the polygraph came into its own. The police will almost never prosecute a man who has been cleared by their own test, and in the military the polygraph is considered conclusive in both pretrial and posttrial stages. (In the military system, judgments of fact can be reviewed in the posttrial stage.) And yet, polygraph results are not admissible in our courts. Reliability is not the real issue; there is no question of the polygraph's scientific reliability in the hands of a competent operator.

It seems to me that the major obstacle is the legal establishment's fear of a device able to pierce falsehood and isolate the truth. Much of the bland perjury that supports a good deal of our litigation would vanish with the prospect of the polygraph hanging over the head of the litigant. In the great majority of cases, an innocent man will leap for the test. A guilty man usually will do just the opposite—he'll raise a covey of objections even though he knows nothing about the technique. The intelligent move would be to make polygraph tests available to all citizens as a means of unpublicized absolvement of suspicion prior to formal pretrial procedures.

Now, the plea of guilty. The current arrangement is a testimonial to hypocrisy. The concept of "I did it and I want to straighten out" has about as much to do with the average guilty plea as purity has to do with politics. To induce a client who did it to plead guilty, the lawyer talks years, not reformation. He has to convince his client that a trial probably will end in conviction and a four- to seven-year sentence, whereas a guilty plea will draw a three-to-five. But a three-to-five isn't going to solve anything for the client, even though it may represent a good job on the lawyer's part.

What I have in mind is a system of earned freedom that could prove effective with all but the most hardened criminals. The convict should be given an opportunity to work, and to generate some kind of income. And he should learn something other than the manufacture of number plates— a trade in which job opportunities in the outside world are somewhat less than superabundant.

At present, the defendant who draws a prison term is for all practical purposes being told that five-to-seven or ten-to-fifteen is what it takes to straighten him out. This is the first step in killing his motivation to come to grips with himself. And when you kill motivation, you might as well kill the human being. It would have to make a difference if he felt he was being put into a system that would help him become a productive citizen— if he could be told that as he demonstrated his improvement, he would be able to *earn* his way into partial confinement and then into freedom.

There would still, of course, be some prisoners who could not be restored to society. I wouldn't advocate, for instance, Albert DeSalvo's outright release under any conditions. I don't think DeSalvo is dangerous, but I'm not about to bet my reputation or my wife's life on it. And I don't believe any good psychiatrist would want him released, either, because we can never say he's cured unless we first find out what was wrong with him—and nobody is making any serious effort to do that. But the great majority of people being destroyed by the penal system would have access to a program that would permit them to wake in the morning with something other than total misery in their hearts. Instead of cycling and recycling through the prisons like soiled laundry, they might be equipped to make it in the outside world.

There is another avenue of change that should be opened if we are to improve our system of criminal law. We have to put more time and effort into training criminal lawyers—whatever training exists at present is largely accidental. When I entered law school, an attorney who later became a judge gave me a book and wrote on the flyleaf: "Dear Lee, as you enter law school, bear this in mind. When I was a young man, not skilled, and overmatched by my opponents, I lost many cases that I should have won. But as I became older and more skilled and my opponents showing up were tyros, I won many cases that I should have lost. So in the end, justice was done." His intent was lighthearted, but the inscription's truth is chilling.

An extra year of law school that offered all the criminal law courses the regular curriculum neglects—investigation, cross-examination, trial tactics, summation, brief-writing, and appellate procedures—might help. Afterward, the graduate could spend a year as clerk to a trial judge, a year as an assistant prosecutor, and a year as a nonsalaried aide (some sort of subsidization would have to be arranged) to a defense lawyer. Instead of being confined to office paperwork, he would sit at the lawyer's side in court. Any of these years could be accelerated for a student who already had background experience or who showed an exceptional flair for the law.

There's something else. The would-be criminal lawyer should know about the loneliness of his chosen profession. And about the satisfactions of being a renegade.